Pittsylvania County Court House, Chatham, Virginia
Chatham Court House Built 1853

MARRIAGES

of

PITTSYLVANIA COUNTY, VIRGINIA

1806–1830

Compiled by

KATHLEEN BOOTH WILLIAMS

CLEARFIELD

Reprinted for
Clearfield Company, Inc. by
Genealogical Publishing Co., Inc.
Baltimore, Maryland
1999

Originally published: Danville, Virginia, 1965
Reprinted: Genealogical Publishing Co., Inc.
Baltimore, 1980
© 1965 Kathleen Booth Williams
© transferred to Genealogical Publishing Co., Inc.
Baltimore, Maryland, 1978
All Rights Reserved
Library of Congress Catalogue Card Number 80-68125
International Standard Book Number 0-8063-0903-2
Made in the United States of America

FOREWORD

"Marriages of Pittsylvania County,Virginia, 1806-1830"
follows Mrs. H. A. Knorr's book, "Marriages of Pittsylvania
County, Virginia, 1767-1805" and, for this twenty-five year
period, contains more than 800 more marriages than are
shown for the previous thirty-nine years. This shows how
the population had increased though Henry County had been
taken from Pittsylvania County in 1777.

This book, approved by Mrs. Knorr to the extent that
she worked with me one day in Chatham, was undertaken after
we had received several letters from people in far-away
states who wrote asking WHY were marriages stopped so early
-- "after all, that is more than one hundred and fifty
years ago." So, it is thought well to start where other
books have left off and publish as many marriages as one
can.

The Marriage Register in Chatham, Virginia, for the
years 1806-1830 was copied and then each marriage was check-
ed by the original bond and Minister's Return. In doing
this checking several errors were found in the Marriage Register. This is where the Deputy Clerks helped. When an
error was found a Deputy Clerk was shown the bond and the
Register and she noted in the Register what the correction
should be, such as: The Register had said "Arthur W. Evans"
and the bond said "Arthur W. Eanes." Two or more marriage
bonds were found that had not been listed in the Register
and a Deputy Clerk typed them in. More than two names were
corrected and there were several errors in dates, which
could have been typographical errors.

Sometimes the spellings of names were queer - these
are given as found in the records.

Most bonds are in good condition though some are torn,
and some Minister's Returns have almost scalloped edges,
leaving part of a date only.

Some bonds show the name of the bride's father and
there is no note of consent. Some notes of consent tell
pertinent facts concerning the family such as, when a
grandparent raised a child because the patents were dead or
"not in this county."

Not all Minister's Returns were dated. Some say,"since
my last return." They do give names of the couple but no
date of when the ceremony was performed. Some Ministers
made returns for one year and a part of two other years on
one sheet of paper, and once a Minister reported his mar-

riages for <u>four</u> years on a single sheet of paper. These returns are filed with the bonds the year they reached the Court House. Sometimes a Minister said he married a couple <u>prior</u> to the date of the bond. Could this be because he had lost his notes and was reporting from memory? Such instances are noted in parenthesis.

The following Ministers sent in Returns:

Joel T. Adams - Baptist
Nathan Anderson
Eben Angel - Baptist
Abner Anthony
Joel Ashworth
John Atkinson
James Beck - Baptist
Richard B. Beck
William Blair - Baptist
Thomas Boaz - Baptist
Edwin G. Cabaniss (E.G.)
Jarrot W. Cook, Jr.
William Davis
Crispen Dickenson (Dickinson)
Griffith Dickenson (Dickinson)
Elias Dodson
George Dodson
Richard Elliott - Baptist
Ira Ellis - Methodist
Joseph Hatchett
Willis Hopwood
Robert Hurt

John Jenkins - Baptist
John W. Kelly
John Leigh
Nathan (Nathaniel) Lovelace
Orson Martin (also Orin)
Clement McDonald (C.M.)
John G. Mills - Baptist
A. D. Montgomery
Shadrack Mustain (Musteen)
James Nelson - Baptist
David Nowlin - Baptist
Thomas Payne - Methodist
William S. Plummer (Plumer)
James Reid - Methodist
Milton Robertson (M.)
W. Robertson
Thomas Sparks
Thomas Still - Methodist
John C. Taylor
John Terry - Presbyterian
Arnold Walker
Peyton Welch

Not all of these Ministers lived in Pittsylvania County.

I wish to express my appreciation to Mr. Samuel W. Swanson, Clerk of Pittsylvania County Circuit Court, and the following Deputy Clerks: Julian N. Harris, Roma B. Felts, Nancy S. Bumgarner, Carolyn W. Pickeral, Emilie R. Watlington, Ann D. Adams and Adylene C. Crider for their courtesy and help at all times. Often it seemed they would do more than duty demanded. Also, I thank Mrs. H. A. Knorr for the day she worked with me in Chatham and her other expressions of kindness.

Kathleen Booth Williams

MARRIAGES OF PITTSYLVANIA COUNTY, VIRGINIA

1806 - 1830

2 October 1829. Abihu AARON and Margaret R. Blair, dau. of Samuel Blair who consents. Sur. Israel Fuller. p. 93

16 December 1816. William ABBETT and Tempy Owen. Sur. Julius Owen. p. 60

19 September 1825. Brooks ABBOTT and Sally Owen. Sur. Julius Owen. p. 82

8 November 1825. Henry ABBOTT and Susan Hardy, dau. of Jesse Hardy who consents. Sur. James B. White. p. 82

20 July 1816. Jesse ABBOTT and Polley Watson. Sur. William Watson. Married 21 July by the Rev. Shadrack Mustain. p. 60

11 February 1817. Francis ABSTON and Mary Bruice who gives her own consent. Sur. Robert Farmer. Married 12 Feb. by the Rev. Shadrack Mustain who says Mary Bruce. p. 62

19 August 1820. John F. ABSTON and Elizabeth Bruce, who signs her own consent. Sur. Frederick Bruce. Married 23 Aug. by the Rev. Shadrack Mustain. p. 70

13 January 1818. William ABSTON and Nancy Irby, dau. of William R. Irby who consents. Sur. Laban Farmer. Married by the Rev. Griffith Dickinson "since my last return." p. 65

5 May 1826. William ABSTON and Sarah Dove, dau. of George Dove who consents. Sur. Frederick Bruce. Married 10 May by the Rev. Eben Angel. p. 85

8 November 1808. Elkanah ADAMS and Sally Meade, dau. of James Meade. Sur. Silvester A. Vaden. Married by the Rev. Thomas Payne who says "8 October 1808." p. 44

21 November 1824. Gabriel ADAMS and Francis Moorefield. Sur. Stokeley Adams. Edward Moorefield signs the certificate. No relationship given. p. 79

15 June 1812. Green ADAMS and Nancy Thomas. Sur. William Thomas. Married 18 June by the Rev. Thomas Boaz. p. 52

5 August 1824. Harrison ADAMS and Milley Terrell. Sur. Ezra Hill. Jessea Terrell signs the certificate. Married 5 Aug. by the Rev. John Leigh, M. G., Halifax County. p. 79

15 July 1811. James ADAMS and Mary Womack, dau. of Allen Womack. Sur. Robert Adams. Married 16 July by the Rev. Griffith Dickinson. p. 49

28 March 1814. John ADAMS and Alice Astin. Sur. William Astin, Jr. William Astin signs the certificate. p. 56

8 November 1820. John ADAMS and Charity James who signs her own consent. Sur. John Bayes. Married 9 Nov. by the Rev. Griffith Dickinson. p. 70

19 August 1822. Johnson ADAMS and Lucy S. Williams. Sur. David C. Williams. Married 27 Aug. by the Rev. Griffith Dickinson who says Lucy L. Williams. p. 74

13 February 1809. Nathan ADAMS and Sally Murphy, dau. of James Murphy who is Surety. Married 16 Feb. by the Rev. Thomas Payne. p. 46

5 March 1824. Patterson ADAMS and Edith Rumley, who signs her own consent. Sur. Amos Watson. Married 5 March by the Rev. Ira Ellis. p. 79

13 November 1815. Peter ADAMS and Polly Astin, dau. of William Astin who consents. Sur. Will Astin. (Junr. in top of bond.) Married 16 Nov. by the Rev. Thomas Sparks. p. 57

26 December 1807. Redman ADAMS and Mary Polly Grigsby, dau. of Moses Grigsby who consents. Sur. Jamerson Corbin. Married by the Rev. David Nowlin. Returned in 1808. p. 42

26 December 1827. Samuel ADAMS and Tamson A. Dix, who signs her own consent. Sur. Peter Barksdale. Married 26 Dec. by the Rev. William Blair. p. 87

8 February 1825. Stokely ADAMS and Winifred Vaden, dau. of Sylvester A. Vaden who consents. Sur. James A. Vaden. p.82

16 August 1823. Thomas ADAMS and Frances Tribble. Married by the Rev. Shadrack Mustain. Minister's Return. p. 77

29 December 1824. William ADAMS and Lucy Jones, who signs her own consent. Sur. Byrd Yates. p. 79

21 April 1817. Edward ADKERSON and Polley Farris. Sur. Nathaniel Farris. p. 62

9 August 1822. James ADKINS and Polly Elliott. Sur. James Hodges. Peter Parrish, whose consent says he adopted Polly, signs the certificate. Married -- Aug. by the Rev. Ira Ellis. p. 74

10 November 1828. John W. ADKINS and Haridice Reynolds.
Sur. Anderson Adkins. John D. Reynolds, father of Haridice,
and Henry Adkins, father of John W., sign the certificate.
Married 12/13 Nov. by the Rev. Orson Martin. p. 90

18 January 1830. Joseph ADKINS and Bathena Martin. Sur.
Joel Martin. Married 20 Jan. by the Rev. Orson Martin.p.95

15 July 1809. Owen ADKINS and Isabel Harris, dau. of John
Harris who consents. Sur. James Hines. p. 46

7 June 1830. Ralph ADKINS and Sophia Parrish. Sur. Isham
Griffy. Married 7 June by the Rev. Richard B. Beck. p. 95

13 September 1824. Wyatt ADKINS and Phebe Oakes. Sur. William Oakes. Catherine Oakes consents. Henry Adkins consents for his son, Wyatt. p. 79

17 July 1816. Allen AKIN and Susan Echols. Sur. Obediah
Echols. Married by the Rev. David Nowlin "since my last return." Return dated 1821. p. 60

19 July 1819. Armistead AKIN and Elizabeth Lewis, who signs
her own consent. Sur. David C. Williams. Married by the
Rev. David Nowlin. p. 68

25 December 1815. George ALEXANDER and Nancy Morton, who
signs her own consent. Sur. Levi Garrett. p. 57

29 December 1808. Faunteroy ALLEN and Judith Tarleton Woodson. Sur. B. Woodson. William and Mary Townes sign the certificate. No relationship stated. p. 44

17 November 1807. James ALLEN and Nancy Dyer. Married by
the Rev. Thomas Payne. Minister's Return. Recorded in 1808
Entered twice, pp. 42 and 43

27 January 1812. James G. ALLEN and Polly Bradley. Sur.
Reubin Hall, "who made oath that Daniel Bradley gave his free
and voluntary consent." (This is on back of bond.) Married
29 Jan. by the Rev. William Blair. p. 52

20 September 1824. James R. ALLEN and Nancy Thompson. Sur.
Reubin Hopkins. p. 79

8 December 1814. Lewis B. ALLEN and Mary C. Jones, dau. of
Richard Jones who consents. Sur. Joseph Barnett. p. 56

18 July 1809. Littleton ALLEN and Susanna Minter, who
writes her own consent as "of age." Sur. Othniel Minter.
. p. 46

21 December 1829. Meridith B. ALLEN and Mary H. Cox, dau. of Elizabeth S. Cox who says Mary, her daughter, is of age and has no other guardian. Sur. William R. Harefield. Married 24 Dec. by the Rev. Orson Martin. p. 93

21 April 1814. Moses ALLEN and Jane Thomas. Sur. James Thomas. Married 26 April by the Rev. Thomas Boaz. p.56

14 December 1819. Robert ALLEN and Tabitha Wells. Sur. John Wells. p. 68

9 November 1825. Henry ALTICK and Catharine Campbell. Sur. Jacob. Zink. p. 82

29 January 1829. Shadrack ALVIS and Frances Bennett. Sur. Walden Bennett. p. 93

1 November 1825. Francis AMOS and Anna Adkins, dau. of William Adkins who consents. Sur. Francis Lacy. p. 82

30 August 1819. Banister ANDERSON and Elizabeth Thompson. Sur. John Thompson. Washington Thompson consents. No relationship stated. Married 4 September by the Rev. John Jenkins. p. 68

19 December 1826. Churchell ANDERSON and Rebecca Thompson. Sur. John S. White. Washington Thompson signs the certificate. Married 21 Dec. by the Rev. William Blair who says Churchill Anderson and Rebecca W. Thompson. p. 85

22 January 1812. Jacob ANDERSON and Fanny Green, who gives her own consent. Sur. Will Anderson. (William up in bond.) p. 52

10 October 1810. John ANDERSON and Lucy Walden. Married by the Rev. Griffith Dickinson. Minister's Return. p. 47

19 December 1826. Jonas ANDERSON and Polly S. Jones. Sur. Jn⁰ P. Wilkinson. Thomas Jones signs the certificate saying, "Polly Sandige Jones has been living with me for the last eleven years and I have every right to believe that she is 21 years of age and consents to marriage." p. 85

12 November 1822. Joseph ANDERSON and Susannah Bohannon, dau. of Joseph Bohannon who consents. Sur. Joel Marrable. p. 74

2 June 1830. Joseph E. ANDERSON and Manerva Caroline Terry, dau. of Daniel Terry who consents. Sur. Hartwell Motley. Married 3 June by the Rev. Griffith Dickinson. p. 95

18 December 1815. Thomas ANDERSON and Chloe Glascock, dau. of Eliza Glascock who consents. Sur. Thomas Glascock. Married 21 December by the Rev. John Jenkins. p. 57

26 February 1824. Thomas ANDERSON and Sarah P. Tunstall. Married by the Rev. William Blair. Minister's Return.p.79

20 November 1815. William ANDERSON and Elizabeth Mottley, dau. of Elizabeth Mottley who consents. Sur. Robert Dupey. Married 21 Nov. by the Rev. John Jenkins. p. 57

17 December 1825. Charles ANGEL and Martha Vaughan, who signs her own consent. Sur. Emanuel Wayne. Married 25 Dec. by the Rev. Eben Angel. p. 82

16 December 1811. Nicholas ANGEL and Amey C. Taylor, dau. of Cornelius Taylor who is Surety. Married 3 October by the Rev. Thomas Boaz. p. 49

19 April 1813. Daniel ANGLIN and Edey Abbett. Sur. John Anglin. Married 22 April by the Rev. Thomas Boaz. p. 54

2 September 1824. William A. ANTHONY and Sarah Echols. Sur. David Echols. p. 79

17 April 1810. Isaac APHER and Polley Taylor. Married by the Rev. Thomas Payne. Minister's Return. p. 47

4 March 1825. Thomas D. ARCHER and Nancy Cahall, dau. of Peter Cahall who consents. Sur. John Cahall. p. 82 (A double wedding? See William C. Archer.)

4 March 1825. William C. ARCHER and Kitty Cahall, dau. of Peter Cahall who consents. Sur. John Cahall. p. 82 (A double wedding? See Thomas D. Archer.)

26 December 1825. Henry ARNN and Mary Robertson, dau. of John Robertson, Jr. who consents. Sur. David Robertson. p. 82

29 May 1819. George ARNOLD and Nancy Bailes. Sur. Joshua Saunders. Elizabeth Bailes, mother of Nancy, and Nancy, herself, sign the certificate. Married 28 August by the Rev. John Jenkins. p. 68

12 November 1820. George ARON, Jr. and Frances Donaldson, dau. of James Donaldson who consents. Sur. Robert Shelton. Married 22 Nov. by the Rev. William Blair who says George Aaron. p. 70

14 January 1822. Baldin ARTHUR and Nancy Bybee, dau. of Joseph Bybee who consents. Sur. James E. Kelly. Married 4 April by the Rev. Shadrack Mustain. p. 74

13 April 1820. Coleman ARTHUR and Polley Barber, dau. of Joseph Barber who consents. Sur. Reuben Barber. Married 13 April by the Rev. Shadrack Mustain. p. 70

31 January 1814. James ARTHUR and Sally Keesee, dau. of Jesse Keesee who consents. Sur. Booker Keesee. Married 10 February by the Rev. Griffith Dickinson. p. 56

11 May 1822. Joab ARTHUR and Milly Goard. Sur. Cornelius Towler. Married by the Rev. John W. Kelly. (Minister says 1 May.) p. 74

19 March 1822. John ARTHUR and Nancy Bennett. Sur. Palmerin Bennett. Married 6 June by the Rev. John W. Kelly. p. 74

11 March 1811. William ARTHUR and Sally Foster, dau. of Molley Barber who consents. Sur. David Parker. p. 49

19 December 1826. James ASHBY and Lucinda Sikes. Sur. Holmes Gwinn. Joab Sikes signs the certificate. p. 85

17 January 1822. George ASTIN and Margaret Millner. Married by the Rev. James Beck. Minister's Return. p. 74

25 July 1816. James ASTIN and Sally Jones, dau. of William Jones who consents. Sur. Peter Tiffin. p. 60

23 October 1818. William ASTIN and Anne. P. Harrison, dau. of Ro. Harrison who consents. Sur. Josiah W. Harrison. p.65

20 October 1815. Henry ATKERSON and Lucy Davis, dau. of Francis Davis who consents. Sur. Jerome Rossan. p. 57

14 November 1821. Charles W. ATKINSON and Nancy Willis, dau. of Joel Willis who consents. Sur. Brackton Atkinson. Married by the Rev. David Nowlin. p. 72

18 May 1807. Edmund ATKINSON and Winnifred Martin. Sur. Leonard Dove. p. 42

8 February 1823. Harrison P. ATKINSON and Jamime Laprade, granddaughter of Benjamin Laprade who says he raised her. Sur. John Laprade. p. 77

5 October 1826. Henry W. ATKINSON and Mary Carter. Sur. Richard I. Shelton. p. 85

29 December 1828. James B. ATKINSON and Eadey Riddle. Sur. Hawker Rice. p. 90

5 February 1811. Nathaniel ATKINSON and Martha Henry, dau. of Mary Henry who consents. Sur. Benjamin Henry, who testifies as to Martha's age. Married 6 Feb. by the Rev. Joseph Hatchett who says Nathaniel Adkinson. p. 49

19 September 1825. Owen ATKINSON and Fanny Campbell. Sur. Jacob Zink. p. 82

3 August 1826. Champness AUSTIN and Betsy B. Gover, who
signs her own consent. Sur. Harrison Covington. Married 4
Aug. by the Rev. Orson Martin. p. 85

31 October 1826. Champness AUSTIN and Elizabeth W. Austin.
Sur. Daniel B. Austin. Stephen Austin consents for himself
and wife. p. 85

24 August 1809. William AUSTIN and Polley S. Hankins. Sur.
Jeremiah Walker. William and Polley sign their own consents.
Polley signs "Polley Smith Hankins." Married by the Rev.
Thomas Still. p. 46

20 January 1812. Thomas BAGERLY and Lois Still, dau. of
Thomas Still who consents. Sur. David Baggerly. Married
29 Jan. by the Rev. Thomas Sparks. p. 52

-- ---- 1809. David BAGGERLY and Thaly Sparks, dau. of Thomas Sparks who consents. Sur. Samuel Murphy. p. 46

17 October 1808. Elijah BEGGERLY and Polley Burnett, dau.
of Gilbert Burnett who consents. Sur. Laban Grisham. Married 20 Oct. by the Rev. William Blair. p. 44

13 March 1818. Thomas BAGGERLY and Visey Gammon, dau. of
William Gammon who consents. Sur. John Baggerly. p. 65

18 June 1807. Charles BAILEY and Ann Clark. Sur. Tunstall
Shelton. Married 7 July by the Rev. Griffith Dickenson.
p. 42

11 April 1812. James BAILEY and Susanna Neal. Sur. John
Neal. No relationship given. Married 15 April by the Rev.
Griffith Dickinson. p. 52

15 November 1826. Elisha BAILISS and Mildred Wright. Sur.
Robert Wright. Married 20 Nov. by the Rev. Eben Angel who
says Bayliss. p. 85

2 February 1813. Samuel BALL and Polly Hedrick, dau. of
Philip Hedrick who requests the license. Sur. George Hedrick. Married 6 Feb. by the Rev. Joseph Hatchett. p. 54

21 September 1825. Gerard BANKS, Jr. and Sarah Smith, dau.
of Thomas Smith, whose consent says " Gerard Banks, Jr., of
Halifax." Sur. Alexander Jackson. p. 82

17 February 1816. Coleman BARBER and Anna Eddes, dau. of
John Eddes who consents. Sur. Preston G. Eds. p. 60

4 November 1816. Coleman BARBER and Anna Waggoner. Sur.
George Craft. Married 10 Nov. by the Rev. Shadrack Mustain.
p. 60

8

19 November 1814. David BARBER and Nancy McBride. Sur.
William Simpson. Mar. 24 Nov. by the Rev. Griffith Dickinson who says David Barbour. p. 56

6 November 1806. Elisha BARBER and Jane Mitchell. Married by the Rev. Griffith Dickinson. Minister's Return. p. 40

13 November 1815. Elisha BARBER and Sarah Edds, dau. of John Edds who consents. Sur. Preston G. Edds. p. 57

12 September 1828. James BARBER and Frances Irby. Sur.
William Irby. William Irby signs the certificate. Married 15 Sept. by the Rev. Eben Angel. p. 90

-- ---- 1807. Jeremiah BARBER and Phebe McCullock. Married by the Rev. John Jenkins. Return dated 21 Dec.1807. p. 42

28 July 1830. Jeremiah BARBER and Nancy Worsham. Married by the Rev. Eben Angel. Minister's Return. p. 95

6 January 1820. Joel BARBER and Rebecka Markham, who signs her consent as Rebecker J. Markham. Sur. James Whitehead.
Married 11 Jan. by the Rev. Griffith Dickinson. p. 70

7 September 1811. John BARBER and Mourning Hudson, dau. of Sally Hudson. Sur. William Barber. Married by the Rev.
William Nowlin. Returned in 1813. p. 49

1 October 1829. John BARBER and Martha Ragland. Married 1 Oct. by the Rev. Griffith Dickenson. p. 93

12 May 1828. Joseph BARBER and Anna Dalton. Sur. William Doss. Married 20 June by the Rev. Eben Angel. p. 90

26 October 1816. Matthew BARBER and Susanna Thurman, dau. of Molley Thurman who consents. Sur. Thomas Irby. Married 1 Nov. by the Rev. Shadrack Mustain. p. 65

12 April 1824. Shadrack BARBER and Polly Farmer, dau. of Laban Farmer who consents. Sur. Robert Farmer. Married 13 April by the Rev. Griffith Dickinson. p. 79

27 March 1818. William BARBER and Elizabeth Goard, dau. of Jemima Goard who requests the license. Sur. Elijah Towler.
Married 28 March by the Rev. Shadrack Mustain. p. 65

5 December 1827. William BARBER and Mary Jenkins. Married by the Rev. Griffith Dickinson. Minister's Return. p. 87

17 June 1816. Caleb BARBOUR and Betsy Custard. Sur. John Barbour. Married 19 Aug. by the Rev. John Jenkins. p. 60

17 January 1814. Asa BARKER and Sarah Harris. Sur. Moses Barker. Elizabeth Harris signs the certificate. No relationship given. Married 28 Jan. by the Rev. William Blair. p. 56

6 January 1826. Clark H. BARKER and Susan Bohannon, dau. of Nathaniel Bohannon who consents. Sur. Thomas Overby. Married 13 Jan. by the Rev. William Blair. p. 85

14 March 1823. Elisha BARKER and Rebecca Crawford. Sur. Abraham Rorer, Jr. p. 77

16 July 1830. George BARKER and Elmyry Gipson, who signs her own consent. Sur. William W. Tuggle. p. 95

12 November 1823. Green BARKER and Susan Hiler, dau. of Mary Hiler who consents. Sur. William Tuggle. p. 77

7 October 1825. James BARKER and Elizabeth Goodman, who signs her own certificate. Sur. David Goodman, who says Elizabeth is of age. p. 82

8 December 1814. John BARKER and Mourning Robertson. Married by the Rev. David Nowlin. p. 56
There is no date on the Rev. David Nowlin's Return. The date given was taken from Robertson data by Mr. W. B. Sours.

16 August 1809. Thomas BARKER and Jenny Harp. Sur. William Elliott. Married by the Rev. Thomas Sparks who says Jean. p. 46

26 December 1828. Thomas BARKER and Anna Arthur, granddaughter of Jesse Keesee who says, "an orphan child that I have raised and am the nearest connection she has in this part of the country." Sur. John Chatten. p. 90

15 December 1823. Beverly I. BARKSDALE and Christina W. Faris, dau. of Amos Faris who consents. Sur. Henry Faris. p. 77

22 November 1823. Claiborne BARKSDALE and Harriet T. White, dau. of John White, whose request for the license says Dr. Claiborne W. Barksdale. Sur. John L. White. p. 77

21 December 1829. Peter BARKSDALE and Sarah M. Easley, dau. of Robert Easley who consents. Sur. David Logan. p. 93

30 December 1820. Richard H. BARKSDALE and Sarah Shields. Sur. William Shields. Married by the Rev. John Jenkins. p. 70

13 January 1813. William H. BARKSDALE and Lucy Shields. Sur. Thomas Shields. p. 54

18 October 1819. Shubel T. BARNARD and Sarah C. Adams. Sur. Charles S. Adams. Married by the Rev. Griffith Dickinson. p. 68

14 February 1823. Smith BARNARD and Frances Chisum, dau. of James Chisum. Sur. Hezekel P. Smithson. Married 21 Feb. by the Rev. William Blair. p. 77

3 January 1809. John BARNES and Frances Burch, dau. of John Burch who consents. Sur. Dandridge Burch. p. 46

25 September 1815. Samuel BARNES and Jane Scott, dau. of Niven (?) Scott who consents. Sur. Jeremiah Scott. p. 57

18 March 1810. Nathaniel BARNET and Elizabeth Sutherlin. Married by the Rev. William Blair. Minister's Return. p. 47

30 September 1816. Joseph BARNETT and Polly Newbill, dau. of John Newbill who consents. Sur. Stephen T. Woodson. Married by the Rev. William Blair on 3 October. p. 60

1 April 1811. Robert BARNETT and Nancy Brown, dau. of Henry Brown who consents. Sur. Daniel Brown. Married 18 April by the Rev. Griffith Dickinson. p. 49

21 December 1808. Thomas BARNETT and Polley Sutherlin, dau. of Thomas Sutherlin who consents. Sur. Joseph Burnett. Married by the Rev. George Dodson. p. 44

16 August 1826. George BARRETT and Mary Walker, who gives her own consent as "of age". Sur. John Wilson. Married 19 Aug. by the Rev. Griffith Dickinson. p. 85

17 December 1827. William BARRETT and Nancy Wright. Sur. John Barrett. Nancy signs her certificate as "a free woman of age"; George right also signs. Married 21 Dec. by the Rev. Griffith Dickinson. p. 87

18 February 1812. John DARROW and Sally Walker. Sur. Vincent Walker. No relationship stated. Married by the Rev. Griffith Dickinson. (Minister says Feb. 11). p. 52

14 June 1822. Arthur DAUGH and Frances Sutherlan, dau. of Mary Sutherlan who consents. Sur. William H. White. p. 74

13 February 1827. John BAXTER and Sarah Willis. Married by the Rev. William S. Plumer. Minister's Return. p. 87

22 May 1806. Abednigo BAYES and Tabitha Jennins. Married by the Rev. Griffith Dickinson. Minister's Return. p. 40

15 July 1811. Beverly BAYS and Nancy Bays who writes her own consent. Sur. Hubbard Farmer. p. 49

4 July 1818. Isham BAYS and Polley Taylor. Sur. Obediah Taylor. Married "in 1818" by the Rev. David Nowlin. p.65

19 April 1819. John BAYS and Polly Hatchett. Sur. Edward Hatchett. Married 22 April by the Rev. William Blair. p. 60

15 February 1808. Josiah BAYES and Lettice Mayes, dau. of Elizabeth Mayse who consents. Sur. Fleming Mase. p. 44

3 September 1827. Joshua BAYS and Lucinda Owen. Sur. David Owen. Married 6 Sept. by the Rev. John W. Kelly. p. 88

21 October 1822. Joshua BEAL and Frances Neal. Sur. Stephen Neal. Married 24 Oct. by the Rev. Griffith Dickinson. p. 74

20 December 1814. William BEAL and Nancy Lea, dau. of Matthew Lea who consents. Sur. Stephen Lea. p. 56

1 December 1815. Warner Beasley and Elizabeth Burton, dau. of Nancy Burton who consents. Sur. James Nance. Married 11 Dec. by the Rev. Thomas Sparks. p. 57

25 January 1819. Charles BEAVER and Polley Newman. Sur. Henry Newman. Married 25 Jan. by the Rev. Joel Ashworth who says, "within a few days after this date." p. 68

26 January 1829. Edwin R. BEAVERS and Elizabeth B. Carter. Sur. William Carter. p. 93

18 July 1825. John F. BEAVERS and Elizabeth Soyars. Sur. James Soyars. Married -- July by the Rev. William Blair. p. 82 (Minister's Return is torn.)

4 November 1812. Joseph BEAVERS and Lettice Railey. Sur. William McNealy. Married 6 Nov. by the Rev. William Blair. p. 52

8 November 1817. James BECK and Lucy H. Dickenson. Sur. John Fowlks. William Dickenson, Guardian of Lucy, and Lucy herself, sign the certificate. Consent dated: Nottoway County, Virginia, Sept. 25, 1817. Married 20 Nov. by the Rev. William Davis. p. 62

15 July 1811. Richard B. BECK and Lucy Devin, daughter of Elizabeth Devin whose consent says that she, Elizabeth, is widow of Joseph Devin, Deceased. Sur. James Beck. p. 49

17 September 1816. Samuel BECK and Joannah Parrish, dau. of Abram Parrish who consents. Sur. Richard B. Beck. Married 8 October by the Rev. James Beck. p. 60

10 March 1830. William BECK and Irena Stone. Sur. Samuel Beck. William Beck, Guardian of Ireney Stone, signs the certificate. Married 12 March by the Rev. Orson Martin. p. 95

8 December 1830. David BEEN and Elizabeth Martin. Married by the Rev. Clement M. McDonald. Minister's Return. p. 95

10 October 1814. Elisha BELL and Sarah Baber, dau. of Joice Baber (father), who consents. Sur. Joseph West. Married by the Rev. Nathaniel Lovelace. Return made in 1815. p. 56

19 April 1819. Abner BENNETT and Nancy Edwards. Sur. Coleman Edwards. Married 13 May by the Rev. Shadrack Mustain. p. 68

2 June 1817. Bartlett BENNETT and Polly Brown. Sur. David Roarer. Married 3 June by the Rev. Shadrack Mustain. p. 62

8 January 1811. Dodson BENNETT and Polley Wright, dau. of James S. Wright who is Surety. p. 49

6 February 1823. John BENNETT and Ann Linsey. Sur. John Ratliff. Married 6 Feb. by the Rev. William Blair. p. 77

20 December 1812. Lewis BENNETT and Polly Towler. Sur. William Towler. No relationship stated. Married 21 Dec. by the Rev. Joseph Hatchett. p. 52

23 February 1822. Reubin BENNETT and Polly Tosh, dau. of George Tosh who consents. Sur. John Tosh. Married 1 March by the Rev. Ira Ellis. p. 74

8 March 1820. Thomas BENNETT and Clary Dalton. Sur. William Dalton. Married 8 March by the Rev. Shadrack Mustain. p. 70

17 September 1817. Walden BENNETT and Tabitha Dove. Sur. Jarrett P. Dalton. p. 87

13 December 1817. William BENNETT and Mildred Bobbett. Sur. Peter Bennett. Married 13 Dec. by the Rev. Shadrack Mustain. p. 62

15 December 1825. William BENNETT and Mary Linsey. Married 15 Dec. by the Rev. William Blair. p. 82

12 December 1826. Winston BENNETT and Elizabeth Berger. Sur. John Berger. p. 85

18 January 1810. Selby BENSON and Nancy Osborn. Married by the Rev. William Blair. Minister's Return. p. 47

16 February 1829. Daniel BERGER and Elizabeth S. Jones.
Sur. William Graves. John Jones signs the certificate.
No relationship stated. Married 26 Feb. by the Rev. Cris-
pen Dickenson. p. 93

-- ---- 1809. William BERGER and Nancy Lewis. Married by
the Rev. Elias Dodson. Minister's Return. (This return
is in the 1809 package but not dated.) p. 46

6 October 1825. Alfred BETHEL and Martha B. Sullivan.
Sur. William H. Tunstall. Married 6 Oct. by the Rev. Clement McDonald. p. 82

26 February 1810. Joshua BETTERTON and Mary West. Married by the Rev. Griffith Dickinson. Minister's Return.
p. 48

19 December 1808. Pierce BILLINGS and Elizabeth Dennison,
dau. of Richard Dennison who consents. Sur. James Soyars.
Married 8 February 1809 by the Rev. Thomas Sparks. p. 44

9 August 1827. Pierce BILLINGS and Calvy Gray, dau. of
Narby Gray who consents. Sur. John Gray. p. 87

11 February 1817. Christopher BINGHAM and Rody Mays.
Sur. Nathaniel Faris. Married 15 Feb. by the Rev. Shadrack Mustain who says Rhoda Mays. p. 62

21 December 1816. Lemuel BIRTHRIGHT and Polly S. Black,
dau. of Susanna Black whose note says, "she is without
father or guardian." Sur. Reuben G. Dews. Married 26
Dec. by the Rev. Griffith Dickinson. p. 60

14 February 1816. John BLACK and Margaret Dearing. Married by the Rev. Griffith Dickinson. Minister's Return.
p. 60

21 April 1815. Leroy BLACKBOURN and Patsey M. Lewis. Sur.
Littleberry Lewis. Married by the Rev. David Nowlin. p.57

31 January 1828. Russell BLACKWELL and Judith Prewit, dau.
of Absolem Prewet who consents. Sur. John Jackson. p. 90

11 January 1814. John BLADES and Delphy Bradley, dau. of
Daniel Bradley who consents. Sur. Reubin Hall. Married
11 Jan. by the Rev. William Blair. p. 56

15 October 1827. Drury BLAIR and Chloe T. Coleman, dau.
of Chloe Coleman who consents. Sur. Johnson Coleman.
Married 10 November by the Rev. William Blair. p. 87

14 August 1810. John BLAIR and Salley Wade. Married by
the Rev. William Blair. Minister's Return. p. 47

8 September 1827. John F. BLAIR and Christian Keen, dau. of John Keen who consents. Sur. Charles Keen. Married 13 Sept. by the Rev. William Blair. p. 87

29 November 1813. Joseph BLAIR and Jane Matthews who writes her own consent. Sur. Samuel Thomas. Married 2 December by the Rev. William Blair. p. 54

26 July 1810. Samuel BLAIR and Polley Reynolds. Married by the Rev. William Blair. Minister's Return. p. 47

29 August 1809. Benjamin BLAKELY and Rachel Thomas, dau. of John Thomas. Sur. John Bowlin. Married 31 Aug. by the Rev. Thomas Boaz. p. 46

15 December 1824. Francis BLANKS and Fanny Duncan. Sur. Nathaniel Duncan. p. 79

3 August 1826. Henry BLANKS and Nancy Wyatt, dau. of James Wyatt who consents. Sur. Joel Blanks. p. 85

27 December 1826. Henry BLANKS, Jr. and Louisa Barksdale, dau. of Eliza Barksdale who consents. Sur. Claiborne B. Barksdale. p. 85

18 December 1820. James BLANKS and Jane Bruce. Sur. Joseph Blanks. Mary Farmer, guardian of Jane, signs the certifi- cate. Married by the Rev. John Jenkins. p. 70

25 December 1826. Joel BLANKS and Nancy M. Compton. Sur. Isaiah Compton. Married 4 January 1827 by the Rev. John W. Kelly. p. 85

27 September 1823. William BLANKS and Mary Blanks who signs her own consent. Sur. David Owen. David Owen and John Far- Mer testify that Mary is 21. Married 27 Sept. by the Rev. Griffith Dickinson. p. 77

16 November 1818. Charles BLUNT and Jane H. Johnson, dau. of Nancy Johnson who consents. Sur. Geo. W. Johnson. Mar- ried by the Rev. David Nowlin. p. 65

24 September 1821. Edmund A. BOAZ and Elizabeth Booker. Sur. Richard E. Booker. p. 72

6 October 1830. Isaac BOAZ and Easther Stow. Sur. James M. Stow. Married 9 Oct. by the Rev. Orson Martin. p. 95

-- ---- 1823. James BOAZ and Sarah Booker. Sur. Richard E. Booker. License requested by Richard E. Booker. No re- lationship stated. Edmond A. Boaz consents. p. 77 (Bond and consent are mutilated.)

4 January 1826. John BOAZ and Mildred Breedlove. Sur. James Boaz. William Beck, guardian of John Boaz, and Richard Breedlove, who consents for Mildred, sign the certificate. p. 85

2 September 1811. Thomas BOAZ and Phoebe Boaz. Sur. David Boaz. Married 5 Sept. by the Rev. Thomas Boaz. p.49

2 February 1816. Thomas BOAZ and Barbary Inman, dau. of William and Betsy Inman who consent. Sur. Henry Inman. p. 60

18 August 1806. William BOAZ and Suriah Bullington. Sur. Robert Bullington. Married 25 September by the Rev. William Blair. p. 40

4 October 1824. William BOAZ and Nancy Nelson. Sur. John Nelson. p. 79

6 February 1827. William BOBBETT and Nancy Rice. Sur. Macager Bennett. Charles Bobet and Benjamin Rice consent. Married 9 Feb. by the Rev. Shadrack Mustain. p. 87

9 December 1815. Thomas BOBBITT and Milley Dalton. Sur. Lewis Dalton. Married 20 Dec. by the Rev. Shadrack Mustain who says Milley is daughter of Lewis Dalton. p. 57

18 October 1819. Booten BOHANNON and Nancey Slayden. Sur. Samuel Slayden. James Slayden signs the certificate. No relationship stated. Married 21 September by the Rev. William Blair. p. 68

5 January 1825. James W. BOLING and Sarah Barber. Sur. Coleman Barber. p. 82

22 April 1817. Will BOLING and Lucy Pace. Sur. Thos. G. Tunstall. p. 62

17 November 1824. Smith BOLLING and Ann Thomas. Sur. William Holt. James Thomas signs the certificate. No relationship stated. p. 79

11 September 1806. William BOLLING and Nephana Hodges. Sur. Edmund Hodges. Jesse Hodges requests the license be issued. No relationship given. Married by the Rev. Richard Elliott who says Nephanon Hodges. p. 40

11 February 1823. George W. BOLLINGER and Lucinda Wingo. Married by the Rev. William Blair. Minister's Return. p.77

23 September 1823. Merriwether BOLTON and Nancy T. Price, dau. of Major Price, Sr., who consents. Sur. Pleasant Walker. Married 13 Nov. by the Rev. William Blair. p. 77

28 September 1830. George BOOKER and Elenor Murphy, dau. of Abigail Murphy whose consent says, "my daughter Eleaner." Sur. Terrell Hopper. Married 7 October by the Rev. William Blair. p. 95

15 November 1824. John BOOKER and Nancy Reynolds who signs her own certificate. Sur. James Blair. p. 79

17 March 1823. Richard E. BOOKER and Sally Boaz, who signs her own certificate. Sur. William Beck. p. 77

23 August 1825. Stephen BOOKER and Henrietta Bohannon, dau. of Nancy Bohannon who consents. Sur. Ludwell Bohannon. p. 82

3 July 1816. Berry BOOTH and Nancy Booth. Sur. William Atkinson. John Booth, grandfather of Berry, and Nancy (the bride) sign the certificate. John Booth, Jr. and Mary Booth say Nancy is in her 23rd year. p. 60

18 May 1818. John BOOTH and Mary ODeneal. Sur. Philip Harp. p. 65

3 May 1820. John BOOTH and Elizabeth Brown, who signs her own certificate. Sur. Winston Brown. Married 9 May by the Rev. William Blair. p. 70

21 July 1828. Lawson BOOTHE and Mary Jones. Sur. Phillip Elliott. James Elliott signs the certificate as "acting for Miss Mary Jones, her parents not being alive", gives consent. p. 90

5 July 1813. Thomas BOOTH and Elizabeth K. Geesling. Sur. William Spencer. Sarah Geesling and Epaphroditus Booth sign the certificate. p. 54

16 March 1812. Samuel M. BOOTHE and Rachel Harp. Sur. Adams Sutherlin. Married 19 March by the Rev. Thomas Sparks who says Merady Boothe. (Was he called by his middle name?) p. 52

24 December 1822. William BOOTH and Jemima Lane. Sur. William Hall. Married -- Dec. by the Rev. Ira Ellis. p. 74

2 December 1817. James BORDEN and Polley Eanes. Sur. William P. Tate. p. 62

17 June 1822. James BOSWELL and Polly Yattes. Sur. Samuel Yattes. Married 27 June by the Rev. Griffith Dickinson. p. 74

5 February 1819. John BOTNER and Malinda Watson. who signs her own certificate. Sur. William Farthing. Married 6 Feb. by the Rev. William Blair. p. 68

13 January 1829. William BOULDING and Susanna Campbell. Sur. Creed T. Shelton. p. 93

20 April 1830. Thomas BOULTON and Susan L. Waller. Married by the Rev. William Blair. Minister's Return. p. 95

26 March 1806. Ozias BOW and Sally Oakes. Sur. Robert Oakes. Married by the Rev. Willis Hopwood. p. 40

15 April 1829. John BOWEN and Joanna Craft. Sur. George Craft. Married 5 May by the Rev. Crispen Dickenson. p. 93

29 August 1815. James BOWLIN and Frankey Dyer, dau. of Haymon Dyer. (He signs Hamon Dyer when he requests the license.) Sur. Haymon Dyer. Married 31 Aug. by the Rev. Thomas Boaz. p. 57

28 ---- 1806. John BOWLING and Hannah Jackson. Sur. Ephriam Jackson. Married by the Rev. Richard Elliott. p. 40 (Bond torn.)

6 November 1815. Thomas BOYD and Elizabeth Stamps, dau. of William Stamps who requests the license be issued. Sur. Marshall Waddill. Married 9 Nov. by the Rev. William Blair. p. 57

19 December 1825. Nacy BOZWELL and Susan Yeates, dau. of Samuel Yattes who consents. Sur. Banister Hardy. Married by the Rev. Griffith Dickinson who says Nacey Boswell. p. 82

21 December 1829. Samuel BRADLEY and Frances Slayton. Sur. Thomas Slayton. Married 24 Dec. by the Rev. William Blair. p. 93

24 December 1827. Henry BRADNER and Betsy Jones, who gives her own consent. Sur. William Headspeth. p. 87

18 December 1826. John C. BRADNER and Henrietta Craft. Sur. George Craft. Married 21 Dec. by the Rev. John W. Kelly. p. 85

14 December 1824. James BRANCH and Ann Farthing. Sur. Abner Farthing. p. 79

5 November 1821. Asa BRANSON and Nancy A. Jefferson. Sur. John Jefferson. Married 8 Nov. by the Rev. James Beck. p. 72

2 April 1818. George BRANSON and Rebecca Mahan. Sur. James Branson. Married 2 April by the Rev. James Beck. p. 65

21 October 1816. James BRANSON and Elizabeth Cook. Sur. Harmon Cook. Married 24 Oct. by the Rev. Shadrack Mustain. p. 60

29 May 1812. Christopher BRAY and Juley V. Adkins, who gives her own consent. Sur. George Stovall. p. 52

27 April 1824. David W. BREEDLOVE and Mary R. Still. Sur. Richard P. Breedlove. James Still signs the certificate. No relationship given. p. 79

28 November 1825. Samuel BREWER and Mary A. Pritchett. Sur. John M. Inge. William Pritchett signs the certificate. No relationship given. p. 82

30 October 1815. William BREWER and Patsy Jefferson. Sur. Samuel A. Jefferson. Married by the Rev. David Nowlin. p. 57

10 November 1806. Nelson BRIENT and Polley Pettey, dau. of Davis Pettey who consents. Sur. Zebulon Scates. Married 12 Nov. by the Rev. William Blair who says Nelson Briant. p. 40

26 January 1822. Joseph BRIMM and Sally Drane, dau. of William and Nancy Drane who consent. Sur. William Oakes. Married 29 Jan. by the Rev. James Beck. p. 74

16 December 1816. John BRISCOE and Agness P. Ware, dau. of William Ware who consents. Sur. Notley W. Briscoe. p. 60

9 October 1817. Robert BROADNAX and Ann R. Wilson. Sur. Thos. G. Tunstall. Married 14 Oct. by the Rev. Ira Ellis. p. 62

4 December 1806. Leonard BROOKS and Polley Fuller, dau. of Zachariah Fuller who consents for himself and wife. Sur. Brittain Fuller. Married 11 Dec. by the Rev. William Blair. p. 40

20 November 1815. Samuel BROOKS and Martha Griffey, widow of Nathan Griffey, deceased, who signs her own consent. Sur. William Adkins. Married by the Rev. Shadrack Mustain. (Minister says on Nov. 19.) p. 57

20 December 1827. Smith BROOKS and Nancy M. Gunter, dau. of Thomas Gunter who consents. Sur. Allen Caldwell. Married 20 Dec. by the Rev. William Blair. p. 87

-- ---- 1807. Alexander BROWN and Polley Fontaine, dau. of Elizabeth Fontaine who consents. Sur. William Beavers. Married 24 December by the Rev. William Blair. p. 42 (This bond has only 1807 for a date.)

29 May 1828. Biggers BROWN and Catharine Smith, dau. of Joseph Smith who consents. Sur. Thomas Smith. p. 90

21 September 1818. Bird BROWN and Henrietta Brown. Sur. Richard Wright. Married 22 Sept. by the Rev. William Blair. p. 65
Consent:
    "To the Clerk of Pittsylvania Court -
                        Sir this will be your
Justification for Issuing License for my Daughter Henrietta Brown to Inter marry with Bird Brown and also my consent for my son Bird Brown to Intermarry with her the said Henrietta Brown. Given under our hands this 19th day of September 1818.
Wit: William Payne   Langston Brown
     Richd Brown   Rebecah X Brown"

23 December 1824. Bird T. BROWN and Frances Shelton, dau. of Thomas Shelton who consents. Sur. William Shelton. Married 27 Dec. by the Rev. William Blair. p. 80

13 October 1819. Brazton BROWN and Rebecca Donnelson, dau. of Richard Donnelson who consents. Sur. John Madding. Married 16 December 1819 by the Rev. William Blair. p. 68

9 October 1812. Burwell BROWN and Polly Holder. Sur. William Hall. Married 6 November by the Rev. William Blair. p. 52

9 February 1829. Burwell BROWN and Polley Barnett, who writes her own consent. Sur. William Hall. p. 93

16 October 1822. John BROWN, Jr. and Ann D. Craddock, who signs her own consent. Sur. Jesse Pitts. p. 74

30 March 1812. Landon BROWN and Elizabeth Gover, dau. of John Gover who consents. Sur. Nelson Phillips. p. 52

14 December 1829. Mordicai BROWN and Elinder Smith. Sur. Obadiah H. Brown. Married 23 Dec. by the Rev. William Blair who says Elianor Smith. p. 93

23 May 1819. Obediah BROWN and Sally Prewit. Sur. Austin Harriss. Married 1 June by the Rev. William Blair. p. 68

22 November 1808. Robert BROWN and Susanna Still, dau. of Thomas Still who consents. Sur. Josiah Still. p. 44

20

12 October 1810. Vincent BROWN and Milley Reynolds. Married by the Rev. William Blair. Minister's Return. p. 47

29 September 1806. Wyatt BROWN and Nancy Curtis, dau. of Reubin Curtis who consents. Sur. Arthur Cross. Married 2 October by the Rev. William Blair. p. 40

22 April 1816. Coleman H. BRUCE and Jane Roach. Sur. Burdett Roach. Married 22 April by the Rev. Shadrack Mustain. p. 60

25 November 1823. Coleman BRUCE and Elizabeth R. Swinny, dau. of James Swinney who consents. Sur. Thomas Irby. Married 27 Nov. by the Rev. Shadrack Mustain. p. 77

18 January 1819. Frederick BRUCE and Polley Abston. Sur. Francis Abston. Married 21 Jan. by the Rev. Shadrack Mustain. p. 68

18 January 1830. George BRUCE and Betsey Ann Lovelace. James Lovelace requests the license. Sur. Michael P. Tribble. p. 95

16 January 1828. Meredith BRUCE and Elizabeth Walden who writes her own consent. Sur. Charles P. Dalton. Married 20 Jan. by the Rev. Eben Angel. p. 90

18 December 1806. William BRUCE and Polly Eads. Married by the Rev. Griffith Dickinson. Minister's Return. p. 40

8 November 1824. William BRUCE and Susanna Dews, dau. of Reuben G. Dews who signs the certificate. Sur. John Tucker. Married 11 Nov. by the Rev. Shadrack Mustain. p. 79

5 December 1818. Isaac BRUMFIELD and Letty Mayhue. Sur. Henry Mayhue. Married by the Rev. Griffith Dickinson. p. 65

8 July 1823. James W. BRUMFIELD and Tallithecum Hoskins, who writes her own consent. Sur. Isaac Brumfield. Married 10 July by the Rev. Griffith Dickinson. p. 77

21 June 1827. Thomas H. BRUMFIELD and Ludey Mayhew. Sur. Henry Mayhew. p. 87

27 May 1817. William B. BRUMFIELD and Susanna Oakes. Sur. John Williams. p. 62

10 July 1813. Charles BRYANT and Nancy Orrender. Sur. Thomas Chambers. Married 15 July by the Rev. William Blair. p. 54

10 February 1824. Jesse S. BRYANT and Elizabeth Barker, dau. of Moses and Nancy Barker who consent. Sur. Larkin Lewis. Married by the Rev. David Nowlin. p. 79

24 March 1830. Jesse S. BRYANT and Keziah Chaney, dau. of Charles Chaney who consents. Sur. Samuel Chaney. p. 95

30 October 1816. William BRYANT and Pheby Shelton. Sur. David Shelton. p. 60

24 November 1818. William BRYANT and Elizabeth Adams, dau. of Redmon Adams who signs the certificate. Elizabeth also signs. Sur. Redmon Adams. Married 26 Nov. by the Rev. William Blair. p. 65

23 December 1818. William BUCK and Elizabeth H. Williamson. Sur. Wm. Watson. John Williamson consents. No relationship given. Married by the Rev. Griffith Dickinson. p. 65

1 November 1811. William BUFORD and Susanna Robertson Shelton, dau. of Vincent Shelton who consents. Sur. Booker Shelton. Married 2 Nov. by the Rev. Griffith Dickinson. p. 49

7 August 1824. James BULLINGTON and Anna Herndon. Sur. Moses Herndon. Married 10 Aug. by the Rev. Richard B. Beck. p. 79

5 November 1823. John BULLINGTON and Susanna Branson, dau. of Jonathan Branson who consents. Sur. Pleasant Mahan. p.77

2 December 1822. Josiah BULLINGTON and Sarah Mahon. Sur. Pleasant Mohon. p. 74

31 December 1808. Robert BULLINGTON and Arrey Adams, dau. of Luke Adams. Arrey signs her own consent. Sur. William Bullington. p. 44

2 December 1815. Robert BULLINGTON and Nancy Harvey. Sur. Ellis Wilson. p. 57

31 December 1824. Benton BUMPASS and Elizabeth P. Harris, dau. of Bezaleel and Elizabeth Wier who consent. (Consent says Bezaleel Wier, Senr.) Sur. Bezaleel Wier, Senr. Married 18 January 1825 by the Rev. William Blair. p. 79

30 May 1829. Henderson BUMPASS and Susan Harris. Sur. Benton Bumpass. L. M. Claiborne, guardian, signs the certificate. (Doesn't say whose guardian.) p. 93

18 January 1825. Benton BUMPAS and Eliza Harris. Married by the Rev. William Blair. Minister's Return. p. 82

7 March 1815. John BURCH and Fanny Welden. (Weldon?) Sur. Jonathan Weldon. p. 57

3 February 1827. Robert BURCH and Manerva Raney, dau. of Mary Raney who consents. Sur. John Barnes. p. 87

11 January 1830. Henry BURGESS and Judea Earls, dau. of Thomas Earls who consents. Sur. Clement S. Farmer. Married 13 Jan. by the Rev. Richard B. Beck. p. 95

5 February 1811. William BURGESS and Rhoda Chaney. Married by the Rev. Elias Dodson. Minister's Return. p. 49

17 October 1808. Barnett BURNETT and Elizabeth Campbell, who writes her own consent. Sur. Benjamin Burnett. p. 44

28 September 1812. Benjamin BURNETT and Betsey Harvey. Sur. Thomas Burnett. No relationship given. Married 30 Sept. by the Rev. Thomas Boaz. p. 52

20 September 1813. Godfrey BURNETT and Massey Twedwell, dau. of Benjamin Twedwell who consents. Sur. Thomas Cooper. Married 30 Sept. by the Rev. William Blair. p. 54

2 August 1825. James BURNETT and Rebecca Nicholas, dau. of Chas. Nicholas who requests the license. Sur. Stokely Farthing. Married 4 Aug. by the Rev. Griffith Dickinson. p. 82

14 January 1826. Malekijah BURNETT and Sarah Shelton. Sur. John Burnett. p. 85

16 March 1816. Thomas BURNETT and Seeny Dallis, dau. of Robert Dallis who consents. Sur. Terry Dallis. p. 60

21 December 1829. Thomas BURNETT and Polly Strattin. Sur. Thomas Strattin. Married 24 Dec. by the Rev. William Blair. p. 93

24 January 1808. William BURNETT and Pheby Roland. Married by the Rev. Griffith Dickinson who says Barnett. (Minister's Report says married "June 24, 1808.") p. 44

16 September 1816. Edward BURNETT and Nancy Johnson. Sur. Wm. B. Alexander. p. 60

17 May 1826. Edmond BURTON and Susanna Peerman. Married by the Rev. William Blair. Minister's Return. p. 85

19 January 1829. James BURTON and Nancy Thomas, dau. of Henson Thomas who consents. Sur. Samuel Beck. p. 93

18 February 1830. John BURTON and Lucy Pass. Married by the Rev. A. D. Montgomery. Minister's Return. p. 95

23 October 1806. William BURTON and Anna Harris, dau. of
John Harris, Senr. Sur. John Harris, Jr. Married 4 November by the Rev. Joseph Hatchett. p. 40

27 January 1827. William BUSTLE and Edith Robertson. Sur.
James Allen. Married 29 Jan. by the Rev. William Blair.
p. 87

20 December 1819. Jonathan BUTLER and Rebecca Douglas, dau.
of Mary Douglas who signs the certificate. Rebecca also
signs. Sur. William Rogers. Married 23 Dec. by the Rev.
John Jenkins. p. 68

26 October 1821. Barney CAHALL and Eleanor Hall, who signs
her own certificate. Sur. Clement Wilson. Married 26 Oct.
by the Rev. James Beck. p. 72

18 September 1817. John C. CALHOUN and Sally Bustle. Sur.
Elisha Billins. p. 63

13 July 1818. John B. CALLAHAN and Martha Thompson, dau. of
Jennings Thompson who consents. Sur. Pyrant Thompson. Married 29 July by the Rev. William Blair. p. 65

12 March 1808. Samuel CALLAND, Jr. and Elizabeth C. Johnson,
dau. of Richard Johnson whose consent says, "my Daughter
Elizabeth Chaney Johnson." Sur. James Hinton. p. 44

20 March 1815. Henry CALLOWAY and Millicent Hailey. Sur.
Joseph E. Hailey. p. 58

17 February 1812. James CALLOWAY and Catharine M. Markham,
who writes her own consent. Sur. James Whitehead. Married
by the Rev. David Nowlin. p. 52

29 July 1811. Daniel CAMERON and Ruth Rowland, dau. of
Jesse Rowland who consents. Sur. Charles Nichols. Married
by the Rev. Thomas Payne. (Minister says 30 July.) p. 50

28 April 1807. John CAMERON and Sarah Lewis, who writes her
own. consent. Sur. James Moore. Married 29 April by the
Rev. Thomas Payne. p. 42

17 November 1827. William H. CAMP and Catharine M. Whitehead. Sur. James Whitehead. Married 13 December by the
Rev. Griffith Dickinson. p. 88

4 April 1822. Galaway CAMPBELL and Maria Getton. Sur. William Tuggle. p. 74

10 May 1821. John CAMPBELL and Susanna Shelton. Sur.
Daniel Shelton. Married -- May by the Rev. Ira Ellis. p.72

17 February 1810. William CAMPBELL and Sarah Ball, dau. of John Ball. Married by the Rev. Joseph Hatchett. Minister's Return. p. 48

18 December 1815. William CAMPBELL and Sally Raleigh, who signs her own consent. Sur. William McNealey. Married 18 Dec. by the Rev. Shadrack Mustain. p. 57

25 February 1825. Johnson CANDLER and Lucy W. Holt, who writes her own consent. Sur. Absolom Farmer. Married 3 March by the Rev. John G. Mills. p. 82

3 December 1829. John CARMICAL and Lucy Burgess, who writes her own consent. Sur. Robert Carmical. Married 6 Dec. by the Rev. William Blair. p. 93

4 January 1809. John CARNS and Fanny Burch. Married by the Rev. William Blair. Minister's Return. p. 46

20 December 1812. Augustin H. CARTER and Rebecca Soyars. Sur. James Soyars. No relationship stated. p. 52

3 November 1815. Charles E. CARTER and Nancy Morris, who signs her own certificate. Sur. John Barnes. Married 6 Nov. by the Rev. Thomas Boaz. p. 57

28 October 1809. Christopher L. CARTER and Polley Sawyers, dau. of James Sawyers. Sur. James Sawyers. p. 46

24 September 1827. Edward H. CARTER and Harriet L. Ragsdale. Sur. Thomas Ragsdale. p. 88

22 January 1827. Henry CARTER and Malinda Wilson, dau. of Polley Wilson whose consent says Henry Carter of Charlotte County. Polley also signs the certificate. Sur. John Durham. Married 27 Jan. by the Rev. Eben Angel. p. 88

28 April 1823. Jesse CARTER and Sally W. Muse, dau. of Thomas Muse who consents. Sur. Thomas Carter. p. 77

1 December 1806. Joseph CARTER and Nancey Robertson, dau. of Christopher Robertson, Senr., who in his consent, says his daughter, Nancey, is of age. Nancey writes her own consent on the same piece of paper. Sur. Jennings Thompson. p. 40

18 October 1814. Miller CARTER and Polly Grimes. Sur. Richard Dennison. Married 20 Oct. by the Rev. William Blair. p. 56

25 June 1812. Paschal CARTER and Elizabeth Durrett, dau. of Mary Durrett who consents. Sur. Levin Carter. Married 25 June by the Rev. William Blair. p. 52

28 November 1829. Rawley W. CARTER and Nancy M. Walton, dau. of Jesse Walton who consents. Sur. Pleasant K. Walton. Rawley W. Carter, Junr. is written up in the bond. Married 3 December by the Rev. George Stevens. p. 93

16 December 1811. Robert CARTER and Rebecca Winn. Sur. Thomas Stewart. Married 24 Dec. by the Rev. William Blair. p. 50

18 December 1820. Stewart CARTER and Celia Vass, dau. of Greenberry Vass who consents. Sur. Pleasant Vass. p. 70

20 October 1807. Thomas CARTER and Elizabeth Pierce. Sur. James Elliott. p. 42

26 September 1827. Thomas CARTER and Bathina Shaw. Sur. Jesse Shaw. Married 28 Sept. by the Rev. Clement McDonald. p. 88

25 April 1829. Thomas CARTER, Jr. and Sarah H. Giles. Sur. Ephriam Giles. p. 93

27 December 1823. Thomas CARTER, Jr. and Elizabeth Lilly, dau. of William A. Lilly who authorizes the license be issued. Sur. John Pinnell. Married -- Dec. by the Rev. Ira Ellis. p. 77

21 January 1809. John CASEY and Phebe Ragsdale, dau. of John Ragsdale, deceased. Sur. Thomas Elliott. Married 10 February by the Rev. Thomas Sparks. p. 46

9 November 1810. Jesse CASSADA and Anna Harness. Married by the Rev. William Blair. Minister's Return. p. 48

28 November 1815. John CAVENDER and Elizabeth Compton, dau. of Jeremiah Compton who consents. Sur. Edmond Chumbley. p. 58

20 June 1807. Nathan CHAFFIN, Jr. and Nancy Adams, dau. of George Adams. Sur. Sylvester Adams. p. 42

3 January 1826. Elijah CHAINEY and Sally Hall, who gives her own consent. Sur. Reubin Chainey. Married 12 Jan. by the Rev. William Blair who says Elijah Chaney. p. 85

6 August 1814. Moses CHAINEY and Sally Polly, *a (Colly)* who gives her own consent. Sur. John Hailey. Married by the Rev. George Dodson who says Moses Chaney. p. 56

14 April 1822. William CHAINEY and Elizabeth Bradley. Sur. Samuel Bradley. Married 30 April by the Rev. William Blair. p. 74

26 September 1809. Allen CHANDLER and Frances Parrish, dau. of Abram Parrish. Sur. Matthew Parrish. Married by the Rev. William Blair. (Minister says 4 September.) p. 46

15 January 1827. William CHANDLER and Martha B. White, dau. of Hamilton White who consents. Sur. James B. White. Married 16 Jan. by the Rev. William S. Plummer. p. 88

-- ---- 1809. Joseph CHANEE and Nancy Shelton. Married by the Rev. Elias Dodson. Minister's Return. p. 46

28 December 1811. Abraham CHANEY and Nancy Donalson. Married by the Rev. Elias Dodson. Minister's Return. p. 50

17 April 1815. Ezekial CHANEY and Polly Hill. Sur. Joseph Hill. Married 20 April by the Rev. George Dodson. p. 58

15 November 1830. Isiah CHANEY and Sarah Chaney, who signs her own consent. Sur. Reuben Chaney. Married 16 Nov. by the Rev. John Leigh who says Josiah Chaney. p. 95

3 February 1824. Jonas CHANEY and Nancy Hittson. Sur. William Johnson. Alexander Hillson (Hittson?) signs the certificate. No relationship given. Married 5 Feb. by the Rev. William Blair. p. 80

21 January 1822. Joseph CHANEY and Lucy Chaney. Sur. Moses Chaney. Married 23 Jan. by the Rev. William Blair. p. 74

4 November 1822. Reubin CHANEY and Nancy Burch, dau. of John Burch, Senr. who signs the certificate. (He signs with a mark.) He says, "we are willing." Sur. John Burch. (He signs his name.) p. 74

20 April 1829. Singleton CHANEY and Mary Ford, dau. of Elisha and Rebecca Ford who consent. Sur. Gerald Ford. Married 20 April by the Rev. John Leigh. p. 93

6 March 1815. William CHANEY and Nancy Polly, dau. of Sally Chaney. Sur. John Hailey, who writes the certificate for Salley Chaney and Nancy. Married by the Rev. George Dodson. (Moses Chainey married Sally Polly in 1814.) p. 58

8 November 1806. William CHAPMAN and Delila Spencer. Sur. Jesse Shaw. Married by the Rev. Thomas Sparks. p. 40

4 April 1816. William CHAPMAN and Elizabeth Fisher. Sur. Barksdale Fisher. Robert Chapman, father of William, and Barksdel Fisher, father of Elizabeth, consent. p. 60

16 December 1828. Nathaniel CHATTEN and Elizabeth Mottley. Sur. John Chatten. Thomas Chatten, father of Nathaniel, consents. p. 90

20 October 1829. John CHATTIN and Elizabeth Mattox. Sur. Samuel B. Mattox. p. 93

18 January 1813. Joseph CHATTIN and Jincey Myers. Sur. William Myers. Married 21 Jan. by the Rev. William Blair. p. 54

5 May 1829. William CHATTIN and Lucinda Walden, granddaughter of Milly Keesee whose consent says that both of Lucinda's parents are dead. Sur. John Chattin. Married 7 May by the Rev. Crispen Dickenson. p. 93

1 March 1810. William CHESHER and Amelia Betterton. Married by the Rev. Griffith Dickinson. Minister's Return. p. 48

11 November 1817. Dudley CHICK and Sally Wayne, dau. of Joseph Wayne who consents. Sur. William Denning. Married by the Rev. Griffith Dickinson, "since my last return." This return dated 1819. p. 63

10 September 1827. Joshua CHILDRES and Tabitha Haymore, dau. of John Haymore who consents. Sur. William Jones. p. 88

24 March 1818. John Wm. CHILDRESS and Phebe Midkiff. Sur. Thomas Turley. Abraham Midkiff says, "I have no objections." No relationship stated. Married 25 March by the Rev. Shadrack Mustain. p. 65

17 December 1830. Franklin P. CHILES and Ann E. White, dau. of Haml. White, who consents. (Hamilton White, Jr. witnesses this consent.) Sur. Thos. G. Tunstall. Married 23 Dec. by the Rev. Edwin G. Cabaniss, Baptist. p. 95

16 October 1827. John CHILTON and Elizabeth Epperson. Sur. John Travis, Jr. Francis Epperson consents. No relationship given. p. 88

4 February 1814. James CHISNHALL and Polly Oliver. Sur. Robert B. Atkins. p. 56

15 November 1830. John W. CHISUM and Lettice R. Fackler, dau. of George Fackler who consents. Sur. Samuel Soyars. Married 16 Nov. by the Rev. William Blair. p. 95

20 December 1826. Obadiah CHUMBLEY and Dicey Short. Sur. Robin Short. Married 25 Dec. by the Rev. Eben Angel. p. 85

10 October 1820. John CHUMBLY and Sarah K. Rowland. Sur. Nimrod F. Rowland. John and Elizabeth Rowland, Sarah's parents, consent, and Sarah, also, signs the certificate. Married 12 Oct. by the Rev. Griffith Dickinson. p. 70

11 December 1826. Christopher CITY and Rachel Miller. Sur. James Miller. Married 22 January 1827 by the Rev. Shadrack Mustain. p. 85

22 December 1818. Leonard CLAIBORNE and Letitia W. Clark, dau. of William Clark who requests the license be issued. Sur. William S. Clark. p. 65

28 October 1815. William CLANTON and Polly Thornton, dau. of Rowland Thornton who consents. Sur. Jesse Wills. p. 57

29 September 1817. James H. CLARK and Nancy W. Coleman. Sur. Stephen Coleman. p. 63

17 October 1817. John CLARK and Rhoda Hamrick, dau. of David Hamrick who signs the certificate. Sur. William Hamrick. p. 62

20 March 1815. Warren CLARK and Rebecca Frizzle, dau. of Abraham Frizzle who consents. Sur. Jacob Norton. p. 58

25 December 1823. William CLARK and Elizabeth Hardy who gives her own consent. Sur. Philip Hawker. p. 77

22 December 1809. Leonard CLARKE and Ann Snoddy, dau. of John Snody who consents. Sur. George Cook. Married by the Rev. George Dodson. p. 46

19 November 1811. George W. CLEMENT and Lettice Smith, dau. of John Smith. Sur. Ralph Smith. Married 1 Dec. by the Rev. Joseph Hatchett. p. 50
(The bond says Lettice Smith. In the Register, written over this, in pencil, is Stella Smith.)

21 September 1829. Abram CLEMENTS and Martha Ann Callaway. Sur. Henry C. Ward. p. 93

14 May 1807. Daniel CLEMENTS and Wilmoth Irby. Married by the Rev. Griffith Dickinson. Minister's Return. p. 42

3 November 1828. John CLIFT and Catharine Jacobs. Sur. Henry Jacobs. Married 4 Nov. by the Rev. Richard B. Beck. p. 90

14 July 1829. John M. CLOPTON and Mary W. Terry. Sur. Benjamin F. Terry. William L. Terry signs the certificate. No relationship stated. Married 15 July by the Rev. William Blair. p. 93

19 January 1818. Edmund W. COBBS and Polley Worsham, dau. of Elizabeth Worsham who consents. Sur. Selby Benson. p. 65

26 May 1828. John COBBS, Jr. and Mildred Ann Stone, dau. of James H. Stone who consents. Sur. Thomas A. Cobbs. p. 90

22 December 1829. Eli COLE and Mary F. Posey, dau. of Robert Posey who consents. Sur. Joel H. Tanner. Married 23 Dec. by the Rev. William Blair. p. 93

15 December 1828. John S. COLE and Casandra White. Sur. James C. Cole. Casandra, daughter of John White whose consent says, "Doctor John S. Cole and my daughter Casandra Caroline." Married 25 Dec. by the Rev. Griffith Dickinson. p. 90

3 September 1809. Daniel S. COLEMAN and Nancy Robertson, dau. of George Robertson. Sur. James Robertson. Married 6 Sept. by the Rev. William Blair. p. 46

21 July 1824. Joel COLEMAN and Milley Robertson, dau. of Christopher Robertson who consents. Sur. Samuel Hutchings. Married 2 August by the Rev. James Beck. p. 70 (Is this a double wedding? See Samuel Hutchings.)

31 October 1827. Johnson COLEMAN and Martha G. Douglass, dau. of John Douglass who consents. Sur. Edward Douglass. Married 6 November by the Rev. Griffith Dickinson. p. 88

11 September 1824. Matthew W. COLEMAN and Mary Goodwin, dau. of Jane Goodwin who consents. Sur. William Mays. p. 80

7 January 1820. Robert COLEMAN and Sarah Crews, dau. of Susannah Crews who consents. Sur. John Crews. Married 13 Jan. by the Rev. Shadrack Mustain. p. 70

4 November 1816. Stephen COLEMAN and Susannah Robertson, dau. of George Robertson who signs the certificate. Sur. Allen Stokes. Married 7 Nov. by the Rev. William Blair. p. 60

23 October 1830. Jacob T. COLES and Nancy Catherine Patton, dau. of James D. Patton whose consent is dated, "Danville, Oct: 22d 1830." Sur. W. H. Tunstall. Married 28 Oct. by the Rev. A. D. Montgomery. p. 95

24 November 1825. Jno. COLES and Louisa M. Payne. Married by the Rev. Griffith Dickinson. Minister's Return. p. 82

27 November 1827. Robert T. COLES and Elizabeth F. Patton. Sur. William H. Tunstall. Married 28 Nov. by the Rev. A. D. Montgomery. p. 88

30 November 1818. Obediah COLLEY and Sarah Willis, dau. of Joel Willis who consents. Sur. Samuel Willis. Married by the Rev. David Nowlin. p. 65

30

18 March 1816. William COLLEY and Patsey Carter. Sur.
Charles E. Carter. Married 30 May by the Rev. William
Blair. p. 60

28 January 1811. Daniel COLLIE and Peggy Dodson, dau. of
George Dodson who consents. Peggy also signs the certifi-
cate. Sur. George Richardson. Married by the Rev. Elias
Dodson. p. 50

6 March 1809. Philip COLLIE and Rhoda Dodson, dau. of
George Dodson who consents. Rhoda also signs the consent.
Sur. John Dodson. Married by the Rev. Elias Dodson. p. 46

31 October 1826. David COLLINS and Margaret Thomas, dau. of
William Thomas who consents. Sur. Abraham Thomas. p. 85

21 February 1820. Hiram COLLINS and Matilda Reynolds. Sur.
John H. Kendrick. p. 70

7 December 1821. Hyram COLLINS and Lucy Atkins. Sur. William Atkins. Married by the Rev. David Nowlin. p. 72

-- ---- 1817. John COLLINS and Wilmoth Seamore. Married by
the Rev. Griffith Dickinson. Minister's Return. p. 62

11 February 1824. Abraham COLSTON and Peachy H. Breedlove.
Sur. David W. Breedlove. Richard Breedlove signs the certificate. No relationship given. p. 80

27 December 1813. John COMPTON and Rebecca Chisnhall. Sur.
John Chisnhall. p. 54

13 November 1813. Levi COMPTON and Elizabeth Epperson.
Sur. John Blanks. p. 54

26 July 1824. William COMPTON and Philida East, dau. of
Thomas East who consents. Sur. Micajah Compton. Married
28 July by the Rev. Griffith Dickinson. p. 80

15 November 1824. James W. CONWAY and Ann Stamps, dau. of
Timothy Stamps who consents. Sur. Beverly Lindsey. Married -- Nov. by the Rev. William Blair. p. 80

15 March 1828. David COOK and Mary W. King. Sur. Peyton
King. p. 90

7 September 1812. Fr. Born Garson COOK and Ruth Butt, dau.
of Elizabeth Butt who consents. Sur. John Clark. p. 52

15 March 1808. George COOK and Phebe Dalton, dau. of Milley
Slayton who consents for "her daughter". Sur. Alexander
Cook. Married by the Rev. George Dodson. p. 44

25 October 1828. James COOK and Susanna Curry, who signs her own consent as "above 21". Sur. Washington Cook. Married 28 Oct. by the Rev. William Blair. p. 90

6 August 1822. John COOK and Sarah Bolling, dau. of Joseph Bolen who consents. Sur. Thomas Muse. Married -- Aug. by the Rev. Ira Ellis. p. 74

16 July 1827. Philip COOK and Elizabeth Earp. Sur. Matthew Earp. p. 88

4 March 1822. Thomas COOK and Nancy Boling, dau. of Joseph Bolen who consents. Sur. Thomas Muse. Married 4 March by the Rev. John W. Kelly. p. 74

23 March 1827. William COOK and Precilla Earp. Sur. Samuel Earp. p. 88

14 November 1811. William H. COOK and Nancy Motley, dau. of Elizabeth Motley who consents. Sur. Floyd Tanner. Married by the Rev. David Nowlin. p. 49

27 August 1806. John M. COOKSEY and Dorcas McMillion, dau. of Joseph McMillion who consents. Sur. Joseph McMillion. Married 28 Aug. by the Rev. William Blair. p. 40

19 December 1825. Sterling S. COOPER and Elizabeth Ramsey, dau. of Hailey S. Ramsey who consents. Sur. Elijah Hughes. Married 24 Dec. by the Rev. Orson Martin. p. 82

14 March 1814. Richard CORAM and Polly Oaks, dau. of William Oakes who consents. Sur. Isaac Oaks. p. 56

17 December 1827. Jackson CORBIN and Elizabeth Owen, dau. of Julius Owen who consents. Sur. William Abbott. Married 25 Dec. by the Rev. Crispen Dickenson. p. 88

8 October 1818. Jamison CORBIN and Sarah Davis, dau. of Benjamin Davis who requests the license be issued. Sur. James Davis. Married 9 Oct. by the Rev. William Blair. p.65

18 December 1806. Thomas CORBIN and Nancy Grigsby. Sur. William Meadows. Thomas Corbin, father of Thomas, consents and says his son is under age. Moses Grigsby, father of Nancy, consents. Married by the Rev. David Nowlin. p. 42

29 January 1822. Shadrack CORDER and Elizabeth Thomas. Sur. James Thomas. Married 31 Jan. by the Rev. James Beck. p. 74

25 April 1816. William H. CORN and Polly Dejarnett. Sur. George Dejarnett. p. 60

5 October 1807. Foushee C. CORNWELL and Betse Cheatham. Sur. William How. Abia Cheatham consents. No relationship stated. Married by the Rev. Elisha Dodson. p. 42

28 December 1811. Samuel CORNWELL and Rhody A. Moore who signs her own consent. Sur. Charles Cornwell. Married by the Rev. George Dodson. p. 50

15 February 1813. Silas C. CORNWELL and Jane Shields. Sur. Pleasant Shields. Married 16 Feb. by the Rev. William Blair. p. 54

23 March 1812. Thompson CORNWELL and Jane Yeaman. Sur. John Yeaman. No relationship stated. Married 26 March by the Rev. William Blair. p. 52

1 April 1816. William G. CORNWELL and Elizabeth Yeaman, dau. of John Yeaman who consents. Sur. Silas C. Cornwell. Married 4 April by the Rev. George Dodson. p. 60

17 December 1827. Peter G. COUSINS and Edna Stone. Sur. Isaac Stone. p. 88

13 December 1830. Robert COUSINS and Mariah Smith. Married by the Rev. A. D. Montgomery. Minister's Return. p. 95

18 November 1825. Willis G. COUSINS and Elizabeth Royall, dau. of Eliza Royall who consents. Sur. Solomon Fuller. p. 82

23 December 1826. Allen H. COVINGTON and Elizabeth Wells, dau. of John Wells who requests the license be issued. Sur. George W. Eanes. p. 85

17 September 1821. George COVINGTON and Anna Osbourn who signs her own certificate. Sur. James Harman. Married 23 Sept. by the Rev. Richard B. Beck. p. 72

20 September 1824. Harrison COVINGTON and Peggy Gover who signs her own certificate. Sur. John Garrett, Jr. Married 20 Sept. by the Rev. Richard B. Beck. p. 80

2 December 1810. Isham COX and Lucy Farmer. Married by the Rev. Griffith Dickinson. Minister's Return. p. 48

14 June 1823. Isham COX and Susanna Saunders. Sur. Matthew Barber. Jane Saunders requests the license be issued. No relationship given. Married 18 June by the Rev. Shadrack Mustain. p. 77

5 January 1809. Robert COX and Sally Alexander, dau. of William Alexander who consents. Sur. William Spencer. Married 6 Jan. by the Rev. Thomas Payne. p. 46

15 January 1827. Samuel COX and Mary A. C. Sutherlin. Sur. Adams Sutherlin. Married 25 Jan. by the Rev. William Blair. p. 88

19 March 1807. Thomas COX and Sarah Bruce. Married by the Rev. Griffith Dickinson. Minister's Return. p. 42

24 January 1814. Asa CRADDOCK and Nancy Pitts, dau. of Lucy Pitts. Sur. John T. Craddock. Lucy Pitts writes: "Nancy is under age. Please issue this marriage license and you will oblige me and my father who is guardian of all my children." John Brown, as guardian, signs the certificate. Married by the Rev. Nathaniel Lovelace. p. 56

26 February 1821. Edmond CRADDOCK and Elizabeth Pitts, dau. of Lucy Pitts who consents. Sur. Coleman Pitts. Married 1 March by the Rev. Griffith Dickinson. p. 72

29 May 1816. Samuel CRADDOCK and Caty Foust. Sur. Jacob Foust. Married 30 May by the Rev. James Beck. p. 60

18 January 1819. Samuel CRADDOCK and Susanna Foust, dau. of Jacob and Eve Fous who consent. Sur. Michael Foust. p. 68

28 March 1828. William CRAIGHEAD and Susannah Maxy. Married by the Rev. Abner Anthony. Minister's Return. p. 90

19 December 1811. Aaron CRANE and Frankey Right, dau. of Milley Right who consents. Sur. Philip Brice. Married 24 Dec. by the Rev. William Blair. p. 49
(The Register designates Milley Right as "father".)

21 February 1820. Henry CRANE and Elizabeth McNeeley. Sur. William McNeeley. Married 24 Feb. by the Rev. Shadrack Mustain. p. 70

21 February 1820. Jacob CRAYN (Crane?) and Nancy Debo. Sur. Philip Debo. Married 22 Feb. by the Rev. Shadrack Mustain. p. 70

5 August 1814. James CRANE and Nancy Dennison. Sur. Richard Dennison. p. 56

22 July 1819. Grief CRAWFORD and Nancy Short. Sur. Thomas Parsons. Lucy Bush signs the certificate. No relationship stated. Married July 1819. by the Rev. Ira Ellis. p. 68

21 March 1813. Christopher CREAMER and Nancy Parsons. Sur. John Parsons. Married 1 April by the Rev. Griffith Dickinson. p. 54

34

18 December 1821. Robert CREASY and Polly Erven Beck, dau. of Robert Beck whose consent says Robert Creasy is of Henry County. Sur. William Beck. p. 72

27 October 1806. William W. CRENSHAW and Susanna Walker. Sur. David Walker. Married 30 Oct. by the Rev. William Blair. p. 40

8 December 1829. Andrew CREWS and Lucy Neal. Sur. Abraham Neal. p. 93

29 March 1828. George W. CREWS and Tabitha O. Collins. Married by the Rev. Griffith Dickinson. Minister's Return. p. 90

13 March 1830. John CREWS and Sarah Tankersly who writes her own consent. Sur. Baldwin D. Arthur. Married by the Rev. Eben Angel. p. 95

6 April 1809. William CREWS and Elizabeth Abston. Married by the Rev. Griffith Dickinson. Minister's Return. p. 46

10 February 1810. David CRIDER and Polley Vance, dau. of David Vance. Married by the Rev. Joseph Hatchett. Minister's Return. p. 48

15 June 1807. Samuel CRIDER and Polley Debo, dau. of Philip Debo who consents. Sur. William Dalton. Married 30 June by the Rev. Joseph Hatchett. p. 42

4 January 1814. William CRIDER and Celah Young, dau. of Peyton Young who consents. Sur. Henry Crider. Married 6 Jan. by the Rev. Joseph Hatchett. p. 56

5 December 1811. Henry CROFF and Nancy Yeates. Sur. Charles Yeates. Married 11 Dec. by the Rev. Joseph Hatchett. p. 50

4 May 1814. Henry CROFF and Aggy Polly who writes her own consent. Sur. David Croff. p. 56

15 July 1812. Edmund CROSS and Elizabeth Napier. Sur. Moses Allen. p. 52

25 February 1822. Langley CROWDER and Fanny Hanks, dau. of Thomas Hanks. Sur. William Hanks. Married by the Rev. Orin Martin. p. 74

24 January 1812. Alexander CUNNINGHAM and Patsey M. Wilson, dau. of John Wilson who consents. Sur. Robert Wilson. p. 52

30 September 1830. John CURRY and Elizabeth Jones, dau. of Lewis Jones who consents. Sur. Washington Jones. Married 26 October by the Rev. William Blair. p. 95

15 January 1821. William CURTIS and Susanna Lewis, dau. of Charles Lewis who consents. Sur. Warren Clark. Married 16 Jan. by the Rev. William Davis. p. 72

24 October 1826. Daniel D. CUSTARD and Susannah Berger. Sur. John Berger. Married 26 Oct. by the Rev. Shadrack Mustain. p. 85

30 July 1817. John CUSTARD and Catharine Rorer. Sur. John Rorer. Married 31 July by the Rev. Shadrack Mustain. p. 62

16 October 1826. George W. DABBS and Elizabeth W. Coleman. Sur. Daniel Coleman. Married 19 Oct. by the Rev. John W. Kelly. p. 85

24 January 1816. Robbin DALEY and Elizabeth Glasco. Married by the Rev. Thomas Sparks. Minister's Return. p. 60

20 November 1826. Jabez L. DALLAS and Elizabeth P. Wells. Sur. Thomas Burnett. Thomas and Nancy Hines, guardians of Elizabeth, request the license be issued. p. 85

17 March 1817. Merideth DALLIS and Sally Blair. Sur. James Blair. Married 1 April by the Rev. William Blair. p. 63

11 November 1817. Terry DALLIS and Polley Boaz. Sur. David R. Boaz. Married 27 Nov. by the Rev. James Beck. p. 63

11 September 1819. Benjamin DALTON and Elizabeth Pickerall. Sur. Joseph Midkiff. Married 26 Sept. by the Rev. Shadrack Mustain. p. 68

14 March 1828. Booker DALTON and Nancy Mayhew. Sur. Henry Pickeral. p. 91

21 October 1820. Coleman DALTON and Dolly Shelton. Sur. Richard Shelton. Married 26 Oct. by the Rev. Shadrack Mustain. p. 70

3 June 1826. David DALTON and Mary Walden. Sur. Thomas Dalton. Jesse Keesee writes, "Mary is orphan of Henry and Maryann Walden, they both being dead; she is over 21, and a granddaughter of mine." Married 4 June by the Rev. Shadrack Mustain. p. 85

-- ---- 1817. Edward DALTON and Lydda Neal. Married by the Rev. Griffith Dickinson. Minister's Return. p. 63

36

6 February 1824. Edward DALTON and Nancy Bruce. Sur. Jesse
Abston. John Bruce signs the certificate. No relationship
given. Married 10 Feb. by the Rev. Griffith Dickinson.
p. 80

5 January 1807. George DALTON and Nancy Parsons Keese.
Sur. Francis McGlasson. Married by the Rev. Joseph Hatchett. (Minister says 10 January 1808.) p. 42

2 July 1818. Henry DALTON and Nancy Owen. Sur. James Owen.
Married by the Rev. Griffith Dickinson. p. 65

3 July 1812. James DALTON and Polly Clever. Sur. James
Pickeral. Married 3 July by the Rev. Joseph Hatchett. p. 52

12 March 1828. Jarratt P. DALTON and Mary T. Waddleton.
Sur. John A. Watlington. p. 91
Mary's name was evidently misspelled when the bond was written because John's name was spelled "Waddleton" in the top
of the bond. He signed "Watlington."

19 February 1810. John DALTON and Frankey Witcher. Sur.
John Witcher. Married by the Rev. David Nowlin. p. 48

22 November 1826. John DALTON and Coley V. Mattox. Sur.
Coalman D. Bennett. Married 24 Nov. by the Rev. John W.
Kelly. p. 85

18 September 1826. Jonathan DALTON and Rebecca Dalton.
Sur. Benjamin Dalton. Married 26 Sept. by the Rev. Shadrack Mustain. p. 85

15 June 1826. Lacey DALTON and Jane Pickeral, dau. of Thomas Pickeral who consents. Sur. John M. Hudson. p. 85

18 January 1819. Littleberry DALTON and Nancey C. Camp,
dau. of George Camp who consents. Sur. William Dalton.
Married 21 Jan. by the Rev. Shadrack Mustain. p. 68

5 January 1812. Littleberry DAULTON and Fanny Dove. William Dove, Jr. signs the certificate. No relationship
stated. Sur. Drury Mustain. Married 6 Jan. by the Rev.
Griffith Dickinson who says Littleberry Dalton. p. 52

17 July 1809. Samuel DALTON and Sudy Mustain, dau. of Avery
Mustain who consents. Sur. Henry Gosney. Married 27 July
by the Rev. Griffith Dickinson. p. 46

27 April 1826. Samuel DALTON and Catharine Pickerall. Sur.
Thomas Pickerall. Married 4 June by the Rev. Shadrack Mustain. p. 85

28 January 1823. Thomas DALTON and Nancy Taylor, dau. of Milley Taylor whose consent says, "she being of lawful age." Sur. Jarrett P. Dalton. Married 29 Jan. by the Rev. Griffith Dickinson. p. 77

10 January 1807. William DALTON and Rachel Bennett who writes her own consent. Sur. Henry Jacobs. Married 14 Jan. by the Rev. Joseph Hatchett who says, "this night" he performed the ceremony "by candle light." p. 41

19 February 1821. John DANGERFIELD and Sally Cook. Sur. Harmon Cook. Married by the Rev. John W. Kelly. (Minister says 14 February.) p. 72

4 January 1808. William DANGERFIELD and Dorothy Henry, dau. of Francis Henry who consents. Sur. John Huffman. Married by the Rev. David Nowlin. p. 44

27 August 1823. George DANIEL and Rhoda Thompson who signs her own certificate as of age and "parents not in this part of the country." Sur. Thomas Marshall. Married 2 September by the Rev. Richard B. Beck. p. 77

3 January 1826. Hezekiah G. DANIEL and Mary L. Watkins, dau. of Benjamin Watkins who consents. Sur. John W. Atkinson. p. 85

25 October 1819. Jordan DANIEL and Eddy Skates, who signs her own certificate. (Uses a mark.) Sur. James Hays. Married by the Rev. Griffith Dickinson who says, Eddy S. Keatts. p. 68

8 October 1807. Benjamin DAVIS and Catharine Gilbert, dau. of Jeremiah Gilbert who consents. Sur. George Gilbert.p.42

22 December 1823. Benjamin DAVIS and Winifred Yeaman. Sur. John Yeaman. Married 25 Dec. by the Rev. William Blair. p. 77

17 April 1815. Daniel DAVIS and Lydia Boaz. Sur. Shadrack Boaz. Married 27 April by the Rev. Thomas Boaz. p. 58

28 July 1821. Francis DAVIS and Mary Merritt, who signs her own certificate. Sur. Thomas Moody. Married --July 1821 by the Rev. Ira Ellis. p. 72

30 September 1822. Garret DAVIS and Ann Thompson. Sur. Robert Cook. Married 1 October by the Rev. Griffith Dickinson. p. 75

4 November 1822. James DAVIS and Kerren Tanner, dau. of Thomas Tanner who consents. Sur. Jeremiah White, Jr. Married 6 Nov. by the Rev. William Blair. p. 75

24 December 1822. John DAVIS and Frances Harvey. Sur. Richard Harvey. p. 75

1 October 1825. John DAVIS and Winifred Carter. Sur. Thomas Carter. p. 82

15 December 1828. John DAVIS and Sarah Terry, dau. of David and Lettuce Terry who consent. Sur. John Terry. Married by the Rev. William Blair. (Minister says 28 October). p. 90

15 May 1815. Jordan DAVIS and Rachel Abston, dau. of John Abston who consents. Sur. Laban Farmer. Married 25 May by the Rev. Griffith Dickinson who says, "Jordon R. Davis." p. 58

21 October 1811. Joshua DAVIS and Sally Green. Sur. Matthew Callahan. Married 31 Oct. by the Rev. Thomas Boaz. p. 50

20 December 1826. Larkin H. DAVIS and Elizabeth Smith, dau. of Joseph Smith who consents. Elizabeth also signs the certificate. Sur. Ewel Smith. Married 21 Dec. by the Rev. William Blair. p. 85

27 September 1827. Micajah DAVIS and Lucy R. Cabaniss. Sur. Israel Davis. Matt and Martha Cabaniss sign the certificate. No relationship given. Married 16 October by the Rev. Edwin G. Cabaniss, Baptist. Return dated: "Franklin, Nov. 5, 1827. p. 88

1 May 1819. Sampson DAVIS and Ann Pruet. Sur. Joseph Pruitt. p. 68

16 August 1823. Thomas DAVIS and Frances Tribble. Sur. Denet Gutrey. David Echols, Guardian of Frances, signs the certificate. p. 77

21 December 1829. Thomas DAVIS and Ann Terry. Sur. David Terry. Married 21 Dec. by the Rev. John Leigh. p. 93

22 November 1824. Thomas DAVIS, Jr. and Elizabeth Sheppard. Sur. William Sheppard. Married 25 Nov. by the Rev. Griffith Dickinson. p. 80

10 February 1817. William DAVIS and Lucy Woodson. Sur. Joseph Davis. Murry Woodson gives consent for his daughter Marry Woodson. p. 63

11 October 1824. William DAVIS and Camelia Craft. Sur. Philip Craft. (In pencil is written, "her father.") p. 80

23 June 1810. Jonathan I. DAWSON and Anne Adams, dau. of John Adams. Sur. Johnson Adams. p. 48

15 December 1817. Gilbert DEAR and Lucea Devin, whose consent says she is daughter of Joseph Devin, deceased. Sur. Richard B. Beck. p. 63

6 September 1827. Willis W. DEAR and Eliza Austin. Sur. Atkinson O. Lovelace. Stephen Austin consents. No relationship stated. Married 6 Sept. by the Rev. Orson Martin. p.88

18 August 1817. William DEARING and Polley Harrison, dau. of Ashworth Harrison who consents. Sur. Joshua Harrison. p. 63

4 September 1824. Barnett DEARMORE and Gillion Shelton. Sur. Allen Smith. John Dearmore signs the certificate. No relationship stated. Gilliam Shelton writes her own consent. Married 8 Sept. by the Rev. William Blair. p. 80

4 December 1821. Bryant DEARMORE and Sarah Slayton, dau. of Lucy Slayton who consents. Sarah also signs as Sarah W. Slayton. Sur. William Shelton. Married 6 Dec. by the Rev. William Blair. p. 72

29 March 1816. John DEARMORE and Elizabeth Wright, who writes her own consent. Sur. Silvester Vaden. Married by the Rev. David Nowlin. p. 60

12 February 1820. John DEARMORE and Susannah Bustle, who signs her own certificate. Sur. Will Bradley. Married 12 Feb. by the Rev. William Blair. p. 70

6 March 1830. Benjamin DEBO and Locky Dalton. Sur. Coalman D. Bennett. Married 10 March by the Rev. Joel T. Adams. p. 95

21 November 1820. Allen DEBOE and Jincey Love. Sur. Robert Love. Married 23 Nov. by the Rev. Shadrack Mustain. p. 70

17 December 1827. Philip DEBOE, Jr. and Rebecca Custard. Sur. William Custard. p. 88

13 January 1823. Daniel DEJARNETTE and Martha A. Franklin, dau. of Edward Franklin who consents. Sur. John Franklin. Married 16 Jan. by the Rev. Griffith Dickinson who says Danl. Dejarnett. p. 77

20 March 1815. Henry W. DeJARNETT and Lucinda Kemp Buckley. Sur. Jesse Buckley. Married by the Rev. Nathan Lovelace. p. 58

15 October 1813. Stephen DENNISON and Elizabeth Ingram. Sur. Garland Ingram. Married 19 Oct. by the Rev. William Blair. p. 54

16 February 1811. James DEVIN and Temperance COX, dau. of
James S. Cox who consents. Sur. John Devin. Married 19 Feb.
by the Rev. Thomas Boaz. p. 50

16 February 1811. John DEVIN and Polley Hankins, whose consent says, "I am my own Gardien." Sur. James Devin. Married
21 Feb. by the Rev. Thomas Boaz. p. 50

3 November 1823. John DEVIN and Ann Bibb Nowlin, dau. of
David Nowlin who consents. Sur. John Douglass. Married 6
Nov. by the Rev. Griffith Dickinson. p. 77

15 November 1813. William DEVIN and Elizabeth Croff, who
writes her own consent. Sur. John Crider. Married 2
December by the Rev. Thomas Boaz. p. 54

21 August 1824. Ezekiel DEWS and Martha M. Stone, dau. of
Prudence Stone who consents. Sur. William Dews. Married
26 Aug. by the Rev. Shadrack Mustain. p. 80

6 December 1819. William DEWS and Nancy Stone, dau. of Prudence Stone who consents. Sur. Samuel Stone. Married 9
Dec. by the Rev. John Jenkins. p. 68

11 November 1824. William DEWS and Susannah Dews. Married
by the Rev. Shadrack Mustain. Minister's Return. p. 80

1 January 1823. Abner DICK and Nancy Burnett. Sur. Hezekiah Giles. Married 2 Jan. by the Rev. James Beck. p. 77

28 November 1826. Crispin DICKENSON and Christiana Berger,
dau. of Jacob Berger who consents. Sur. Daniel Berger.
Married 31 Dec. by the Rev. John W. Kelly. p. 85

15 March 1824. Griffith DICKENSON and Ann M. Jones, dau.
of Eml. Jones who signs the certificate. Sur. Vincent Dickenson. Married 25 March by the Rev. William Blair. p. 80

11 July 1828. John DICKENSON and Martha M. Baskervill.
Sur. George H. Baskervill. Married 16 July by the Rev. A. D.
Montgomery. p. 90

17 July 1830. Peyton DICKERSON and Catey Terry, who signs
her own consent. Sur. William W. Tuggle. p. 96

-- April 1827. James DILLARD and Sarah Holt, dau. of David
Holt who consents. Sur. John McAlister. Married 8 May by
the Rev. William S. Plummer. p. 88
(Edge of bond mutilated.)

13 July 1819. John DILLARD and Oney Stanley. Sur. Robert
Roland. Married by the Rev. Griffith Dickinson. p. 68

27 January 1810. Lynch DILLARD and Mildred Ward, dau. of
William Ward. Mildred writes her own consent. Sur. Peter
Markham. Married 28 Jan. by the Rev. Griffith Dickinson.
p. 48

29 September 1822. Nicholas DILLARD and Martha Doss, (widow), who signs her own certificate. Sur. Samuel M. Lowell.
Married 9 October by the Rev. Shadrack Mustain. p. 75

20 May 1811. Elisha DISMUKES and Judith Lee, who writes her
own consent. Sur. William Echols. p. 50

7 December 1830. Richard T. DISMUKES and Mary Lucas, who
signs her own consent. Sur. Charles Lucas. p. 96

12 April 1819. John P. DIX and Lydia Dodson. Sur. John
Ratliff. Married 15 April by the Rev. William Blair. p. 68

28 December 1813. Larkin DIX and Sally Haskins, dau. of
John Haskins who consents. Sur. Nathaniel Barnett. Married
28 Dec. by the Rev. William Blair. p. 54

21 January 1809. Thomas DIX and Jane Mickleberry, dau. of
Mary Mickleberry. Sur. Jacob Kirby. Married by the Rev.
George Dodson. p. 46

28 January 1811. William DIX and Patsy Ferguson, dau. of
Lucy Ferguson. Sur. John Ferguson. p. 50

28 March 1814. Littleberry DIXON and Mary Towler, dau. of
Judith Towler who consents. Sur. Landford Dave. p. 56

21 January 1828. Peyton S. DIXON and Nancy Francis, dau. of
Ephriam Francis who consents. Sur. Jesse Strange. Married
14 February by the Rev. Richard B. Beck. p. 90

20 November 1807. John DOBYNS and ----- Kidd. Sur. Moses
Kidd. p. 42

22 March 1825. Benjamin DODD and Betsy E. Harris. Sur.
Peter M. Harris. p. 83

25 October 1819. Allen DODSON and Polly Gardner, dau. of
Hath Gardner. Sur. Bird Dodson. Married 26 Oct. by the
Rev. William Blair. p. 68

9 November 1829. Bennett G. DODSON and Elizabeth Hardy,
dau. of Banister Hardy who consents. Sur. Daniel Taylor.
Married 12 Nov. by the Rev. Crispen Dickenson. p. 93

31 August 1824. Carter C. DODSON and Nancy Myers. Sur.
Elijah Lynch. p. 80

7 June 1825. Charles DODSON and Sarah Stamps, dau. of William Stamps who consents. Sur. Charles Lucy. Married 9 June by the Rev. William Blair. p. 82

17 December 1821. Eli DODSON and Francis S. Davis. Sur. Asa Davis. p. 72

18 November 1811. Elias DODSON, Jr. and Maria Marshall, dau. of Unity Shields , whose note says,"with the consent of her mother Unity Shields." Sur. Pleasant Shields. Married by the Rev. George Dodson. p. 50
(Pleasant Shields married Unity Marshall, widow, in 1810.)

14 February 1820. Elisha DODSON and Nancey Wilson, dau. of Thomas Wilson. Sur. William W. Wilson. Married 17 Feb. by the Rev. James Beck. p. 70

6 April 1825. Elisha DODSON and Catharine Gardner, dau. of Silvany Gardner, (mother), who consents. Sur. Greenville P. Dodson. Married 7 April by the Rev. William Blair. p. 83

24 January 1828. George DODSON and Maro McDaniel, dau. of Ann McDaniel. Sur. Clement McDaniel. Married 26 Jan. by the Rev. Clement McDonald. p. 90

21 November 1825. George L. DODSON and Rebecca Hedspeth, dau. of Lewis Hedspeth who consents. Sur. Greenville P. Dodson. Married 25 Nov. by the Rev. John Leigh. p. 82

19 December 1825. Greenville P. DODSON and Sarah Atkinson, dau. of Josiah Atkinson who consents. Sur. Lewis Simpson. Married 20 Dec. by the Rev. William Blair. p. 83

14 December 1830. Humphrey DODSON and Mary Ann Simpson. Married by the Rev. William Blair. Minister's Return. p.96

1 January 1823. James R. DODSON and Martha Johnson, dau. of Josiah Johnson whose note says, "my daughter is of age." Sur. Matthew Dunn. Married 2 Jan. by the Rev. James Beck. p. 77

20 April 1812. Jethro DODSON and Lucy Slayden, dau. of William Slayden who consents. Lucy also signs the consent. Sur. Daniel Collie. p. 52

26 December 1806. John DODSON and Levina Walters, dau. of Robert Walters who consents. Sur. Lemuel Walters. Married 29 Dec. by the Rev. Elias Dodson. p. 41

20 September 1819. Joseph DODSON and Polley M. Dodson. Sur. Jethro Dodson. William Dodson, father of Polley, and Polley, herself, sign the certificate. Married 29 Sept. by the Rev. William Blair. p. 68

21 September 1819. Joseph DODSON and Martha Davis. Sur. Asa Davis. Married 22 Sept. by the Rev. William Blair. p. 68 (Is this a double wedding? See William Dodson.)

19 December 1812. Obediah DODSON and Susanna Shields, dau. of Pleasant Shields who consents. Sur. John B. Dodson. Pleasant Shields' consent says, "Obediah Dodson of Halifax County and Susannah Shields of Pittsylvania County. p. 52

8 November 1830. Peter DODSON and Aphphia Ingram, dau. of Larkin and Katherine Ingram who consent. Sur. George D. Ingram. Married 11 Nov. by the Rev. William Blair. p. 96

24 November 1824. Presley DODSON and Ann C. Davis, dau. of Asa Davis who consents. Sur. Jesse Atkinson. Married 24 Nov. by the Rev. William Blair. p. 80

3 May 1809. Sampson DODSON and Elizabeth Dodson, dau. of George Dodson who consents. Sur. Clement McDonald. Married by the Rev. George Dodson. p. 46

23 December 1826. Thomas H. DODSON and Elizabeth Myers. Sur. Carter C. Dodson. p. 85

24 January 1807. William DODSON and Mary Fearn. Sur. William Beavers. p. 42

14 August 1815. William DODSON and Judith Dickson. Sur. Benjamin Dickson. No relationship stated. p. 58

21 September 1819. William DODSON and Catharine P. B. Davis. Sur. Asa Davis. Married 23 Sept. by the Rev. William Blair who says Catharine Permala B. Davis. p. 68 (Is this a double wedding? See Joseph Dodson.)

21 November 1826. William E. DODSON and Elizabeth W. Moore, who signs her own consent. Sur. Elisha Dodson. Married 24 Nov. by the Rev. William Blair. p. 85

20 June 1818. Arthur DOSS and Catharine Mayhue. Sur. Henry Mayhue. Married by the Rev. Griffith Dickinson. p. 65

19 February 1806. Asa DOSS and Stacey Simpson, dau. of Thomas Simpson who consents. Sur. Thomas Simpson. Married 25 Feb. by the Rev. Griffith Dickinson, who says Azariah Doss. p. 41

25 June 1813. Azariah DOSS and Mary Neel, dau. of John Neel who consents. Sur. Benjamin Dalton. Married 27 June by the Rev. Griffith Dickinson. p. 54

11 December 1822. Edward DOSS and Nancy Mitchell. Sur.
Charles Angel. Reubin Mitchell, (no relationship given),
and Nancy, herself, sign the certificate. Married 19 Dec.
by the Rev. Griffith Dickinson. p. 74

29 ---- 1812. William DOSS and Patsey Crews. Sur. Andrew
Crews. No relationship stated. (Month not in bond.) p. 52

29 September 1825. William DOSS and Sally Rigney. Sur.
John Rigney. p. 82

12 May 1828. William DOSS and Betsey Barber. Sur. Joseph
Barber. Married 20 May by the Rev. Eben Angel. p. 91

26 March 1818. Peyton DOSWELL and Mary P. Cabell, whose consent says she is of age. Sur. Dabney P. Sneed. p. 65

10 February 1812. James DOUGLAS and Martha McDaniel, who
writes her own consent. Sur. George Douglas. No relationship stated. Married 12 Feb. by the Rev. Griffith Dickinson. p. 52

18 October 1819. John DOUGLAS and Catharine Nowlin, dau. of
David Nowlin who consents. Sur. Wade Nowlin. Married by
the Rev. Griffith Dickinson. p. 68

20 October 1823. John L. DOUGLAS and Sarah L. Terrell, who
signs her own certificate. Sur. Charles H. Lynch. Married
29 Oct. by the Rev. Griffith Dickinson. p. 77

14 December 1824. Samuel DOUGLAS and Mary Davis. Sur.
James B. Rogers. John Jenkins, grandfather of Mary, signs
the certificate saying, "she is under my care." p. 80

5 December 1827. Smith DOUGLAS and Clarissa Ruffin McGrigor, dau. of William McGrigor who consents. Sur. Vincent
M. Lewis. Married 6 Dec. by the Rev. Griffith Dickinson.
p. 88

18 June 1821. Thomas DOUGLAS and Eleanor Black. Sur. John
Douglas. Married by the Rev. David Nowlin. p. 72

14 October 1829. Edward DOUGLASS and Agness W. Womack who
signs her own consent. Sur. Richard White. Married 15 Oct.
by the Rev. Griffith Dickenson, Sr. p. 93

13 January 1813. George DOUGLASS and Temperance Mason, who
writes her own consent as <u>Tempitha</u> Mason. Sur. Philip L.
Grady. Married 19 Jan. by the Rev. Griffith Dickinson. p.54

15 March 1819. Robert DOUGLASS and Patsey Blanks. Sur.
John Blanks. Married 4 September 1819 by the Rev. John
Jenkins. p. 68

2 March 1830. George DOULIN and Catharine Colley, dau. of
Daniel and Peggey Collie who consent. Sur. Thos. G. Tunstall. p. 95

18 June 1827. Booker DOVE and Francis Vaughan who signs her
own certificate. Sur. E. Y. Wimbish. p. 88

18 December 1828. Coleman DOVE and Elizabeth Worsham, dau.
of William Worsham who consents. Sur. Patrick Worsham. Married by the Rev. Eben Angel. p. 90

19 January 1807. Landford DOVE and Nancy Towler, dau. of
Judith Towler who consents. Sur. John Towler. p. 42

1 April 1811. William DOVE and Mary Polley Mustain, dau. of
Avery Mustain. Sur. Avery Mustain. Married 25 April by the
Rev. Griffith Dickinson. p. 50

15 January 1816. William DOVE and Oney Saunders. Sur. Jesse
Saunders. Married 23 Jan. by the Rev. Griffith Dickinson.
p. 60

22 January 1824. William DOVE and Peggy Barrett. Sur. John
Barrett. Married 23 Jan. by the Rev. Griffith Dickinson.
p. 80

10 June 1814. Levin DOWNES and Mary Durratt, dau. of Mary
Durratt who consents. Sur. Paskel Carter. Married 16 June
by the Rev. William Blair. p. 56

18 December 1820. Hezekiah DRAIN and Nancy Tiffin, dau. of
Thomas and Elizabeth Tiffin who consent. Sur. Stephen Walker. Married 21 Dec. by the Rev. James Beck. p. 70

7 August 1826. Andy DRAKE and Polly English. Sur. James
English. p. 85

2 January 1811. Preston DUDLEY and Mary Ann Doss. Sur. Will
Doss. James Doss requests that this license be issued. William Doss makes oath that Mary Ann is "above 21." p. 50

17 November 1830. Thomas DUDLEY and Malitia Tankersly, who
signs her own consent. Sur. Nicholas Dillard. Married by
the Rev. Eben Angel. p. 96

21 December 1830. Wylie R. DUDLEY and Ellender Kelly, dau.
of James Kelly who consents. Sur. Thomas Kelly. p. 96

8 January 1810. William DUFF and Elizabeth Johnson, whose
own consent says she is "upwards of 18 years of age." Sur.
Samuel Meadows. Married by the Rev. John Atkinson. p. 48

14 November 1807. Francis DULEY and Lettey Yates, who signs
her own certificate as Libbey Yates. Sur. Row. Ragland.
Married by the Rev. David Nowlin, Baptist. p. 42

28 December 1818. Elisha DUNBAR and Rachel Parsons. Sur.
Daniel Dunbar. Married 30 Dec. by the Rev. William Blair.
p. 65

20 November 1823. Samuel DUNBAR and Mary Ann Love. Sur.
James K. Love. No relationship given. p. 77

4 February 1823. William DUNBAR and Elizabeth Giles, dau.
of Thomas Giles who is Surety. Married -- Feb. by the Rev.
Ira Ellis. p. 77

14 October 1830. Alexander DUNCAN and Elizabeth George.
Sur. William Chattin. Married 15 Oct. by the Rev. Joel T.
Adams. p. 95

7 September 1818. John DUNCAN and Jane Elliott. Sur.
Hezekiah Smith, Jr. James Watkins, (no relationship given),
and Jane, herself, sign the certificate. James Watkins
writes, "I do hereby certify that Jane Eliot has lived in
my house for several years and that she is of full Age to
Act for her Self." p. 65

13 December 1828. John DUNCAN and Margaret Gregory. Sur.
John Travis. Absalom and Elizabeth McKinzie sign the certificate. Married 26 February 1829 by the Rev. A. D. Montgomery. p. 90

27 September 1824. Nathaniel DUNCAN and Lucy Chattin, who
signs her own certificate. Sur. Silvester Vaden. Silvester Vaden and Edmond Adams say Lucy is over 21. p. 80

2 January 1811. William DUNCAN and Jinney Sparks. Sur.
John Sparks, who testifies Jinney is of age. No relationship stated. p. 50

20 October 1815. Edmund DUNN and Jincy Alexander, dau. of
William Alexander who consents. Sur. William B. Alexander. Married 26 Oct. by the Rev. Thomas Boaz. p. 58

2 November 1818. James DUNN and Martha Fuller. Sur. George
Fuller. Nancy Fuller signs the certificate. No relationship stated. Married 3 Nov. by the Rev. James Beck. p. 65

4 February 1809. Matthew DUNN and Betsey Jackson, dau. of
Ephram Jackson who consents. Sur. Thomas Matthews. Married 4 Feb. by the Rev. Thomas Boaz. p. 46

10 April 1823. Richard R. DUNN and Susannah Parrish. Sur.
John R. Parrish. p. 77

18 December 1815. Thomas DUNN and Anna Fuller. Sur. James Pearson. Zachariah Fuller signs the certificate. No relationship stated. p. 58

15 February 1816. Thomas DUNN and Anney Fuller. Married by the Rev. James Beck. Minister's Return. p. 60

22 December 1808. Walters DUNN and Judah Parrish, dau. of Peter Parrish. Judah gives her own consent as "of age." Sur. Thomas Matthew. Married 23 Dec. by the Rev. Thomas Boaz. p. 44

29 December 1810. Edmund DUPUY and Elizabeth G. Steels. Married by the Rev. Griffith Dickinson. Minister's Return. p. 48

16 December 1822. Stephen DUPUY and Winifred Proctor, who signs her own certificate. Sur. William Ferguson. Married 16 Dec. by the Rev. William Blair. p. 74

25 October 1819. William H. DUPUY and Agness P. Ware, dau. of William Ware who consents. Sur. William R. Adams. Married 25 Oct. by the Rev. Thomas Sparks. p. 68

9 August 1825. John DURHAM and Sally Hawker, dau. of Ambus and Cloary Hawker who consent. Sur. James Hawker. Married 9 Aug. by the Rev. John Leigh. p. 82
(Ambrose Hawker and Cloe Murray were married in 1891. See page 14 of the Register.)

10 January 1820. John DURRAM and Jincey Wilson, dau. of Nancy Wilson who, in his request that the license be issued, says his daughter is of age. Sur. Robert T. Gregory. Married by the Rev. Griffith Dickinson on Jan. 13, and says John Durham and Jinney Wilson. p. 70

25 November 1822. Coleman DYER and Louisa Shelton, dau. of Leroy Shelton who consents. Sur. George Dyer. Married 12 Dec. by the Rev. James Beck. p. 75

28 March 1818. Jonathan DYER and Peggy Bryant. Sur. (None given.) Married by the Rev. William Blair. (Minister says 24 March.) p. 65

15 May 1815. Abraham EANES and Catharine Wells, who signs her own certificate as "of age." Sur. William Eanes. p. 58

21 April 1828. Abraham S. EANES and Casandra Covington, who writes her own consent. Sur. John Garrett, Jr. p. 91

5 June 1819. Arthur W. EANES and Elizabeth Riddle. Sur. Thomas Riddle. Elener Eanes, mother of Arthur, signs the certificate saying her son is under age. p. 68

28 April 1823. Joseph H. EANES and Ann W. Cobbs, dau. of Charles Cobbs who consents. Sur. Walton Cobbs. p. 77

12 January 1824. Matthew EARP and Lucy Earp. Sur. Nicholas Earp. Married 15 Jan. by the Rev. Orson Martin. p. 80

4 September 1819. Philip EARP and Sally O'Neal. Sur. John O'Neal. p. 68

-- ---- 1806. Briant EASLEY and Molley Farguson. Married by the Rev. Richard Elliott. Minister's Return "for the year 1806." p. 41

6 November 1821. John S. EASLEY and Agness C. White, dau. of John White who consents. Sur. Howson S. White. p. 72

30 October 1823. William A. EASLEY and Tabitha H. Stone. Married by the Rev. Griffith Dickinson. Minister's Return. p. 77

13 September 1826. Asa EAST and Elizabeth Templeton. Sur. Thomas East. Martin Templeton signs the certificate. Married 14 Sept. by the Rev. Griffith Dickinson. p. 85

22 December 1828. Thomas EAST and Elizabeth West, dau. of Joseph West who consents. Sur. James Templeton. Married 23 Dec. by the Rev. Griffith Dickinson. p. 91

6 September 1830. Coleman ECHOLS and Louisa Robertson. Sur. Nathaniel Wooding. Married 7 Sept. by the Rev. Crispin Dickenson. p. 96

22 December 1830. Joel H. ECHOLS and Sarah W. Anthony. Sur. W.H.Tunstall. Married 23 Dec. by the Rev. William Blair

22 December 1829. Joel W. ECHOLS and Nancy Hodge, dau. of Fleming Hodge who consents. Sur. Morton Hodge. p. 93

19 March 1828. Nowlin ECHOLS and Mary Slayton, who signs her own consent as "of age." Sur. James W. Conway. Married 20 March by the Rev. William Blair. p. 91

15 April 1816. Obediah ECHOLS and Agness Clement, who signs her own certificate. Sur. Bryant W. Nowlin. Married by the Rev. David Nowlin. p. 60

21 October 1816. William ECHOLS and Sally Hailey. Sur. James Soyars. Married 24 Oct. by the Rev. John Jenkins. p. 60

14 December 1824. Winn ECHOLS and Judith F. Wilkinson, who signs her own certificate. Sur. Fredk. T. Wilkinson. Married 14 Dec. by the Rev. William Blair. p. 80

5 February 1829. James EDDS and Lucy Abston, dau. of Francis Abston who consents. Sur. Francis Abston. Married by the Rev. Eben Angel. p. 93

12 December 1818. Preston G. EDDS and Susan Aron. Sur. Isaac Aron. Married 17 Dec. by the Rev. James Beck. p. 66

31 December 1827. Thomas EDDS and Jane Wallace. Sur. William Abston. Josefa Edds, father of Thomas, and Jain Wallace, herself, sign the certificate. Married 6 January 1828 by the Rev. Eben Angel. p. 88

9 April 1816. Thomas EDMONDS and Delila Darby. Sur. Lewis Ralph. Married 10 April by the Rev. Thomas Sparks. p. 60

15 October 1823. Samuel EDMUNDSON and Mary Johnson. Sur. Richard Johnson. Married Oct. 1823 by the Rev. Ira Ellis. p. 77

15 January 1821. Daniel C. EDWARDS and Jincy Dalton. Sur. George Craft. Married 8 February by the Rev. Shadrack Mustain. p. 72

20 February 1828. Gidion EDWARD_ and Martha Gilbert. Sur. David L. Keen. James Gilbert requests the license be issued. His note witnessed by David L. Keen and Elisha Keen. Married 20 Feb. by the Rev. Abner Anthony. p. 91

16 February 1824. William C. EDWARDS and Sabinda James. Sur. William Hutchings. p. 80

8 September 1824. George ELLIOTT and Catharine Uhles. Sur. George Ules. p. 80

11 March 1822. Hiram ELLIOTT and Susan Royall, dau. of Elizabeth Royall who consents. Sur. Nathaniel R. Royall. p. 75

30 June 1810. James ELLIOTT and Nancy Galding. Sur. Andy Galding. Married 4 July by the Rev. Thomas Boaz. p. 48 On the back of the bond: "Andy Galding the security to the within bond and Brother to the within named Nancy Galding this day made oath before me Deputy Clerk for the Court of said County, that the said Nancy Galding is above the age of Twenty one years." Signed "E-- Rawlins."

7 November 1829. James ELLIOTT and Polly Coward, who gives her own consent. Sur. William Elliott. p. 93

13 August 1809. John ELLIOTT and Lettice Holland, dau. of Catherine Holland. Sur. John Nelson. Married 17 Aug. by the Rev. Thomas Boaz. p. 46

31 December 1821. John ELLIOTT and Susanna May, dau. of
Susanna May who consents. Sur. Nathaniel Elliott. p. 72
(Is this a double wedding? See Nathaniel Elliott.)

-- ---- 1806. Jonathan ELLIOTT and Lucy Parrish. Married
by the Rev. Richard Elliott. p. 41
See Jonathan Elliott 1807.

15 August 1807. Jonathan ELLIOTT and Lucy Parrish. Sur.
Peter Parrish. p. 43
See Jonathan Elliott - 1806.

31 December 1821. Nathaniel ELLIOTT and Jane May, dau. of
Susanna May who consents. Sur. John Elliott.
(Is this a double wedding? See John Elliott.)

16 January 1815. Philip ELLIOTT and Elizabeth Gordan. Sur.
Levy Watts. p. 58

11 October 1814. Robert ELLIOTT and Sally Chesher. Sur.
William Chesher. Married 13 Oct. by the Rev. Shadrack
Mustain. p. 56

19 November 1809. Thomas ELLIOTT and Sally Ward. Sur. Thomas Elliott. Married 23 Nov. by the Rev. Thomas Boaz. p. 46

4 February 1812. Thomas ELLIOTT and Rhoda Justice, dau. of
Elizabeth Justice who consents. Sur. William Taylor. Married 6 Feb. by the Rev. Joseph Hatchett. p. 52

6 April 1829. Allen EMMERSON and Darcas Johnson. Sur.
Joshua Smith. p. 93

18 July 1814. Henry EMMERSON and Betsey Chesher. Sur. William Chesher. Married 21 July by the Rev. Shadrack Mustain.
p. 56

15 February 1819. Henry EMMERSON and Nancy Smith. Sur.
Joshua Smith. Married 25 Feb. by the Rev. James Beck. p.68

15 May 1809. James EMMERSON and Milley Adams, dau. of
Elijah Adams who is Surety. Married 16 May by the Rev. William Blair. p. 46

18 June 1806. John EMMERSON and Patsey Jackson. Sur. Fontain Price. Ephraim Jackson sonsents. No relationshil
shown. Married by the Rev. Richard Elliott. p. 41

20 September 1830. Samuel EMMERSON and Sally Holley. Sur.
James Emmerson. Married 22 Sept. by the Rev. Richard B.
Beck. p. 96

14 October 1816. William EMMERSON and Betsy Aron. Sur.
Jacob Aron. Married 18 Oct. by the Rev. James Beck. p. 60

16 December 1822. Stephen ENGLISH and Martha R. Lumpkin.
Sur. Moore Lumpkin. p. 75

6 January 1814. Anthony EPPERSON and Elizabeth Napier. Sur.
John Witcher. Married "since June 1813" by the Rev. David
Nowlin who says Elizabeth Napper. p. 56

18 May 1820. John EPPERSON and Rebecca Guinn, dau. of Jesse
Gwin who consents. Sur. William Thomas. Married 23 May by
the Rev. William Blair. p. 70

-- ---- 1807. Littleberry EPPERSON and Elizabeth Beale.
Married by the Rev. John Jenkins. Minister's Return dated
21 December 1808. p. 43

3 November 1806. John ESTES and Susanna Walker, dau. of
William Walker who consents. Sur. John Wade. p. 41

9 March 1816. Thomas ESTIS (Estes?) and Elizabeth Walker.
Sur. William Walker. p. 60

17 April 1820. William ESTES and Susan H. Shelton, dau. of
Thomas Shelton who consents. Sur. Robert H. Shelton. Married 20 April by the Rev. William Davis. p. 70

3 February 1817. James EUDALEY and Nancey Fallen, who signs
her own certificate. Sur. Isaac Gardner. p. 63

22 December 1815. Robert EUDALEY and Elizabeth Glasgow.
Sur. Herod Worsham. Robert Glasgow signs the certificate
saying Elizabeth is of age. No relationship stated. p. 58

14 December 1830. Benjamin EVANS and Sarah H. Shelton, dau.
of Henry Shelton who consents. Sur. Shadrack Wright. Married 16 Dec. by the Rev. William Blair. p. 96

14 August 1819. Champness EVANS and Elizabeth Reynolds, dau.
of Jesse and Sarah Reynolds who consent. Sur. David Evans.
Married 26 Aug. by the Rev. William Blair. p. 68

6 August 1810. David EVANS and Sally Reynolds, dau. of
Jesse Reynolds who consents. Sur. Richard Wright. Married
9 Aug. by the Rev. William Blair. p. 48

5 July 1819. Jacob EVANS and Bashaba Davis. Sur. Robert
Evans. p. 68

21 October 1822. Joseph EVANS and Seeney Slaydon, who signs
her own certificate. Sur. Thomas Slaydon. Married 22 Oct.
by the Rev. William Blair. p. 75

15 November 1819. Robert EVANS and Polley King. Sur.
Royall King. Married 17 Nov. by the Rev. William Blair.
p. 68

7 October 1816. William EVANS and Martha Mahan, who signs
her own certificate as "Marthey." Sur. Thomas Mahan. p. 60

4 September 1810. George FACKLER and Polley White, dau. of
Jer. White who consents. Sur. Josiah Forguson, Jr. p. 48

17 December 1829. Littleberry FALLEN and Ann E. Townes,
dau. of Robert Townes who consents. Sur. Paschal W. Ragsdale. Married 22 Dec. by the Rev. A. D. Montgomery. p.93

26 February 1827. William FALLEN and Elizabeth E. Philips.
Sur. Matthew Haley. Lovelace Haly, guardian of Elizabeth,
consents. p. 88

31 January 1825. Hugh FALLIN and Leannah Walters, dau. of
Arthur Walters who consents. Sur. Alexander I. Walters.
Married 3 February by the Rev. William Blair, who says Hugh
Fallen. p. 83

18 March 1816. William FALLING and Lucy Mills. Sur. Martin
Wilson. Anthony Mills signs the certificate. No relationship stated. Married 21 March by the Rev. William Blair.
p. 60

12 April 1830. Amos FARIS, Jr. and Jane Faris. Sur. James
B. Faris. Danl. Johns, guardian of Jane, consents. Married
15 April by the Rev. Griffith Dickenson, Sr. p. 96

20 July 1829. Henry W. FARIS and Prudence Stone, who gives
her own consent. Sur. Joseph Stone. Married 30 July by
the Rev. Griffith Dickenson. p. 93

17 May 1830. James B. FARIS and Nancy Scruggs, dau. of
Drury Scruggs who consents. Sur. Daniel Johns. p. 96

3 March 1829. George FARLEY and Ann M. Farley, dau. of
James Farley who consents. Sur. William B. Seamore. p. 93

27 December 1827. Arthur FARMER and Elizabeth Arnold. Sur.
Elisha Balas. Married 27 Dec. by the Rev. Griffith Dickinson. p. 88

16 April 1827. Clement S. FARMER and Elizabeth Garrett,
dau. of Thomas Garrett who consents. Sur. James Haislip.
Married 23 April by the Rev. Richard B. Beck. p. 88

19 September 1825. James A. FARMER and Rebecca J. Nowlin,
dau. of David Nowlin who consents. Sur. John Devin. p. 83
(Is this a double wedding? See William W. Farmer.)

18 December 1820. John FARMER and Jane Woodson. Sur. Allen Woodson. p. 70

-- ---- 1821. John FARMER and Jane Woodson. Married by the Rev. David Nowlin, "since my last return." This return made in April 1822. p. 72   See John Farmer, 1820.

16 October 1823. Marlin FARMER and Sarah Motley, who signs her own certificate. Sur. Obadiah P. Terry. Married by the Rev. David Nowlin. p. 77

5 January 1812. Newton FARMER and Sarah Ham. Sur. Thomas Hays. p. 52

11 April 1823. Newton FARMER and Sarah Woodson, dau. of Allen Woodson, Jr. who consents. Sur. Stephen D. Woodson. Married by the Rev. David Nowlin. p. 77

12 February 1818. Robert FARMER and Tabitha Bruce, dau. of Tabitha Bruce who requests the license be issued. Sur. Frederick Bruce. Married 15 Feb. by the Rev. Shadrack Mustain. p. 66

19 September 1825. William W. FARMER and Martha Woodson, dau. of Jane Woodson who consents. Sur. James A. Farmer. p. 83
(Is this a double wedding? See James A. Farmer.)

-- ---- 1808. Stephen FARRIS and Mary Whitehead, whose consent says she is widow of Cary Whitehead. Sur. John Patterson. p. 44
(NOTE: day and month left blank on the bond.)

10 January 1826. George FARSON and Jane Chainey, dau. of Charles Chainey who signs the certificate. Sur. Samuel Chainey. Married 18 Jan. by the Rev. William Blair. p. 85

30 December 1809. Abner FARTHING and Delilah Watson, dau. of William Watson, Sr. Sur. William Watson, Jr. Married 22 Jan. by the Rev. Thomas Payne. p. 46

15 December 1828. James FARTHING and Susan Farthing. Sur. Abner Farthing. Married 18 Dec. by the Rev. Griffith Dickinson. p. 91

26 November 1823. Joab FARTHING and Elizabeth Farthing. Sur. Abner Farthing. Married 27 Nov. by the Rev. Griffith Dickinson. p. 77

4 March 1823. John FARTHING and Rebecca Farthing. Sur. John Farthing, Sr. Married 5 March by the Rev. Griffith Dickinson. p. 77

2 March 1810. Lemuel FARTHING and Nancy Reardin. Sur.
James Murphy. Landy Farthing, father of Lemuel, consents. p. 48

27 September 1827. Maynard FARTHING and Susanna Camron.
Sur. John Nichols. Chloye Cameron's consent says she raised
Susannah Cameron from and infant. p. 88

6 March 1807. Richard FARTHING and Elizabeth Parsons. Sur.
Dudley Farthing. Married 9 March by the Rev. Thomas Payne.
p. 43

13 January 1821. Richard H. FARTHING and Dorothy Farthing.
Sur. John Farthing. Married 16 Jan. by the Rev. Griffith
Dickinson. p. 72

6 March 1815. Sandy S. FARTHING and Rebecca Farthing. Sur.
Abner Farthing. No relationship stated. Married 8 March by
the Rev. Griffith Dickinson. p. 58

5 January 1825. Stokely FARTHING and Milly Burnett, dau. of
John Burnett who consents. Sur. Malchijah Burnett. p. 83

20 April 1825. William B. FARTHING and Elizabeth I. Shelton,
who signs her own certificate. Sur. Leroy G. Shelton. p. 83

30 August 1819. Beverly FERGUSON and Ann Williams. Sur.
David C. Williams. Married by the Rev. David Nowlin. p. 68

12 March 1825. Billington Y. FERGUSON and Mary Epperson,
dau. of Francis Epperson who consents. Sur. Bere. C. Gardner. Married May 1825 by the Rev. William Blair. p. 83
(Edge of the Minister's Return is torn.)

18 April 1825. Edmond FERGUSON and Nancy Whitehurst, dau.
of William Whitehurst who consents. Sur. Samuel Ferguson.
Married April 1825 by the Rev. William Blair. p. 83
(Edge of Minister's Return is torn.)

27 October 1821. Henry H. FERGUSON and Elizabeth Millner,
dau. of Wmfon. Millner who consents. Sur. Reubin Hopkins.
Married 23 November by the Rev. James Beck. p. 72

30 December 1828. James FERGUSON and Mary Wilkinson. Sur.
Bere C. Gardner. Judith Echols, mother of Mary Wilkinson,
and William Williams, guardian of Mary, sign the certificate. p. 91

4 January 1806. Joel FERGUSON and Betsey Slown. Sur. Samuel Haley. Thomas Blake writes consent for "my Daughter-
in-law Betsey Slown." p. 41

12 December 1807. John FERGUSON and Sally Hopwood. Sur. Moses Echols. Married 17 Dec. by the Rev. William Blair. p. 43

19 June 1820. Joseph FERGUSON and Aggy Wier. Sur. Joseph Motley. Married 13 July by the Rev. William Blair. p. 70

23 January 1821. Josiah FERGUSON and Nancy Holder, who signs her own certificate. Sur. Richard Johnson. Married 23 Jan. by the Rev. Ira Ellis. p. 72

31 October 1820. Lovell FERGUSON and Susan Walrond. Sur. Francis C. Walrond. John Walrond signs the certificate. No relationship stated. p. 70

-- ---- 1821. Lovel FERGUSON and Susan Walrond. Married by the Rev. David Nowlin, "since my last return." This Return dated April 15, 1822. p. 72 (See Lovell Ferguson, 1820.)

18 May 1818. Robert FERGUSON and Bartia Newbell, dau. of John Newbel who consents. Sur. John M. Dix. p. 66

31 October 1825. Spencer FERGUSON and Elizabeth Travis. Sur. Richard Travis. p. 83

21 December 1822. Tunstall FERGUSON and Susanna Woodson, dau. of Murray Woodson who consents. Sur. John Davis. p. 75

9 October 1827. William FERGUSON and Rose Ann Dunbar. Sur. Daniel Dunbar. p. 88

6 January 1814. John FERRELL and Polley Beasley, dau. of Stephen Beasley. Sur. Warner Beasley. p. 56

5 October 1817. Lorenzo FERREN and Elizabeth Hatchett. Sur. William Hatchett. Married by the Rev. William Blair. (Minister's Report says September 5.) p. 63

1 February 1817. William FIELDER and Elizabeth Turley. Sur. James Turley. Married 6 Feb. by the Rev. Shadrack Mustain. p. 63

19 December 1808. Abraham FINLEY and Rachel Bardin. Sur. James Bardin. No relationship given. Married 27 Dec. by the Rev. William Blair. p. 44

8 March 1814. Robert FINLEY and Polly Neal, who writes her own consent. Sur. Nathaniel Walker. Married 10 March by the Rev. Thomas Boaz. p. 56

20 March 1815. Peter FINNY and Anna Walker. Sur. William Walker. Married by the Rev. Thomas Boaz. (Minister says 21 February.) p. 58

56

56

24 February 1823. David FIRESHEETS and Sarah Anderson, dau.
of Jacob Anderson who consents. Sur. Jesse Anderson. p. 77

14 December 1825. Frederick FIRESHEETS and Nancy Galloway,
who signs her own consent. Sur. Caleb Anderson. Married
22 Dec. by the Rev. John Leigh. p. 83

30 October 1826. Joshua FISHER and Selena Burnett, dau. of
William Burnett. Sur. John Burnett. William Burnett, who
says his daughter is 21, Bazzel Fisher, who says his son
Joshua is an only son and 21, and Selina, herself, sign the
certificate. Sur. John Burnett. p. 85

29 May 1821. Uriah FISHER and Elizabeth Coe, who signs her
own consent. Sur. David Glenn. Married 29 May by the Rev.
Griffith Dickinson. p. 72

21 October 1811. David FitzGERALD and Lucy Terry, dau. of
John Terry who consents. Sur. Jesse Hardey. Married by
the Rev. elias Dodson. p. 50

19 August 1811. Garrett FITZGERALD and Susanna Terry, dau.
of Barton Terry, Sr., who consents. Sur. John Holloway.
Married by the Rev. Elias Dodson. p. 50

7 January 1830. James FITZGERALD and Harriet L. Anderson,
dau. of Nathan Anderson who consents. Sur. Charles Keen.
p. 96

17 August 1818. Jesse FITZGERALD and Frances Lewis. Sur.
John Holloway. Married by the Rev. David Nowlin. p. 66

18 November 1811. John FITZGERALD and Jane Pratley, dau.
of George Pratley who consents. Sur. Wm. Burgess. Married 18 December by the Rev. William Blair. p. 50

20 October 1817. Samuel FITZGERALD and Nancy Anderson, dau.
of Jacob Anderson who consents. Sur. David Anderson. p. 63

18 September 1826. Samuel FITZGERALD and Emily Anderson.
Sur. Bannister Anderson. Married 21 Sept. by the Rev. Griffith Dickinson. p. 85

16 December 1806. Thomas FITZGERALD and Nancy Vaughan, dau.
of Henry and Fanny Vaughan who consent. Sur. Leonard Fitzgerald. p. 41

21 February 1820. Walter FITZGERALD and Mary C. Goolsby,
who signs her own certificate. Sur. William Linn. p. 70

12 April 1813. William FITZGERALD and Sally Jones, dau. of
Thomas B. Jones who consents. Sur. Richard Jones. Married
by the Rev. David Nowlin. p. 54

4 May 1811. John FLETCHER and Seeney Compton, dau. of Frankey Compton who consents. Sur. Robert Grant. p. 50

18 January 1813. John FLIPPIN and Catharine Pell, dau. of Henry Pell who consents. Sur. Joseph Flippin. Married 22 Jan. by the Rev. William Blair. p. 54

15 March 1819. Josiah FLIPPIN and Judith Atkinson, dau. of Josiah Atkinson who consents. Sur. Charles Atkinson. Married 22 March by the Rev. William Blair. p. 68

18 January 1813. Samuel FLIPPIN and Nancy Meadows, dau. of Joab Meadows who consents. Sur. Joseph Flippin. Married 21 Jan. by the Rev. William Blair. p. 54

17 July 1815. Samuel FLIPPIN and Patsy Lawson, who signs her own certificate. Sur. Lewis Downes. p. 58

29 April 1822. Thomas FLIPPIN and Rhody Stamps, dau. of William Stamps who authorizes the bond be issued. Sur. Jesse Atkinson. p. 75

10 May 1811. Robert B. FONTAINE and Nancy Terry, dau. of Benjamin Terry, Sr. who consents. Sur. E. Rawlins. (Eldred Rawlins is up in the bond.) Married by the Rev. David Nowlin. p. 50

17 December 1809. Thomas B. FONTAINE and Nancy Williams, dau. of Salley Williams who consents. Sur. T. Wilkinson, Jr. p. 46

17 November 1823. Thos. B. FONTAINE and Anna Watkins. Sur. James Watkins. Married by the Rev. David Nowlin who says Ballard Fontain. (Was Ballard his middle name?) p. 77

30 November 1829. John FOUSE and Ruth Ann Dent. Sur. George Arnn. Thomas Dent signs the certificate. Relationship not stated. Married 4 December by the Rev. Richard B. Beck. p. 93

6 December 1806. John FOUST and Susanna Whitsell, dau. of Harmon and Catherine Cook, who consent. Sur. William Newton. Harmon Cook was Susanna's step-father. He married Catherine Whitsell in 1805. See page 38 in the Register. p. 41

26 December 1827. Michael FOUST and Susannah Daniel. Sur. George Daniel. p. 88

21 February 1820. Anderson FOWLKES and Sarah Soyars. Sur. James Soyars. Married 24 Feb. by the Rev. James Beck. p.70

29 November 1824. James FOWLKES, Jr. and Sally Robertson, dau. of Christopher Robertson, Sr. who consents. Sur. Peter Robertson. p. 80

10 December 1813. John FOWLKES and Sarah Dickinson. Sur. Miles Holt. Married 15 Dec. by the Rev. William Blair. p.54

27 November 1827. Robert B. FOWLKES and Mary Dews, who gives her own consent. Sur. Ezekiel Dews. p. 88

17 February 1817. David FRALICK and Lucy Thompson. Sur. William Thompson. Married by the Rev. Shadrack Mustain. p. 63

13 July 1808. George FRALICK and Peggy Yates, dau. of Charles Yates. Sur. Charles Yates. p. 44

11 September 1822. Boyd FRANCIS and Jane Cox. Sur. Isham Petty. Boyd Francis and Jane Cox, herself, sign the certificate. p. 75

15 October 1821. Corbin H. FRANCIS and Polly Boaz. Sur. Thomas Boaz. p. 72

20 December 1827. Harrison FRANCIS and Frances Brumfield. Sur. Thomas K. Brumfield. p. 88

1 November 1825. Robert FRANKLIN and Phoebe Tolbart, dau. of Samuel and Judah Beach, whose consent says, "Robert, a free man of color,and Phoebe, a free girl of color." Sur. John Polly. p. 83

16 August 1819. Tarlton W. FRANKLIN and Elizabeth G. Shelton, dau. of Tunstall Shelton who consents. Sur. Pleasant Murphy. Married by the Rev. Griffith Dickinson. p. 68

18 February 1824. William C. FRANKLIN and Elizabeth Robertson, who signs her own certificate. Sur. William Winn. p. 80

23 November 1817. Jno. B. FRAVILLE and Mary Ann Gregory. Sur. William Lewis. p. 63

16 December 1825. John FREEMAN and Polley Battles, dau. of James Battles whose consent says Polly is under 21 and "John Freeman, a free man of color." Sur. William Tuggle. p. 83

26 May 1829. James FRENCH and Sarah B. Henry, dau. of Martha Henry who consents. Sur. James W. Henry. p. 93

10 January 1829. Jarvis FRIOU and Sally I. Stimson, dau. of Solomon Stimson who consents. Sur. Henry Stimson. p. 93

13 December 1815. Reubin FRITHER and Francis Grigsby. Sur. George W. Tyree. Moses Grigsby signs the certificate. No relationship stated. Married by the Rev. David Nowlin. p. 58

28 February 1825. Boaz FRIZZELL and Elizabeth Mitchell.
Sur. John Mitchell. p. 83

28 September 1826. Absolom FULLER and Nancy P. Robertson,
dau. of Christopher Robertson, Jr. who consents. Sur.
Israel Fuller. p. 85

29 March 1808. Britton FULLER and Nancy Pearson, dau. of
Richard Pearson who consents. Sur. John M. Pearson. Married 19 April by the Rev. William Blair. p. 44

14 October 1816. Britton FULLER and Sally Clark. Sur. John
M. Hanks. Sally Clark signs the certificate saying both are
of age. No relationship given. Married 15 Oct. by the Rev.
James Beck. p. 60

15 January 1828. Isaac FULLER and Martha Nuchols. Sur.
Levi Nuchols. p. 91

10 January 1818. Jesse FULLER and Polley Hundley, dau. of
Caleb Hundley who consents. Sur. William Hundley. Married
13 Jan. by the Rev. James Beck. p. 66

26 January 1827. Jonathan FULLER and Mourning Nuckols, dau.
of Milly Nuckols who consents. Sur. Levi Nuckols. p. 88

3 November 1828. Joseph FULLER and Polly Hanks. Sur. Langley B. Crowder. Thos. Hancks, Sr. consents. Married 7 Nov.
by the Rev. Richard B. Beck. p. 91

23 November 1825. Solomon FULLER and Nancy O. Harris, dau.
of Samuel Harris whose consent says, "Capt. Solomon Fuller."
p. 83

29 November 1820. Timothy FULLER and Elizabeth Hundley, dau.
of Caleb Hundley. Sur. William Hundley. Married 29 Nov. by
the Rev. James Beck. p. 70

4 December 1829. Zachariah FULLER and Betsy Nuckols. Sur.
Levy Nuckols. Married 17 Dec. by the Rev. Richard B. Beck.
p. 93

15 December 1823. Abner FULTON and Pamealy Coleman. Sur.
Spilsby Coleman. Chloe Coleman, mother of Pamealy, says her
daughter is of age, and Pamealy writes her own consent.
p. 77

20 March 1828. Nathaniel W. FUQUA and Nancy H. Tucker. Sur.
Pleasant Tucker. p. 91

23 August 1816. John FURGUSON and Susa Shelton, who writes
her own consent. Sur. Beverly Shelton. p. 60

23 November 1819. Joseph GAFFORD and Caroline M. Watson, dau. of John H. Watson who consents. Sur. William Gafford. p. 69

23 May 1826. Charles GALLOWAY and Sarah W. Michaux, dau. of Richard Michaux who consents. Sur. Richard Michaux. p. 85

15 October 1807. Drury GAMMON and Nancy Smith, dau. of Thomas Smith who consents. Sur. Talefferro Carter. Married 20 Oct. by the Rev. William Blair. p. 43

4 November 1811. James GAMMON and Elizabeth Harper, dau. of James Harper who consents. Sur. Drury Gammon. Married by the Rev. Thomas Sparks. p. 50

16 July 1829. John GAMMON and Catharine Pierce. Sur. James Astin. George Mays, guardian of Catharine, consents. p. 93

21 March 1814. William GAMMON and Polly Pearce. Sur. Jeffry Astin who "makes oath that Zadock Pearce gave his consent for the marriage of the within Wm. Gammon and Polly Pearce." p. 56

30 December 1825. Bere C. GARDNER and Nancy S. Ferguson, dau. of William Ferguson who consents. Sur. Henry W. Ferguson. Married 5 January 1826 by the Rev. William Blair. p. 83

12 June 1814. Daniel GARDNER and Mary Shields, dau. of Pleasant Shields who consents. Sur. Silas Cornwell. Married 16 June by the Rev. William Blair. p. 56

26 January 1807. Edward GARDNER and Patsy H. Shelton, dau. of Thomas Shelton who consents. Sur. William Ragland. Married by the Rev. George Dodson. p. 43

21 December 1813. George GARDNER and Mary Atkinson, dau. of Josiah Atkinson who consents. Sur. Charles W. Atkinson. Married 22 Dec. by the Rev. William Blair. p. 54

29 August 1821. Heath GARDNER and Anna Gardner, who signs her own consent. Sur. William Mitchell. Married 30 Aug. by the Rev. William Blair. p. 73

20 September 1830. Silvany GARDNER, Jr. and Sarah S. Blair, dau. of William Blair who consents. Sur. Josiah Blair. Married 23 Sept. by the Rev. Griffith Dickinson, who says Silvan Gardner. p. 96

7 November 1825. Stephen GARDNER and Catharine Fitzgerald, dau. of Jane Fitzgerald whose note says Catharine is of age. Sur. Christopher Fitzgerald. Married 10 Nov. by the Rev. William Blair. p. 83

22 September 1812. James GARLAND and Mary Clark, dau. of William Clark who consents and is Surety. Married 24 Sept. by the Rev. Griffith Dickinson. p. 52

14 March 1821. Alexander GARRETT and Mary Vaughan, who signs her own certificate. Sur. Hilton D. Walker. Married 15 March by the Rev. Griffith Dickinson. p. 72

12 January 1815. Isaac GARRETT and Elizabeth Ward. Sur. Jonathan Elliott. p. 58

29 May 1820. Isaac GARDNER and Nancy W. Williams, dau. of Charles Williams who consents. Sur. Joel Harville. p. 70

1 November 1809. John GARRETT and Sally Covington, dau. of Fanny Covington. Sally writes her own consent. Sur. David Covington. Married 2 Nov. by the Rev. Thomas Still. p. 46

26 October 1814. John GARRETT and Jean Edwards. Sur. James Pearson. Jean Edwards and James Edwards sign the certificate saying both John and Jean are of age. p. 56

3 February 1830. John GARRETT and Nancy Mahan. Sur. Pleasant Mahan. Married 9 Feb. by the Rev. William Blair. p. 96

15 March 1808. Joseph GARRETT and Polley Reiger, whose consent is signed Polly Rieger. Sur. John Garrett. Married 20 March by the Rev. William Blair. p. 44

25 November 1812. William GARRETT and Maria Marshall, who writes her own consent. Sur. William Marshall. No relationship given. Married 1 December by the Rev. Thomas Boaz. p. 52

15 January 1816. Thomas GATES and Salley Richardson. Sur. John Richardson. Thomas and Luce Richardson sign the certificate. No relationship stated. Married 17 Jan. by the Rev. William Blair. p. 60

28 July 1809. James GATEWOOD and Mary Beavers, dau. of William Beavers. Sur. William Dodson. p. 46

6 December 1814. William GAULDIN and Isbell McDaniel, dau. of Randolph McDaniel. Randolph McDaniel and Isbell sign the certificate. Sur. Samuel Gauldin. p. 56

8 February 1813. Samuel GAULDING and Chloe McDaniel. Sur. Moses McDaniel. p. 54

14 September 1817. James GEORGE and Sarah Hamrick. Sur. Jordan George. Sitha Hamrick signs the certificate. No relationship stated. p. 63

29 December 1823. John GEORGE and Sally Hatchett. Sur. Archibald Hatchett. Edward Hatchett signs the certificate. No relationship given. Married by the Rev. Ira Ellis. p. 77

7 September 1819. Robert GEORGE and Sally Owen, dau. of Obed Owen who consents. Sur. William Owen. Married 25 Sept. by the Rev. Thomas Sparks. p. 68

21 May 1810. Charles GIBSON and Sarah Atkinson, dau. of William Atkinson. Sur. Nathaniel Carter. Thomas Geo. Gibson consents. Married by the Rev. Joseph Hatchett. p. 48

19 March 1817. James GIBSON and Elizabeth Taylor. Sur. William Adkins. Thos. Geo. Gibson signs the certificate. No relationship stated. p. 63

24 October 1826. James GIBSON and Polley Martin. Sur. John Gibson. p. 85

15 February 1830. James GIBSON and Lucy Willis. Sur. Micajah Willis. p. 96

24 December 1816. John GIBSON and Peggy Taylor. Sur. Joseph Taylor. Married 25 Dec. by the Rev. Shadrack Mustain. p. 60

25 February 1827. Cornelius GILBERT and Eliza C. Stone, dau. of William H. Stone who consents. Sur. William Stone. Married 1 March 1827 by the Rev. Griffith Dickinson. p. 88

27 June 1827. John GILBERT and Lucy Witcher, dau. of Reuben Witcher who consents. Sur. William Witcher. Married 28 June by the Rev. Abner B. Anthony. p. 88

6 December 1827. Preston D. GILBERT and Wilmuth Gilbert. Sur. Preston Gilbert. Themuel Gilbert signs the certificate dated Franklin County, Virginia, December 2, 1827. Married 6 Dec. by the Rev. Abner B. Anthony. p. 88

22 September 1806. Ephriam GILES and Nancy Chattin, dau. of John Chattin, Sr. Sur. John Chattin. Married 23 Sept. by the Rev. William Blair. p. 41

10 January 1824. Ephriam GILES, Jr. and Wilmoth Walrond. Sur. Stephen Giles. John Walrond signs the certificate. No relationship given. Married by the Rev. David Nowlin. p. 80

9 December 1815. Hezekiah GILES and Mary Watson. Sur. William H. Watson. Married 12 Dec. by the Rev. Shadrack Mustain. p. 58

16 July 1821. James A. GILES and Elizabeth Giles. Sur. John Giles. Married 19 July by the Rev. William Blair. p.72

9 September 1815. John GILES, Jr. and Susanna Riddle. Sur. Stephen Giles. Married 9 Sept. by the Rev. William Blair. p. 58

13 May 1830. John GILES and Louisa Dunbar. Sur. Elisha Dunbar. Married 13 May by the Rev. Crispin Dickenson. p. 96

21 December 1829. Johnson GILES and Parthenia W. Payne. Sur. John L. Payne. William Payne signs the certificate. No relationship given. Married 22 Dec. by the Rev. William Blair. p. 93

16 February 1830. Joseph GILES and Mary Lyon. Married by the Rev. A. D. Montgomery. Minister's Return. p. 96

-- ---- 1806. Thomas GILES and Lucy Easley, dau. of Thomas Easley. Sur. Stephen Giles. Married 27 Dec. by the Rev. William Blair. p. 41

18 December 1820. Vaden H. GILES and Frances Chattin. Sur. John Chattin. Married 20 Dec. by the Rev. William Blair. p. 70

11 January 1819. William GILES and Judith Jones. Sur. Sanford Jones. Married 13 Jan. by the Rev. William Blair. p. 68

28 January 1828. William B. GILES and Ann Payne. Sur. Reuben B. Payne. Giles Payne consents. No relationship given. p. 91

-- December 1827. Alexander GILLESPIE and Lina Stewart. Sur. George Lumpkins. Nancy Lumpkin, mother of Alexander Gillespie,consents for her son. p. 88

29 November 1828. Robert B. GILLIAM and Ann Marie Noble, dau. of John Noble who consents. Sur. W. H. Tunstall. p. 91

17 October 1825. Samuel S. GILMORE and Dianna Trigg. Sur. Samuel Patton. Walter Fitzgerald, guardian of Dianna, consents. p. 83

19 December 1809. James GILPIN and Polley Brooks. Sur. James Woodall. James and Polley write their own consents. Married 31 Dec. by the Rev. Thomas Boaz. p. 46

18 January 1819. Geo. John GLASCOCK and Anna P. Coleman. Sur. Daniel Coleman. Married by the Rev. Griffith Dickinson. p. 68

6 May 1814. Thomas GLASCOCK and Sarah Coleman, dau. of
Daniel Coleman. Sur. Daniel Coleman. p. 56

21 October 1818. James GLASGOW and Susannah High. Sur.
Freeman High. Married 22 Oct. by the Rev. William Blair.
p. 66

18 October 1819. Henry D. GLASS and Elizabeth W. Echols.
Sur. Obediah Echols. Married 21 Oct. by the Rev. John
Jenkins. p. 69

27 April 1812. John L. GLENN and Tabitha Thompson, dau. of
John Thompson who is SURETY. Married 30 April by the Rev.
Joseph Hatchett. p. 52

13 November 1821. Terry GLENN and Polly Whitehead, dau. of
Richard Whitehead who requests the license be issued. Sur.
John S. Glenn. Married 15 Nov. by the Rev. Griffith Dick-
inson. p. 73

30 July 1828. Bluford GOAD and Sophea Turley. Sur. Spencer Turley. p. 91

13 February 1817. John GOAD and Caty Dalton. Sur. William
Towler. Married 13 Feb. by the Rev. Shadrack Mustain. p. 63

17 July 1815. Andrew GOARD and Polly Jacobs. Sur. Henry
Jacobs. Married 26 July by the Rev. Peyton Welch. p. 58

13 October 1806. James GOARD and Peggy Shockley. Sur.
Thomas Shockley. p. 41

23 January 1816. James GODRID and Juriah McHaney, widow.
Sur. Jordan R. Davis. Thomas Davis signs the certificate.
No relationship stated. Married 24 Jan. by the Rev. Grif-
fith Dickinson. p. 60

17 June 1816. William GODSEY and Francis Haizlip, dau. of
William Haizlip who consents. Sur. Landon I. Bishop. p.60

5 December 1811. Henry GOFF and Nancy Yeates. Sur. Charles
Yeates. Married by the Rev. Joseph Hatchett. p. 50

5 August 1819. Peyton GOING and Rhoda Shackleford. Sur.
Garland Shackleford. p. 68

21 April 1821. William GOING and Susanna Bruce. Sur. William Abston. Anna Going, mother of William, and Thomas
Bruce, father of Susanna, each request the license be
issued. Married by the Rev. Shadrack Mustain. p. 72

11 July 1818. Meredith P. GOODMAN and Patsey S. Shelton.
Sur. Coleman Shelton. Married by the Rev. Griffith Dickinson. p. 66

15 December 1818. Robert GOODMAN and Susanna Mahon. Sur. Thomas Mahon. p. 66

19 October 1829. James GOODWIN and Casandre Thacker. Sur. John M. Hart. p. 93

9 December 1830. William GOODWIN and Susanna Wright, dau. of Richard P. Wright. Sur. John D. Wright. Married 14 Dec. by the Rev. William Blair. p. 96

16 November 1829. Richard L. GOSNEY and Nancy Tiffin. Sur. Robert Townes. Married 26 Nov. by the Rev. A. D. Montgomery who says Richard S. Gosney and Mary Tiffen. p. 93

24 December 1829. Turner GOSNEY and Susan Thornton, dau. of Moses Thornton who consents. Sur. Leonard H. Thornton. Married 31 Dec. by the Rev. Richard B. Beck. p. 94

5 November 1829. William GOSNEY and Mary Roach. Sur. Henry Roach. Married 10 Nov. by the Rev. Crispen Dickenson. p.94

14 December 1813. John GOVER and Nancy Brown, dau. of Daniel Brown who consents. Sur. Lowden Brown. p. 54

21 December 1829. Christopher GOWAN and Lucinda Barber. Sur. William Barber. Married by the Rev. Eben Angel. p. 93

22 November 1809. James GRANT and Elizabeth Rowland, dau. of John Rowland, Sr. Sur. John Rowland. Married 23 Nov. by the Rev. Griffith Dickinson. p. 46

17 February 1817. James GRANT and Anna Swepston, who signs her own certificate. Sur. Zachariah Irby. p. 63

-- ---- 1816. John S. GRANT and Anney Pulliam. Sur. Drury Pulliam. p. 60   (Day and month not given in the bond.)

6 January 1819. William GRANT and Patsey Barksdale, dau. of Molly Barksdale who consents. Sur. Wm. H. Barksdale. Married 4 Sept. by the Rev. John Jenkins. p. 68

29 October 1812. Philip L. GRASTY and Jane W. Clark, dau. of William Clark who consents. Sur. William S. Clark. Married 29 Oct. by the Rev. Griffith Dickinson. p. 52

18 August 1817. William GRAVELLEE and Patsey Tucker, who signs her own certificate. Sur. Coulson Tucker. Married 21 Aug. by the Rev. James Beck. p. 63

2 March 1830. Samuel GRAVELLY and Delilah Warren. Sur. Sanders Warren. Jesse and Sarah Warren consent. No relationship stated. Married 3 March by the Rev. Orson Martin. p.96

17 January 1829. Jesse GRAVELY and Elizabeth Warren, who writes her own consent. Sur. Saunders Warren. p. 93

17 March 1822. McCoyle GRAVEN and Mary H. Stone, dau. of Prudence Stone who consents. Sur. William Hall. Married 28 March by the Rev. Griffith Dickinson. p. 75

2 May 1811. Barzilla GRAVES and Frances Williams, dau. of Sarah Williams. Sur. John Henry. p. 50

16 May 1818. James GRAVES and Dinney Witcher. Sur. John Witcher. Married 21 May by the Rev. Shadrack Mustain. p.66

8 May 1817. John GRAVES and Mildred George. Sur. Hugh George. Married 9 May by the Rev. Shadrack Mustain. p. 63

12 August 1828. Thomas GRAVES and Joanna Witcher. Sur. John Witcher. Married 12 Aug. by the Rev. Abner B. Anthony. p. 91

12 May 1818. William GRAVES and Lucy Berger, dau. of Jacob Berger, Jr., who consents. Sur. Daniel Berger. Married 14 May by the Rev. Shadrack Mustain. p. 66

19 July 1827. Adin GRAY and Nancy Dismong. Sur. John Gray. Nancy Gray, mother of Adin, and Lucinda Dismong, mother of Nancy, consent. p. 88

14 February 1823. Jeremiah GRAY and Elizabeth Morgan. Sur. Robert Gourley. p. 78

19 September 1827. John GRAY and Margaret Quinn, dau. of Peggy Quinn who consents. Sur. Redmond Quinn. p. 88

17 December 1823. William GRAY and Mary S. Kidd, dau. of Jane Silcock who consents. Sur. Amos Silcock. p. 77

18 December 1823. Laban GREEN and Elizabeth Crane. Sur. John T. Crane. Married 23 Dec. by the Rev. William Blair. p. 77

17 December 1818. Nathaniel T. GREEN and Anne Colquhoun, dau. of Patsey Colquhoun whose consent says Ann is under 21. Sur. Berryman Green. p. 66

17 June 1822. Robert GREEN and Susanna Clark, who signs her own consent. Sur. John Green. p. 75

31 August 1829. Seaton GREEN and Frances Camp, dau. of George Camp who consents. Sur. James Camp. Married 1 September by the Rev. Crispen Dickenson. p. 93

16 March 1818. Elisha GREER and Anna Graves. Sur. Peyton Graves. Married 23 April by the Rev. Shadrack Mustain. p.66

8 January 1812. John GREGORY and Elizabeth Astin. Sur.William Astin. No relationship stated. Married 9 Jan. by the Rev. William Blair. p. 52

15 June 1818. John GREGORY and Elizabeth H. Corder. Sur. Clement Pigg. ---- Corder signs the certificate. No relationship stated. Married 17 June by the Rev. James Beck. p. 66

19 February 1827. Richard GREGORY and Elizabeth Pigg. Sur. Nathan Hutchison. p. 88

9 April 1829. William GREGORY and Sarah M. Keatts, who signs her own consent as Sary M. Keatts. Sur. William C. Keatts. Married 9 March by the Rev. Griffith Dickinson. p. 94

19 September 1820. Isham GRIFFITH and Ann Parish, dau. of Darias Parrish who consents. Sur. James Hodges. Married 20 Sept. by the Rev. James Beck. p. 70

19 February 1822. William A. GRIFFITH and Lucy Daniel, dau. of Matthew Daniel. Sur. Ira Ellis. Ira Ellis wrote that Matthew Daniel was too ill to write but authorized him to do so. p. 75

9 December 1823. Willis GRIFFEY and Agness Jones. Sur. Gwilliams McDaniel. Sally Griffey and Buck Jones sign the certificate. No relationship given. Married by the Rev. Ira Ellis who says Willis Griffith. p. 77

1 August 1814. Charles GRIGG and Lucy W. Hamlett, dau. of William Hamlett who consents. Sur. Robert Hamlett. Married 1 Aug. by the Rev. Joseph Hatchett. p. 56

18 September 1826. Jesse A. GRIGGS and Mary Tompkins, dau. of Edw. Tompkins who consents. Sur. John Tompkins. Married 24 Sept. by the Rev. William Blair. p. 85

20 February 1809. Peter GRIGGS and Axeye Jesse, who writes her own consent. Sur. Isaac Morton. p. 46

5 February 1817. Barksdale GRIGSBY and Polly Corbin, dau. of William Corbin, deceased. Sur. Redmon Adams. Consent of Polley, herself, says she is 22 years old. Moses Grigsby also signs the certificate. p. 63

1 January 1816. Patrick GRIMES and Keziah Parker. Sur. John Moore. Married 2 Jan. by the Rev. Thomas Sparks. p. 60

15 July 1812. Edmund GROSS and Elizabeth Napier. Sur.
Moses Allen. p. 52

29 April 1814. Richard GROSS and Peggy Daniel. Sur. Luke
Mathes. Marey Daniel writes that Peggy is of age and wishes
the certificate issued. No relationship given. p. 56

22 February 1808. William GROSS and Maryan Foust. Sur.
Jacob Foust. p. 44

6 July 1821. David H. GRUBB and Sarah B. Keesee, who signs
her own certificate saying she is 24 years of age. Sur.
Josiah Ferguson, Jr. Married -- July by the Rev. Ira Ellis.
p. 72

10 November 1825. Jesse J. GRUBB and Minta C. Newton. Sur.
William Newton. p. 83

24 November 1812. Samuel C. GRUBB and Susanna Hodges. Sur.
Edmund Hodges. Jesse Hodges signs the certificate. No relationship stated. Married 24 Nov. by the Rev. Thomas Boaz.
p. 52

18 December 1819. Thomas T. GUNN and Elizabeth A. Hailey,
who signs her own certificate. Sur. Archibald Hailey. Married 22 Dec. by the Rev. Ira Ellis. p. 68

26 April 1823. Beverly GUNNELL and Susannah Lacy, who signs
her own certificate as Saley Lacey. Sur. William Farthing.
Married -- April by the Rev. Ira Ellis. p. 78

13 July 1823. William GWILLIAMS and Sally Mitchell. Sur.
Ephraim Potts. p. 78

16 April 1821. Littleberry GWIN and Zeria McDaniel. Sur.
William Atkinson. Married 18 April by the Rev. James Beck,
who says Kezia McDaniel. p. 72

27 March 1826. Anthony D. HADEN and Rebecca Ferguson, dau.
of Covington Ferguson who consents. Sur. Edmund Ferguson.
Married 4 April by the Rev. William Blair. p. 86

5 February 1817. John HADEN, Jr. and Jane H. Shelton, dau.
of Young Shelton who consents. Sur. Lewis Shelton. John
Haden consents for John Haden, Jr. Married 7 Feb. by the
Rev. Griffith Dickinson. p. 63

20 May 1816. William HADEN and Eddy Shelton. Sur. Littleberry Lewis. Married 24 May by the Rev. Shadrack Mustain.
p. 61

3 October 1828. Mordicai HAGOOD and Permela Worsham. Sur.
John Worsham. p. 91

16 January 1815. Edward HAILEY and Sally High. Sur. Freman High. p. 58

15 February 1816. Robert HAIRSTON and Ruth Wilson. Sur. Samuel Hairston. p. 61

22 September 1818. Samuel HAIRSTON and Agness I. P. H. Wilson. Sur. Samuel H. Woods. Robert Hairston signs the certificate. No relationship stated. p. 66

8 November 1828. Samuel HAISLIP and Jane Branson. Sur. John Bullington. William Haislip, father of Samuel, and Jonathan Branson, father of Jane, consent. Married 11 Nov. by the Rev. William Blair. p. 91

13 November 1821. Clifton HAIZLIP and Polly S. Harris. Sur. Peter M. Harris. Married 20 Nov. by the Rev. Richard B. Beck. p. 73

24 April 1811. Lovelace HALEY and Sally Phillips, dau. of Joseph Wood who consents. Sur. Jeremiah Wood. p. 50

1 September 1814. Temple HALEY and Elizabeth Haley. Sur. Vincent Dickinson. Jos. E. Haley, guardian of Elizabeth, signs the certificate. p. 56

20 December 1825. Anderson HALL and Martha C. James. Sur. Spencer Rodden. Jesse James signs the certificate. No relationship given. p. 83

21 December 1826. Anderson HALL and Mary C. James. Married by the Rev. Jarrot W. Cook, Jr. Minister's Return. p. 86

20 December 1819. Benjamin HALL and Martha Walrond. Sur. Reben Walrond. Married by the Rev. David Nowlin, who says "since my last return." Minister's Return on p. 73. Bond on p. 69

15 December 1827. David HALL and Nancy Crews, dau. of William Crews who consents. Sur. William Crews. Married 20 Dec. by the Rev. Eben Angel. p. 88

14 November 1810. George HALL and Liddy Taylor, dau. of Obediah Taylor who is Surety. Married 14 Nov. by the Rev. William Blair. p. 48

19 January 1822. George HALL and Caty Hawker, dau. of Ambrose Hawker. Sur. Anderson Hall and Ambrose Hawker. Married 24 Jan. by the Rev. William Blair. p. 75

17 January 1814. James HALL and Sally Chaney. Sur. Moses Chaney. Married 26 Jan. by the Rev. William Blair. p. 56

70

17 January 1814. James HALL and Sally Chaney. Sur. Moses Chaney. Married 26 Jan. by the Rev. William Blair. p. 56

20 August 1822. James HALL and Apphia Slayden. Sur. Thomas Slaydon. John Hall, father of James, consents. Married 3 September by the Rev. William Blair. p. 75

17 February 1824. John HALL and Elizabeth Moon. Sur. Jesse Grubb, who gives consent for John Hall, of Bedford County to marry Elizabeth Moon who is living with me in Pittsylvania County. No relationship given. Married 17 Feb. by the Rev. Richard B. Beck. p. 80

16 July 1821. Matthew HALL and Polly Shelton. Sur. William H. Hall. Married 16 August by the Rev. William Blair. p. 73

9 December 1818. Oliver HALL and Lucy Carter, who signs her own certificate as "without parents." Sur. Spencer Carter. p. 66

17 January 1820. Richard HALL and Rebecca Abbitt. Sur. Jesse Abbitt. Married 19 Jan. by the Rev. William Blair who says Rebecca Abot. (Abbott?) p. 70

30 January 1823. Samuel HALL and Mary Hoskins, who signs her own consent. Sur. James Hoskins. Married by the Rev. Ira Ellis. p. 78

10. December 1810. William HALL and Rhoda Brown, dau. of Thomas Brown. Rhoda signs her own certificate. Sur. Burwell Brown. Married 25 Dec. by the Rev. William Blair. p. 48

7 December 1826. William HALL and Lucy C. Shaw, who gives her own consent. Sur. Richard I. Shelton. Married 14 Dec. by the Rev. John G. Mills. p. 86

15 December 1817. William H. HALL and Judith Shelton. Sur. Robert Shelton. p. 63

6 March 1821. George W. HALLER and Nancy F. Johnson, dau. of Richard Johnson. Sur. Richard Johnson. Married March 1821 by the Rev. Ira Ellis. p. 73

1 January 1818. Willis HAM and Alcey Farmer, dau. of Mistress Farmer who consents. Sur. Samuel Farmer. p. 66

21 August 1826. Oliver E. HAMBLETON and Mary M. Poindexter, dau. of Gabriel Poindexter who consents. Sur. Giles H. Vaden. Married 14 September by the Rev. John W. Kelly. p.86

25 February 1820. William HAMILTON and Sally Rogers. Sur. Joseph Rogers. William Rogers, father of Sally, and Sally, herself, sign the certificate. Married by the Rev. David Nowlin "since my last return." pp. 71 & 73

15 April 1817. Robert HAMLETT and Elizabeth T. Muse. Sur. Stephen B. Hamlett. Thomas Muse, father of Elizabeth, signs the certificate. p. 63

3 June 1814. Obediah HAMM and Martha Mills. Sur. John Jones. Anthony Mills signs the certificate. No relationship stated. Martha also signs the certificate. Married 5 June by the Rev. William Blair. p. 56

17 November 1810. Spencer HAMMOCK and Sarah Mees, dau. of Caty Mees who consents. Sur. John Mees. p. 48

10 February 1810. Taliaferro HAMMOCK and Elizabeth Vance, dau. of David Vance who consents. Sur. Philip Vance. p. 48

15 August 1825. Samuel HAMPTON and Julia Ann Millner, dau. of Williamson Millner who consents. Sur. Cornelius Millner. p. 83

27 August 1830. Samuel H. HAMPTON and Jane M. Godley, dau. of Rockhill Godley who consents. Sur. Hiram Godley. Married 3 September by the Rev. William Blair. p. 96

1 December 1818. William HANKINS and Milley Dalton. Sur. William Walton. Married 3 Dec. by the Rev. Shadrack Mustain. p. 66

14 December 1807. Vincent HARDEY and Sally Waller. Sur. David Waller. Married 17 Dec. by the Rev. William Blair, who says Vincent Hardy. p. 43

13 April 1806. Stephen HARDEY and Polley Cunningham. Sur. Nathan Cunningham. p. 41

9 May 1808. Banister HARDY and Alsey Yates, dau. of Stephen Yates, Senr. Sur. John Williams. p. 45

24 December 1812. Elisha HARDY and Polly Nelson. Sur. William Nelson. No relationship stated. Married 29 Dec. by the Rev. William Blair. p. 52

17 November 1825. Green HARDY and Oney Hiler. Sur. Green Barker. Mary Hiler signs the certificate. No relationship given. p. 83

19 December 1825. James HARDY and Nancy Davis. Sur. Joseph Davis. p. 83

4 September 1819. Lewis HARDY and Polly Atkinson. Sur. Lewis Atkinson. Married Sept. 1819 by the Rev. Ira Ellis. p. 69

22 January 1812. Obadiah HARDY and Nancy High. Sur. Freeman High. No relationship given. Married 23 Jan. by the Rev. Joseph Hatchett. p. 52

20 December 1830. Robert G. HARDY and Cornelia Francis Corbin. Sur. Thomas Corbin. p. 96

5 February 1809. Solomon HARDY and Willey Madding, dau. of Thomas Madding who consents. Sur. William Lewis. Married by the Rev. Elias Dodson "since my last return." p. 46

16 February 1829. William R. HARFIELD and Mourning H. Cox, dau. of Elizabeth Cox who says, "near of age and has no guardian or agent except myself." Married 26 Feb. by the Rev. Orson Martin. p. 94

3 June 1817. Soloman HARMAN and Elizabeth Evans, who signs her own certificate. Sur. Samuel Harmon. Married 5 June by the Rev. William Blair. p. 63

30 December 1812. James HARMAN and Nancy Love. Sur. Thomas Rawlings. Married by the Rev. David Nowlin. p. 52 (James signs the bond Harman - Harmon is used up in the bond.)

25 March 1823. Charles HARPER and Ann Price, dau. of Daniel Price who consents. Sur. John Price. p. 78

17 February 1818. George HARPER and Patsey Price, dau. of Cutbird Price who consents. Sur. William Price. Married 17 Feb. by the Rev. James Beck. p. 66

10 January 1809. Jacob HARPER and Elizabeth Watson Pulliam, dau. of Drury Pulliam who consents. Sur. David Richards. Married 12 Jan. by the Rev. William Blair. p. 46

14 October 1816. Jacob HARPER and Elizabeth Worsham. Sur. William Worsham. Married 17 Oct. by the Rev. William Blair. p. 61

8 July 1824. Littleberry HARPER and Lucy Hobson, who writes her own consent. Sur. Nathaniel P. Thomas. p. 80

13 January 1826. Nicholas HARPER and Sally Orrender. Sur. Reubin Hall. p. 86

29 September 1828. Robert HARPER and Eliza C. Coleman, dau. of Ste. Coleman who consents. Sur. Stephen M. Coleman. Married 30 Sept. by the Rev. John G. Mills. p. 91

24 December 1822. William HARPER and Sarah W. Coleman, dau.
of Ste. Coleman, whose consent says daughter <u>Sally</u> W. Sur.
Thomas Glascock. p. 75

16 January 1819. Austin HARRIS and Jemima Barker, dau. of
Martha Barker who consents. Sur. Obediah Brown. Married 21
Jan. by the Rev. William Blair. p. 69

21 December 1816. David HARRIS and Polly Lansford. Sur.
Permenas Lansford. Isham Lansford, father of Polly, and
Molley Lansford (no relationship given), sign the certifi-
cate. Married 24 Dec. by the Rev. William Davis. p. 61

11 June 1825. Doctor HARRIS and Permalie Bateman. Sur. Fuller Harris. Married 16 June by the Rev. Richard B. Beck.
p. 83

2 October 1826. George HARRIS and Betsy Green. Sur. James
Green. Married 3 Oct. by the Rev. Richard B. Beck. p. 86

11 September 1829. Grief HARRIS and Fanny Smith, who gives
her own consent. Sur. Leathy Flagg. Married 12 Sept. by
the Rev. A. D. Montgomery. p. 94

14 November 1806. John HARRIS, Jr. and Polley Burton, dau.
of Elisha Burton who is Surety. Married 20 Nov. by the Rev.
Joseph Hatchett, V. D. M. p. 41

6 December 1824. Samuel HARRIS and Martha M. Pritchett.
Sur. John M. Inge. William Pritchett signs the certificate.
No relationship given. p. 80

28 April 1825. Thomas HARRIS and Joanna Terry, whose note
of consent says that both are of age. Sur. Edmund Mahan.
Married 1 May by the Rev. Richard B. Beck. p. 83

18 September 1826. Thomas L. HARRIS and Martha H. Shelton,
dau. of Leroy Shelton who consents. Sur. Samuel Robertson.
p. 86

12 November 1812. William HARRIS and Elizabeth Dyer. Sur.
Hamon Dyer. No relationship given. Married 13 Nov. by the
Rev. William Blair. p. 52

7 November 1818. William HARRIS and Elizabeth Harvey. Sur.
James Lewis. p. 66

3 January 1811. Abner HARRISON and Letty Parsons, dau. of
Joseph Parsons, Jr. Sur. Meredith Parsons. Married by the
Rev. Thomas Payne. p. 50

21 August 1826. Archibald HARRISON and Mildred Davis, dau.
of Joseph Davis who consents. Sur. William Burgess. p. 86

25 September 1821. Joshua HARRISON and Judith C. Turner, dau. of Stockley Turner who consents. Sur. James Foster. Married by the Rev. John Jenkins. p. 73

7 October 1816. Thweatt HARRISON and Frances Farmer, dau. of Isham Farmer who consents. Sur. Absolom Farmer. Married 10 Oct. by the Rev. John Jenkins. p. 61

26 April 1810. Washington M. HARRISON and Catherine Hoskins, dau. of Thomas Hoskins. Sur. Hiriam Hoskins. Married by the Rev. Thomas Sparks. (Minister says 17 April). p. 48

1 September 1810. William HARRISON, Jr. and Susanna H. Ware, dau. of William Ware who consents. Sur. Nathaniel Harrison. p. 48

15 December 1817. John M. HART and Elizabeth Stone. Sur. Isaac Stone. p. 63

21 November 1820. John HARVEY and Henreter Booker. Sur. Richard E. Booker. p. 71

15 December 1828. William HARVEY and Mary Burton. Sur. Isham Burton. p. 91

16 November 1822. Joel C. HARviLL and Betsey Callaham. Sur. Matthew Callaham. p. 75

31 August 1807. Berryman HATCHET and Rachel Shelton, who writes her own consent. Sur. Daniel Shelton. p. 43

15 April 1816. Harrison HATCHETT and Dicey Young, who signs her own certificate. Sur. Archibald Hatchett. Married 18 April by the Rev. Shadrack Mustain. p. 61

20 October 1817. William HATCHETT and Melinda Witcher. Sur. James Witcher. Married 23 Oct. by the Rev. Shadrack Mustain. p. 63

10 October 1807. William HAWKER and Jinny Snoddy, dau. of John Snody who consents. Sur. Philip Hawker. Married by the Rev. George Dodson. p. 43

24 May 1807. Jonathan HAWKINS and Sarah Booth, dau. of William Booth. Sur. William Booth. p. 43

3 December 1816. Mastin HAWKINS and Judith Dickenson. Sur. John Fowlkes. William Dickenson, guardian of Judith, signs the certificate, dated: Nottoway County, Nov. 19, 1816. Married 5 Dec. by the Rev. James Beck. p. 61

6 September 1830. Ambrose HAY and Judith Hall, dau. of John Hall, who authorizes the license be issued saying, "both parties are of age." Sur. James Chism. p. 96

30 September 1822. John HAY and Seany Self, dau. of Thomas Self whose note says, "both are of age and no dissent on either side." Sur. Burwell Self. p. 75

31 January 1820. William HAY and Nancey Wright, dau. of Daniel and Sarah Wright who consent. Sur. John B. Ragsdale. Married 1 February by the Rev. Thomas Sparks. p. 71

3 November 1817. Caleb HAYMES and Oney Brumfield. Sur. William Brumfield. Married by the Rev. Griffith Dickinson. p. 63

17 January 1818. Reubin HAYMES and Sally Bailey. Sur. James Bailey. p. 66

16 November 1807. Robert HAYMES and Lettice Shelton, who writes her own consent. Sur. Coleman Shelton. Married 17 December by the Rev. Thomas Payne. p. 43

7 December 1812. Daniel HAYNES and Sally Moore. Sur. Thomas Moore. No relationship given. Married 17 Dec. by the Rev. Griffith Dickinson. p. 52

7 January 1822. John HAYNES and Catharine Shellhorse, dau. of Barnett Shellhorse who requests the license be issued. Sur. Jacob Shellhorse. Married 8 Jan. by the Rev. Griffith Dickinson. p. 75

21 November 1826. Richard HAYNES and Mary Love. Sur. Robert Love. p. 86

30 July 1817. Ambrose HAYS and Dolley George, dau. of Jordan George who consents. Sur. John Hays. p. 63

21 May 1821. James HAYSLIP and Ann Garrett, dau. of Thomas Garrett, whose note says Ann is "of full age and there is no objection." Sur. William Payne. Married 31 May by the Rev. Richard B. Beck. p. 73

16 November 1829. William HEADSPETH and Susanna Dodson. dau. of John Dodson who consents. Sur. Thomas W. Hill. Married 26 Nov. by the Rev. John G. Mills. p. 94

15 February 1813. George HEDRICK and Druzillar Ball, dau. of John Ball who consents. Sur. Samuel Ball. Married 18 Feb. by the Rev. William Blair, who says Drusilla. p. 54

27 August 1827. George HEDRICK and Jane Bruce, who gives her own consent. Sur. William Crider. p. 88

23 December 1820. John HEDRICK and Susan Midkiff. Sur. Spencer Midkiff. Married Dec. 1820 by the Rev. Ira Ellis. p. 71

13 July 1813. Philip HEDRICK and Catharine Debo. Sur. Philip Debo. Married 16 July by the Rev. Joseph Hatchett. p. 54

7 June 1824. James HENDERSON and Jane F. Dawson, who signs her own certificate. Sur. Brooks Dawson. p. 80

27 January 1807. John HENDRICK and Rebecca Terry, dau. of Thomas Terry who consents. Sur. William Herring. Married by the Rev. George Dodson. p. 43

1 February 1819. Nathaniel HENDRICK and Elizabeth Eudaley, who signs her own certificate. Sur. William Glasgo. p.69

20 December 1812. Benjamin HENRY and Rosanna Terry, who writes her own consent. Sur. Robert Powell. p. 52

2 May 1811. Samuel HENSON and Elizabeth Barber, dau. of William Barber who is Surety. Married 7 May by the Rev. Joseph Hatchett. p. 50

9 September 1824. Moses HERNDON and Nancy Powell. Sur. John W. Powell. p. 80

17 February 1817. David HIGH and Patsey Hendrick, who signs her own certificate. Sur. Edward Hailey. Married 19 Feb. by the Rev. William Blair. p. 63

23 December 1822. Isham HIGH and Caron Dodson, dau. of Micajah and Tabithy Dodson who consent. Sur. Elisha Dodson. Married 25 Dec. by the Rev. William Blair who says Karen. p. 75

20 October 1827. Isham HIGH and Jane Prewett. Sur. John Prewett. Married 24 Oct. by the Rev. Clement McDonald. p. 88

8 July 1830. James HILER and Polly Chiles. Sur. Joshua Chiles. p. 96

17 March 1828. Daniel HILL and Nancy Headspeath, who writes her own consent and signs "Nancy Headspeth. Sur. William Headspeth. Married 18 March by the Rev. John Leigh. p. 91

15 August 1825. Ezra HILL and Mary Terrell. Sur. Jesse Terrell. Married 18 Aug. by the Rev. John Leigh. p. 83

6 January 1807. Jehu HILL and Polley Perkins. Sur. John Seemster. Married 8 Jan. by the Rev. James Nelson. p. 43

14 December 1830. Joseph HILL and Rachel M. Simpson. Married by the Rev. William Blair. Minister's Return. p. 96

16 November 1807. Nathan HILL and Polly Pearson, dau. of Richard Pearson who consents. Sur. Britton Fuller. Married 19 Nov. by the Rev. William Blair. p. 43

15 December 1828. James HINES and Mary Sanders. Sur. Joseph Mays. Married 18 Dec. by the Rev. Crispen Dickenson who says Mary Saunders. p. 91

8 February 1819. Thomas HINES and Nancy Wells, who signs her own certificate. Sur. Richard Holland. p. 69

26 October 1813. William HINES and Elizabeth Curry, dau. of James Curry who consents. Sur. Terry Dallis. Married 4 November by the Rev. Thomas Boaz. p. 54

18 January 1821. Alexander HITTSON and Mary J. Motley. Sur. Joel Motley. William Alexander, guardian of Mary, and Mary, herself, sign the certificate. Married 20 Jan. by the Rev. William Blair. p. 73

26 December 1808. Benjamin HOBSON and Lucy Stamps, dau. of William Stamps who consents. Sur. Edmond Wall. Married 29 Dec. by the Rev. William Blair. p. 44

22 January 1811. Matthew HOBSON and Sarah Wade, dau. of Henry Wade who consents. Sur. John Wade. Married 23 Jan. by the Rev. Griffith Dickinson. p. 50

29 May 1828. Richard M. HOBSON and Mary Ann Payne, dau. of Leanna L. Patton, who consents. Sur. Alfred M. Bethell. Married 29 May by the Rev. A. D. Montgomery. p. 91 (Samuel Patton had married Leaner L. Payne in 1819. p. 69)

27 December 1824. Allen HODGE and Ann Slayton. Sur. John Slaydon. Married 28 Dec. by the Rev. William Blair. p. 80

11 October 1809. Ephriam HODGES and Susanna Doss, dau. of Pattey Doss who consents. Sur. Saml Yeatts. p. 46

30 November 1824. Isham HODGES and Sarah Harvey. Sur. Richard Harvey. p. 80

26 March 1816. James HODGES and Lucy Shelton, dau. of Thomas Shelton who requests that the license be issued. Sur. Thomas S. Shelton. p. 61

18 October 1815. Josiah HODGES and Elizabeth Davis. Sur. Thomas Davis. Married 19 Oct. by the Rev. Griffith Dickinson. p. 58

21 January 1822. Lemuel HODGES and Nancy Pickeral. Sur. Waller Pickeral. Married 21 Jan. by the Rev. William Blair. p. 75

5 February 1809. Lion P. HODGES and Rachel Griffith, dau. of Salley Griffith who consents. Sur. John Nash. Moses Hodges states that Lyon Hodges is 21 years of age. p. 46

18 September 1826. Asa HODNETT and Nancy Stone. Sur. Isaac Stone. p. 86

30 May 1808. Ayres HODNETT and Nancy B. Bates, dau. of Matthew Bates. Sur. Samuel Meadows. David Nowlin, guardian of Nancy, requests the license be issued. Married by the Rev. David Nowlin, Baptist. p. 45

3 May 1819. James HODNETT and Polly Jones, dau. of Thomas B. Jones who consents. Sur. Garrett Davis. Married by the Rev. David Nowlin. p. 69

6 December 1822. John HODNITT and Lucinda M. Davis. Sur. Thomas Woody. Mary Farmer signs the certificate. No relationship given. p. 75

16 August 1813. Jonas HOLAND and Elizabeth Bingham. Sur. Edmond Bingham. p. 54

5 February 1829. Berryman HOLDER and Rebecca Michaux. Sur. George Jones. Married 5 Feb. by the Rev. John H. Watson. p. 94

21 January 1809. Beverly HOLDER and Betsy Tucker, who writes her own consent. Sur. James Moore. Married 21 Jan. by the Rev. Thomas Payne. p. 46

10 January 1828. Elijah HOLDER and Stirah Sea, who writes her own consent. Sur. Arthur Farmer. Married 10 Jan. by the Rev. Griffith Dickinson. p. 91

22 July 1819. James HOLDER and Elizabeth Hamm, dau. of Thomas Hamm who consents. Sur. Willis Hamm. Married 26 August by the Rev. John Jenkins. p. 69

13 December 1812. John HOLDER and Permely Cox, dau. of William Cox who consents. Permely requested the license be issued. Sur. David Own. (Owen?) Married 24 Dec. by the Rev. Griffith Dickinson. p. 52

4 February 1824. Peter HOLDER and Susanna Shaw, dau. of Even Shaw who consents. Sur. William Nelson. Married 5 Feb. by the Rev. William Blair. p. 80

-- ---- 1808. William HOLDER and Polley Saunders. Married
by the Rev. David Nowlin, Baptist. Minister's Return. p. 44

10 December 1812. William HOLDER and Nancy Wood, dau. of
Joseph Wood who consents. Sur. James Wood. p. 52

20 October 1815. William HOLDER and Mary Lewis, (widow),
who writes her own consent. Sur. Elijah Hardy. Married by
the Rev. George Dodson. p. 58

27 November 1816. Richard HOLLAND and Rebecca Inge, dau. of
John Inge who consents. Sur. Samuel Elliott. p. 61

1 November 1809. James HOLLEY and Elizabeth Rafe, dau. of
Lewis Rafe. Sur. John Oneal. Married 2 Nov. by the Rev.
Thomas Boaz. p. 46

12 June 1810. Joel HOLLEY and Sophy Smith. Sur. William
Smith. Thomas D. Smith requests this license be issued and
says Sophy is of lawful age. No relationship given. Married by the Rev. Thomas Boaz on June 14th. p. 48

28 November 1809. William HOLLEY and Milley Anglin, dau. of
Elizabeth Anglin. Sur. William Smith. Married 30 Nov. by
the Rev. Thomas Boaz. p. 47

19 November 1820. Fleming HOLLOWAY and Catharine Slaydon.
Married by the Rev. William Blair. Minister's Return. p. 71

31 August 1827. James HOLT and Elizabeth Dodson, dau. of
William and Rhoday Dodson who consent. Sur. Lazarus Dodson.
Married 5 September by the Rev. Clement McDonald. p. 88

4 December 1815. William HOLT and Phebe F. Smith, dau. of
William Smith who signs the certificate. Sur. William S.
Clark. Married 7 Dec. by the Rev. John Jenkins. p. 58

9 June 1824. Reuben HOPKINS and Sarah W. Easley. Sur. John
Easley. Mary Easley signs the certificate. No relationship
given. Married 10 June by the Rev. James Reid. p. 80

26 December 1818. Elisha HOSKINS and Maria Mason. Sur.
Hyram Hoskins. Hannah Hoskins signs the certificate. No relationship stated. Married by the Rev. Ira Ellis. p. 66
"This is to certify that Maria Mason is the daughter of a
free woman. I have a claim on her service till she arrives
to the age of 21 years. You are at full liberty to grant
license for her to be joined in Matrimony to Elisha Hoskins."
Signed: Ira Ellis.

12 January 1813. Hyram HOSKINS and Anna McDaniel. Sur.
Meredith Harrison. James Hoskins says Anna is over 21. Jos-
eph Holland says Thomas Hoskins, father of Hyram, consents.
Married 19 Jan. by the Rev. William Blair. p. 54

19 October 1816. Hyram HOSKINS and Nancy Hoskins. Sur. Johnson Hoskins. p. 61

24 June 1825. James HOSKINS, Jr. and Polly Crawford. Sur. Richard Hoskins. p. 83

24 December 1823. Richard HOSKINS and Mary Ozburn. Sur. Washington M. Harrison. p. 78

1 June 1821. Spiler C. HOSKINS and Susan Farmer, dau. of Isham Farmer who signs the certificate. Sur. Absolom Farmer. Married by the Rev. John Jenkins. p. 73

13 August 1819. Thomas HOSKINS and Polley Bryant, who signs her own certificate. Sur. John Nichols. Married 14 Aug. by the Rev. Richard B. Beck. p. 69

25 November 1816. William M. HOSKINS and Mildred M. Hall, dau. of William Hall. Mildred signs her own certificate. Sur. Thomas Smith. p. 61

21 February 1809. William HOW and Sarah Taplin. Sur. Redman Fallen. John Daly signs the certificate and says Sarah is of age. Married by the Rev. William Blair. (Minister says July 22, 1809.) p. 46

12 November 1821. Alexander HOWARD and Lettice Stokes, dau. of Allen Stokes who consents. Sur. Nathaniel Robertson. Married 15 Nov. by the Rev. James Beck. p. 73

22 January 1812. William HOWE and Lucy King. Sur. Anderson Gunnell. Married 23 Jan. by the Rev. William Blair. p. 52

26 December 1820. Joshua HOWERTON and Lucy Conaway. Sur. John B. Roy. Married 28 Dec. by the Rev. William Blair, who says Lucy Conway. p. 71

18 April 1825. Daniel P. HUBBARD and Joanna Carter. Sur. Jesse Carter. p. 83

5 December 1817. Hezekiah HUBBARD and Susannah Fuller, dau. of Zachariah Fuller who consents. Sur. Jesse Fuller. Married 16 Dec. by the Rev. James Beck. p. 63

1 January 1812. John HUBBARD and Polly Woodson, dau. of Allen Woodson who consents. Sur. Joseph Woodson. p. 52

28 August 1828. John W. HUDSON and Mildred West. Sur. Isaac Brumfield. p. 91

1 November 1824. Jacob HUFFMAN and Rebecca Pigg. Sur. Clement Pigg. p. 80

15 December 1807. John HUFFMAN and Nancy Townley Dainger-
field, dau. of John and Elizabeth Daingerfield who consent.
Sur. Wm. Daingerfield. Married 17 Dec. by the Rev. Joseph
Hatchett. p. 43

19 February 1816. Michael HUFFMAN and Milley Keesee. Sur.
Jesse Keesee. Married 24 Feb. by the Rev. Shadrack Mustain.
p. 61

28 March 1822. Charles HUGHES and Judith Soyars. Sur. James
Soyars. Married by the Rev. William Blair. (Minister says
27 March.) p. 75

6 January 1812. Allen HUGHEY and Sally Waggoner, dau. of
Martin Waggoner. Sur. Christopher Waggoner. Married 7 Jan.
by the Rev. Joseph Hatchett. p. 52

24 December 1811. Coleman HUGHEY and Sally Debo, dau. of
Philip Debo, Sr. Sur. Abraham Debo. Married 26 Dec. by the
Rev. Joseph Hatchett. p. 50

23 November 1825. James S. HUGHEY and Milly Waggoner. Sur.
Coleman Barber. p. 83

6 May 1810. Caleb HUNDLEY, Jr. and Nancy Hodges, dau. of
Jesse Hodges who is Surety. p. 48

17 April 1826. Charles HUNDLEY and Elender Smith. Sur.
William Smith. p. 86

17 March 1823. Christopher HUNDLEY and Elizabeth Taylor.
Sur. Thomas Dalton. Married 14 May by the Rev. John W.
Kelly. p. 78

21 January 1817. Robert HUNDLEY and Judith Parker. Sur.
William Parker. Married 23 Jan. by the Rev. Shadrack Mustain. p. 63

20 October 1806. Thomas HUNDLEY and Lucy Beck, dau. of Lucy
Beck who writes consent for her daughter Lucy. Sur. Richard
B. Beck. Married 6 November by the Rev. William Blair. p. 41

17 August 1829. Thomas HUNDLEY and Nancy Beck, who writes
her own consent. Sur. Richard B. Beck. Married 8 September
by the Rev. Richard B. Beck. p. 94

2 November 1821. William HUNDLEY and Tabitha Frizzle, dau.
of Isaac Frizzell who consents. Sur. Boaz Frizzell. Married 6 Nov. by the Rev. James Beck. p. 73

17 November 1824. William HUNDLEY and Elizabeth Curry, dau.
of Thomas Curry whose consent says Elizabeth is of lawful
age. Sur. Samuel Cox. p. 80

27 October 1823. Samuel HUNT and Sarah Douglass, dau. of Edward Douglass who authorizes the license be issued. Sur. Thomas Douglass. Married by the Rev. David Nowlin. p. 78

17 September 1810. William C. HURT and Sarah Smith Devin, dau. of Robert Devin who is Surety. Married 25 Sept. by the Rev. Robert Hurt. p. 48

5 October 1814. Benjamin HUTCHERSON and Elizabeth Devin. Sur. Abraham C. Parrish. Married 6 Oct. by the Rev. Thomas Boaz. p. 56

20 December 1830. Benjamin HUTCHERSON and Sabra Oakes, dau. of William Oakes who consents. Sur. George Oakes. Married 22 Dec. by the Rev. Crispin Dickenson. p. 96

20 May 1808. Elijah HUTCHERSON and Jane Plesico, dau. of George Plexco who consents. Sur. Saml. Hutcherson. p. 44

3 December 1815. George HUTCHERSON and Clary Swanson. Sur. Samuel A. Muse. Wm. Swanson, Sr. signs the certificate. p. 58

2 November 1820. Jeremiah HUTCHERSON and Polly King. Sur. William Grof. p. 71

24 February 1817. Nathan HUTCHERSON and Polly Pigg. Sur. Hezekiah Hubbard. Married 25 Feb. by the Rev. James Beck. p. 63

8 September 1830. Nathan HUTCHERSON and Nancy Dunbar. Sur. Elijah Hutchison. Married 9 Sept. by the Rev. William Blair. p. 96

16 November 1811. John HUTCHINGS and Anny B. Williams, dau. of Thomas Williams. Sur. Doctor C. Williams. p. 50 "James M. Williams, the Son of the within named Anne B. Williams, personally signified his consent to the within marriage." Signed: "Wm. Tunstall."

1 December 1824. Robert HUTCHINGS and Mary Carter. Sur. William H. Tunstall. Married 2 Dec. by the Rev. William Blair. p. 80

31 July 1820. Samuel HUTCHINGS and Lucy Robertson. Sur. Joel Coleman. Christopher Robertson, Sr. signs the certificate. (He was her father.) Married 2 August by the Rev. James Beck. p. 71
(Double wedding? See Joel Coleman.)

10 November 1824. Stokely HUTCHINGS and Ann R. Johnson. Sur. William H. Tunstall. Married Nov. 1824 by the Rev. William Blair. p. 80

16 July 1810. Jeremiah HUTCHINSON and Patsey Thacker. Sur. Peter Thacker. p. 48

7 March 1822. Macajah HUTSON and Lucindy Turley. Sur. John Watson. Married by the Rev. Ira Ellis. p. 75

16 January 1815. Edward H. INGE and Sarah Sutherlin. Sur. Peyton Lumpkins. p. 58

19 November 1806. George INGE and Polley Holland, dau. of Kitty Holland. Sur. Samuel Fuqua. p. 41

18 January 1819. John INGE, Sr. and Nancy Harris, who signs her own certificate. Sur. William Pritchett. p. 69

-- ---- 1809. George INGRAM and Mary Mayes. Married by the Rev. Elias Dodson. Minister's Return. p. 47

3 March 1810. George INGRAM and Mary Mayes, dau. of Frances Mayes who consents. Sur. Armistead Mayes. p. 48

21 February 1825. George INGRAM and Elizabeth Terry, dau. of David and Lettice Terry who consent. Sur. Benjamin Hall. Married 1 March by the Rev. William Blair. p. 83

29 November 1813. Lazarus INGRAM and Elizabeth Dodson. Sur. Micajah Dodson. Married by the Rev. Thomas Boaz. (Minister says on November 9th.) p. 54

23 November 1819. Morris INMAN and Lucy Thomas. Sur. Benjamin Thomas. p. 69

21 August 1815. William INMAN and Elizabeth Pike. Sur. Jacob Ryner. Married 21 Aug. by the Rev. Thomas Boaz. p.58

7 February 1829. William H. INMAN and Ruth Stow. Sur. James M. Stowe. William Beck signs the certificate saying Ruth is one of his wards. p. 94

25 June 1817. Shadrack INNMAN and Dorcas Morris. Sur. William Morris. Married 26 June by the Rev. James Beck. p. 63

19 December 1808. Baxter IRBY and Rhoda B. Oliver, who gives her own consent. Sur. Charles Irby. Married by the Rev. David Nowlin. p. 45

10 January 1816. George IRBY and Polly Irby. Sur. Jordan R. Davis. Thomas Davis, grandfather of Polly, signs the certificate. Married 11 Jan. by the Rev. Griffith Dickinson. p. 61

13 January 1818. James IRBY and Martha Keatts, dau. of
Richard Keatts who consents. Sur. John Keatts. Married by
the Rev. Griffith Dickinson. p. 66

11 December 1806. Peter IRBY and Susanna Hillard. Married
by the Rev. Griffith Dickinson. Minister's Return. p. 41

26 October 1818. Thomas IRBY and Oney Thurman, dau. of
Polley Thurman who consents. Sur. Matthew Barber. Married
29 Oct. by the Rev. Shadrack Mustain. p. 66

5 August 1817. William C. IRBY and Sarah Farmer, dau. of
Martin Farmer who consents. Sur. John Lindsey. p. 63

18 April 1829. George B. IVY and Polly Haislip, dau. of
William and Polly Haislip who consent. Sur. William Haislip. Married 19 April by the Rev. Richard B. Beck. p. 94

1 February 1813. Eli JACKSON and Sally Emmerson. Sur.
Henry Emmerson. Married 4 Feb. by the Rev. Thomas Boaz.
p. 54

20 December 1813. James JACKSON and Judith Emmerson. Sur.
Henry Emmerson. Married 30 Dec. by the Rev. William Boaz.
p. 54

15 September 1825. John JACKSON and Sally Blackwell. Sur.
Robert Blackwell. p. 83

21 December 1822. Levi JACKSON and Anna Emmerson. Sur.
John Emmerson. Married 24 Dec. by the Rev. James Beck.
p. 75

13 January 1826. Allen JACOBS and Matilda White, dau. of
Elizabeth White who consents. Sur. Aaron Jacobs. Married
9 February by the Rev. Griffith Dickinson. p. 86

18 December 1809. Claiborne JACOBS and Fanny Dudley, dau.
of Caley (?) Dudley who consents. Sur. Randolph Bobbett.
Married by the Rev. Joseph Hatchett. p. 47

-- October 1823. Henry JACOBS, Jr. and Elizabeth Barker.
Married by the Rev. Ira Ellis. Minister's Return. p. 78

17 May 1824. Henry JACOBS, Jr. and Elizabeth Barber.
Sur. Hezekiah Barber. p. 80

26 May 1825. John JACOBS and Elizabeth Hammock. Sur. Henry
Crane. Henry Jacobs, father of John, gives consent. p. 83

16 March 1818. Washington JACOBS and Milley Meas. Sur.
George A. Edwards. p. 66

21 December 1826. Catlet JAMES and Elizabeth Thompson. Sur.
Pyrant Thompson. p. 86

28 December 1829. Crispin JAMES and Tempe Grant. Sur. Henry
W. Coleman. One parent wrote a consent and failed to sign
it. Witnesses to consent: Anna Grant, Salla Grant, Henry W.
Coleman. Married 29 Dec. by the Rev. Griffith Dickenson.
p. 94

15 July 1813. Wyatt JARRETT and Francis Burnett. Sur. John
Burnett. Married 5 August by the Rev. Thomas Boaz. p. 54

15 February 1808. Alexander JEFFERSON and Elizabeth Smith,
who writes her own consent. Sur. Saml. A. Jefferson. Married 20 Feb. by the Rev. Joseph Hatchett. p. 45

20 April 1829. Alexander JEFFERSON and Polly Mahan. Sur.
John Mahan. p. 94

15 March 1830. Noten JEFFERSON and Elizabeth Carter. Sur.
Nathan Carter. Married 25 March by the Rev. Orson Martin.
p. 96

17 February 1806. Thomas JEFFERSON and Elizabeth Ball.
Sur. John Bell. Married 27 Feb. by the Rev. Joseph Hatchett.
p. 41
"Pittsylvania County
    To any Licensed Minister of the Gospel within the State
of Virginia -- Thomas Jefferson Having performed in my office
what the law Requires These are to License and permit you
to join together in the holy state of matrimony According to
the rites and Ceremonies of your Church the said Thomas
Jefferson
        and Elizabeth Ball
and for so doing this shall be your sufficient Warrant given
under my hand this 17th Day of February 1806.
                        Will Tunstall C P C"
(This is given because the Register had Elizabeth Bell.)

19 January 1807. Thomas B. JEFFERSON and Jane Graves, dau.
of Peyton Graves who consents. Sur. William Swanson, Jr.
p. 43

13 November 1827. William JEFFRIES and Polly Collie, dau.
of Charles and Aggey Collie who consent. Sur. Charles
Collie. p. 89

12 December 1809. John JENKINS and Abitha Chisholm, dau. of
John Chisholm. Married by the Rev. John Terry. p. 47
(License for this marriage is hand-written by Will Tunstall,
in which he says Abitha is daughter of John Chisholm.)

19 September 1808. William JENKINS and Lucy Farmer, dau.
of Marlin Farmer. Sur. Marlin Farmer. Married by the Rev.
David Nowlin. p. 45

12 November 1827. Boden D. JENNINGS and Judith Glass, dau.
of Willis Glass, who requests the license be issued. Sur.
Willis Glass. Married 29 Nov. by the Rev. Griffith Dickinson. p. 89

21 June 1824. Joseph JENNINGS and Susanna Hardy, who writes
her own consent. Sur. William Simpson. p. 80

14 December 1807. Meredith JENNINGS and Tabitha Mustain.
Sur. William Shelton. Married by the Rev. George Dodson.
p. 43

15 September 1823. Obediah JENNINGS and Agnes Richardson,
dau. of Thomas and Luce Richardson who consent. Sur. Elijah
Richardson. Married 16 Sept. by the Rev. John Leigh, of
Halifax County, Virginia. p. 78

5 November 1829. Richard JENNINGS and Susanna A. Weatherford, dau. of Chas. A. Weatherford who consents. Sur. Stephen Dodson. p. 94

17 March 1825. Thomas W. JENNINGS and Nancy Bohannon, dau.
of John Bohannon who consents. Sur. William H. Jennings.
Married 17 March by the Rev. John Leigh. p. 83

18 October 1827. Joseph G. JOHNS and Mary W. Austin, dau.
of Stephen Austin, who consents for himself and "wife."
Sur. Champness W. F. Johnson. p. 89

10 March 1824. Joseph T. JOHNS and Martha Faris, dau. of
Amos Faris, who requests the license be issued. Sur. James
Doss. Married 17 March by the Rev. Shadrack Mustain. p. 80

-- ---- 1823. Abraham JOHNSON and Mary M. Dunn. Sur. Abraham Martin. p. 78   (Bond mutilated.)

29 August 1817. Andrew JOHNSON and Betsy Nelson. Sur. William Madding. Married by the Rev. George Dodson who says
Elizabeth. p. 63

13 March 1820. Arthur JOHNSON and Patsey Rumley, who signs
her own certificate. Sur. John Parsons. Married 13 March
by the Rev. Ira Ellis. p. 71

6 April 1818. Edmund JOHNSON and Frances Wynne. Sur. Silby
Benson. Wm. Linn authorizes the license be issued for this
marriage - signed: "Wm. Linn, Guardian of Frances Wynne."
p. 66

19 November 1811. Giles JOHNSON and Betsey Midkiff. Sur.
William Midkiff. No relationship given. Married by the Rev.
Thomas Payne. (Minister says 23 March.) p. 50

2 August 1823. James I. JOHNSON and Rebecca Eanes. Sur.
Arthur W. Eanes. p. 78

23 November 1815. Martin JOHNSON and Lockey Leftwich. Sur.
Jeremiah Forguson. William Leftwich and Ruffey Leftwich
sign the certificate. No relationship given. p. 58

25 March 1813. Masten JOHNSON and Elizabeth Dodson. Sur.
Daniel Collie. George Dodson, Sr. says Elizabeth, his
granddaughter, is of age and lives with him "and has neither
father nor mother in the County." Elizabeth also signs the
certificate. Married by the Rev. George Dodson. p. 54

16 February 1811. Mastin JOHNSON and Elizabeth Johnson.
Married by the Rev. George Dodson. Minister's Return. p. 50

23 September 1813. Samuel JOHNSON and Francis Rowland.
Sur. Jesse Rowland. Married "since June 1813" by the Rev.
David Nowlin. p. 54

19 December 1808. William JOHNSON and Rebecca Hubbard, dau.
of Reuben Hubbard who consents. Sur. Benjamin Biba. p. 45

13 August 1810. William JOHNSON and Sally Shelhorse. Sur.
Jacob Shelhorse. Married by the Rev. Joseph Hatchett. p. 48
(Jacob Shelhorse testifies before E. Rawlins, D.C., that
Sally was over 21.)

10 October 1814. Woodson JOHNSON and Charlotte Hambrick.
Sur. Josiah Crews. Sitha Hambrick signs the certificate
saying, "the girl is of age." p. 56

16 August 1830. Archibald JOHNSTON and Hetty Yates, who
signs her own consent. Sur. Francis C. Walrond. p. 96

18 October 1830. George W. JOHNSTON and Pauline R. Parrish,
dau. of Susanna Parrish who consents. Sur. Wilson Parrish.
Married 22 Oct. by the Rev. Orson Martin. p. 96

20 January 1830. Alexander JONES and Martha Giles. Sur.
Thomas Giles. Married 22 Jan. by the Rev. William Blair.
p. 96

15 July 1826. Emanuel JONES and Martha Smith. Sur. Thomas
B. Jones. Hezekiah and Marthy Smith sign the certificate.
p. 86

16 February 1811. George JONES and Catherine Smothers, dau. of John Smothers. Sur. Stephen Giles. Married 18 Feb. by the Rev. Joseph Hatchett. p. 50

15 December 1823. Henry JONES and Rebecca Garrett. Sur. William Payne. Married 23 Dec. by the Rev. Richard B. Beck. p. 78

9 June 1813. James JONES and Polley Brown, dau. of Daniel Brown who consents. Sur. John Glover. p. 54

18 June 1827. James JONES and Jane G. Thompson, dau. of Washington Thompson, who requests the license be issued. Sur. Richard I. Shelton. Married 21 June by the Rev. William Blair. p. 89

14 March 1810. John JONES and Ann Nowlin, dau. of Bryan W. Nowlin. Sur. David Nowlin. Married by the Rev. David Nowlin, Baptist. p. 48

7 December 1812. John JONES and Rosanna Boaz. Sur. Shadrach Boaz. No relationship given. Married 15 Dec. by the Rev. Thomas Boaz. p. 52

17 January 1818. John JONES and Sally Watson. Sur. John Watson. Married 18 Jan. by the Rev. William Blair. p. 66

3 December 1825. John JONES and Elizabeth Adkins. Sur. Pleasant Thacker. p. 83

-- ---- 1808. John JONES and Elizabeth Compton. Married by the Rev. Johns Terry, Presbyterian. p. 45

25 November 1822. Joseph JONES and Rebecca Curry. Sur. John Currey. Lewis Jones, father of Joseph, and Thomas Currey, father of Rebecca, consent. Married 3 December by the Rev. Richard B. Beck. p. 75

25 February 1815. Richard JONES and Milley D. Smith. Married by the Rev. Griffith Dickinson. Minister's Return. p. 58

23 April 1822. Richard JONES and Fanny Jones, dau. of Em. Jones who consents. Sur. Thomas S. Jones. Married 1 May by the Rev. Griffith Dickinson. p. 75

17 December 1827. Thomas S. JONES and Ann R. Calland, dau. of Elizabeth C. Calland who consents. Sur. Richard I. Shelton. p. 88

11 December 1826. Edward JORDAN and Sarah F. Lewis. Sur. Joseph Lewis. Elizabeth Lewis, guardian of Sarah, consents. Married 15 Dec. by the Rev. Eben Angel. p. 86

15 April 1811. George JOYNER and Polley Pulliam, dau. of Drury Pulliam, who is Surety. p. 50

-- ---- 1817. Henry C. KEATTS and Unice Bailey. Married by the Rev. Griffith Dickinson. Minister's Return. p. 63

28 May 1819. Henry C. KEATTS and Unis Bailey. Sur. Daniel Shelton. Married by the Rev. Griffith Dickinson. p. 69

13 August 1821. John KEATTS and Polly Keatts, dau. of Charles Keatts who consents. Sur. Randolph Keatts. Married by the Rev. Ira Ellis. p. 73

29 January 1824. John KEATTS and Nancy Faris. Sur. Thomas Faris. Married 30 Jan. by the Rev. Griffith Dickinson. p.80

17 December 1817. Randolph KEATTS and Elizabeth Gregory. Sur. William Payne. Married by the Rev. Griffith Dickinson. p. 63

17 July 1820. Richard G. KEATTS and Tempy C. Shelton, dau. of Tunstall Shelton who consents. Sur. Leroy Payne. Married by the Rev. Griffith Dickinson. p. 71

1 November 1819. William C. KEATTS and Nancy Gregory. Sur. John K. Gregory. William Payne signs the certificate. No relationship given. Married by the Rev. Griffith Dickinson. p. 69

28 September 1821. Elijah KEELING and Lucy Hoskins. Sur. James Hoskins. Married -- Sept. by the Rev. Ira Ellis. p. 73

18 August 1817. Ashford KEEN and Elizabeth Edwards, dau. of Daniel C. Edwards who consents. Sur. David E. Edwards. p. 63

16 February 1807. John KEENE and Nancey Witcher. Sur. Reubin Witcher. Married 6 April by the Rev. Joseph Hatchett. p. 43

27 December 1809. Benjamin B. KEESEE and Susanna Hutchison, dau. of Mary Hutchison who consents. Sur. William Turley. p. 47

21 February 1814. Booker KEESEE and Jane Dove. Sur. George Dove. Married 10 March by the Rev. Griffith Dickinson. p.56

16 April 1811. George KEESEE and Lettice Taylor, dau. of James Taylor who is Surety. Married by the Rev. Thomas Payne. p. 50

19 March 1810. James KEESEE and Sally Parker, dau. of William Parker. Sur. James Parker. Married by the Rev. David Nowlin. p. 48

2 March 1811. John KEESEE and Polley I. Dupuy. Sur. Robert Dupuy. No relationship stated. Married by the Rev. David Nowlin. p. 50

1 February 1827. Richard KEESEE and Susan Clever. Sur. James P. Dalton. p. 89

22 December 1826. William KEESEE and Anna Pickrall, dau. of Richard Pickrel who authorizes the license be issued. Sur. Richard Keesee. Married 28 Dec. by the Rev. Shadrack Mustain. p. 86

25 March 1826. James E. KELLEY and Elizabeth Angel, dau. of Elen Angel who consents. (Mother) Sur. Charles Angel. Married 30 March by the Rev. Eben Angel who says James B. Kelley. p. 86

27 December 1828. John W. KELLY and Ann T. Brown, dau. of John E. Brown who consents. Sur. Lodowick Brown. Married 30 Dec. by the Rev. Griffith Dickinson. p. 91

21 January 1829. Barksdale KENDRICK and Mildred Brightwell, who signs her own consent. Sur. John Richardson. p. 94

23 October 1817. John H. KENDRICK and Elizabeth Reynolds. Sur. William Adkins. p. 63
(Up in the bond is William Adkins, Jr.)

16 December 1816. Benjamin KERBY and Elizabeth Fitzgerald. Sur. John Fitzgerald. Matthew Fitzgerald gives consent. Relationship not stated. p. 61

30 August 1822. John KERBY and Polly Thomas, dau. of James Thomas who requests the license be issued. Sur. Henry Thomas. Married 24 October by the Rev. James Beck. p. 75

8 August 1820. Moses KERBY and Margarett Oakes. Sur. Jesse Oakes. p. 71

4 April 1824. Elijah KERSEY and Seludy Dyer, dau. of Hamon Dyer who consents. Sur. Isham Burton. p. 80

10 January 1817. Norman KERSEY and Elizabeth Harris. Sur. Haymon Dyer. Married 11 Jan. by the Rev. William Blair. p. 63

5 November 1821. Adonijah KEY and Catharine Rosson. Sur. Joram Rosson. Joseph Rosson, father of Catharine, and Molly Rosson (no relationship given), sign the certificate. p. 73

27 October 1810. Isham KIDD and Peggy Cook, dau. of Biddy Cook who consents. Sur. Griffith Dobbins. p. 48

13 September 1812. John KIDD and Sally Walker. Sur. Griffin Dobbins. Married 1 October by the Rev. Thomas Boaz. p. 53

30 August 1806. Moses KIDD and Margaret Chapman, dau. of Robert Chapman who consents. Sur. Joel Ashworth. Married 2 September by the Rev. William Blair. p. 41

17 November 1823. Cason KING and Sarah Lester. Sur. Thomas Lester. John Lester signs the certificate. No relationship given. Married 17 Nov. by the Rev. Shadrack Mustain. p. 78

2 October 1810. Daniel KING and Nancy Vaughan, dau. of William Vaughan who consents. Sur. Thomas T. Vaughan. p. 48

17 November 1809. David KING and Elizabeth Russell. Sur. William Russell. Married by the Rev. Elias Dodson. p. 47

6 December 1824. Jacob L. KING and Jane Thornton, dau. of Rowland Thornton who requests that the license be issued. Sur. James Thornton. p. 80

17 February 1825. Jacob L. KING and Jane Thornton. Married by the Rev. Arnold Walker, who says Jacob is of Henry County, Virginia, and Jane is of Pittsylvania County, Virginia. Minister's Return. p. 83

9 January 1824. James KING and Obedience East. Sur. Ezekiel East. Married 19 Jan. by the Rev. Shadrack Mustain. p. 80

18 January 1810. John KING and Polly Wills, dau. of John Wills. Sur. Francis Gravelly. p. 48

1 November 1815. John KING and Edy Thacker, who signs her own certificate. Sur. Winnie Adkins. Married 1 Nov. by the Rev. Shadrack Mustain. p. 58

27 December 1826. Munford KING and Margaret Watson. Peter Griggs, guardian of Margaret, requests the license be issued. Sur. Hampton Wade. Married 28 Dec. by the Rev. Clement McDonald, who says Seth Munford King. p. 86

16 December 1823. Rice KING and Sarah Gray, dau. of Nancy Gray who consents. Sur. Jeremiah Gray. Married 24 Dec. by the Rev. Richard B. Beck. p. 78

30 October 1809. Robert KING and Frankey Mallicott, dau. of John Malicoat who consents. Sur. William Mulens. p. 47 (Up in the bond is William Mulins.)

16 October 1826. William KING and Gooley H. Brown. Sur. Bird Brown. Married 23 Oct. by the Rev. William Blair. p. 86

23 December 1829. Robert KNIGHT and Mary W. Stamps. Married by the Rev. William Blair. Minister's Return. p. 94

11 July 1825. Thomas KNIGHTER and Sarah Crayne. Sur. John Crayne. Married 12 July by the Rev. Clement McDonald who says Sarah <u>Crane</u>. p. 83

24 December 1811. Francis KINGTON and Fanny Vaughan, dau. of Mary Harmon who consents. Sur. Nicholas Harmon. Married by the Rev. William Blair. p. 50

17 September 1810. Francis H. LACEY and Betsey W. Peerson, dau. of Sherwood Peerson who consents. Sur. Richmond Peerson. p. 48

15 January 1810. George LACY and Dorcas Turley, dau. of John Turley who is Surety. p. 48

29 October 1810. Pleasant LACY and Zepora Turly, dau. of James Turly who consents and is Surety. Married by the Rev. Joseph Hatchett. p. 48

11 March 1809. William LACY and Martha Cocke, who writes her own consent. Sur. Richard Jones. Richard Jones' note says, "Mr. Lacy is a Stranger about the Court House" and he (Richard Jones) will be Security for Lacy. p. 47

22 December 1809. Charles LAND and Elizabeth Rowland, dau. of Jesse Rowland who consents. Sur. Daniel Cameron. Married 26 Dec. by the Rev. Thomas Payne. p. 47

26 October 1824. Demarcas LANE and Polley B. Faris. Sur. James Henderson. John B. Dawson signs the Certificate and says Polley is of age. Relationship not given. Married 28 Oct. by the Rev. Griffith Dickinson. p. 81

28 May 1818. Joel LANE and Sally Hendrick, dau. of Ezekiel Hendrick who signs the certificate. Sur. David Shelton. p. 66

16 December 1807. John H. LANIER and Polley Robertson. Sur. Edw. Robertson. Married (torn) Dec. 1807 by the Rev. William Blair. p. 43

21 October 1822. John H. LANIER and Sarah W. Inge. Sur. William Tunstall. Married 24 Oct. by the Rev. William Blair. p. 75

20 June 1808. Johnson LANSDOWN and Sally Mottley, dau. of
Sally Mottley. Sur. David Mottley. Married by the Rev.
David Nowlin, Baptist. p. 45

21 December 1816. Permenas LANSFORD and Elizabeth Harris,
dau. of Rebekah Harris who requests the license be issued.
Sur. David Harris. Married 26 Dec. by the Rev. William
Blair. p. 61

2 October 1824. Simeon LANSFORD and Cynthia Haizlip, dau.
of William and Mary Haizlip who consent. Sur. Isham Lansford. p. 81

20 October 1806. Thomas LANSFORD and Elizabeth Mitchell.
Sur. William Mitchell. Married 30 Oct. by the Rev. William
Blair. p. 41

4 January 1827. John LAPRADE and Sarah B. Shelton, who
gives her own consent. Sur. Elijah Lewis. p. 89

22 August 1809. James LARRENCE and Susanna Woodall. Sur.
James Woodall. William Larence, father of James, says his
son is of age. Married 31 Aug. by the Rev. Thomas Still,
Methodist. p. 47

24 January 1818. Adam LAW and Letty Law, who signs her own
certificate. Sur. Samuel A. Muse. p. 66

30 May 1816. William LAW and Jincy Witcher, who signs her
own certificate. Sur. Caleb Witcher, Jr. Married by the Rev.
Joel Ashworth, who says "Doc William Law." p. 61

26 March 1806. Benjamin LAWSON and Amy Fuqua, dau. of John
Fuqua who consents. Sur. Harrison Burns. Married by the
Rev. John Terry. p. 41

28 December 1830. Thomas LAYNE and Jane Edds. Married by
the Rev. Griffith Dickenson, Sr. Minister's Return. p. 96

23 December 1821. Thomas LAZENBY and Lucy Stimson, dau. of
Erasmus Stimson, Senr., who consents. (One witness to consent was Erasmus Stimson, Jr.) Sur. Henry Stimson. p. 73

6 June 1808. John LEAGUE and Polley Betterton, dau. of Wm.
Betterton, Senr. Sur. Wm. Betterton, Jr. Married 9 June by
the Rev. Griffith Dickinson. p. 45

4 March 1816. William LEAL and Sarah Owen, who signs her own
certificate saying she is of full age and fatherless. Sur.
Joel Leal. p. 61

13 September 1813. Byrom LEE and Elizabeth West. Sur.
George West. p. 54   (Bryon in Register - he signs Byrom.)

4 June 1823. Augustine LEFTWICH and Mildred A. Ward. Sur. Jacob Anderson. Married 17 June by the Rev. John W. Kelly. p. 78

22 November 1820. William LEFTWICH and Sarah C. Williams. Sur. Robert Cook. I. (or J.) W. Williams signs the certificate. No relationship stated. (Witnesses to consent: Martha Williams and R. W. Williams.) p. 71

31 May 1809. Obediah LEGRAND and Sally Richey, dau. of James Richey. Sur. William Pigg. (There is a consent - but it is too faded to read .) Married by the Rev. Thomas Sparks. (Minister says 25th May.) p. 47

14 June 1819. John LENNOX and Elizabeth Harper. Sur. Jesse Harper. Married 17 June by the Rev. William Blair. p. 69

20 April 1818. Daniel LESTER and Tabitha Keatts, who signs her own certificate. Sur. Nelson Tucker. Married by the Rev. Griffith Dickinson. p. 66

14 August 1815. John LESTER and Anna Minter, dau. of John Minter, whose note says Anna is "of full age." Sur. Anthony Minter. p. 58

21 August 1820. Thomas LESTER and Olive Pierce. Sur. Robert Pierce. p. 71

20 December 1824. Abraham LEWIS and Elizabeth M. Stone, dau. of Benjamin Stone who consents. Sur. John S. Lewis. Married 23 Dec. by the Rev. Griffith Dickinson. p. 81

23 April 1808. Charles LEWIS and Polly High, dau. of Freeman High who is Surety. Married by the Rev. Elias Dodson. List of 1809 says, "since my last return." p. 45

18 October 1824. Charles LEWIS and Martha M. Nance. Sur. William M. Nance. p. 81

22 July 1816. Claibourne LEWIS and Elizabeth A. Henderson, who signs her own consent. Sur. John S. Lewis. Married 25 July by the Rev. Griffith Dickinson. p. 61

18 March 1811. Coleman LEWIS and Elizabeth Williams, dau. of David Williams who is Surety. Married 4 April by the Rev. Griffith Dickinson. p. 50

14 January 1823. Elijah LEWIS and Jane Lewis, dau. of John Lewis who consents. Sur. John M. Lewis. Married 21 Jan. by the Rev. Griffith Dickinson. p. 78

19 December 1825. Elisha LEWIS and Lucinda Warf, dau. of James Warf who consents. Sur. Holmes Gwinn. Married 22 Dec. by the Rev. William Blair. p. 83

11 May 1812. James LEWIS and Polley Harris, who writes her
own consent. Sur. Moses Thornton. Married 21 May by the
Rev. Thomas Boaz. p. 53

19 April 1819. James M. LEWIS and Elizabeth King. Sur. Peyton King. Married 22 April by the Rev. William Blair who
says Elizabeth N. King. p. 69

15 October 1830. Joseph LEWIS and Keturah P. Harrison, dau.
of Robert Harrison, who requests the license be issued. Sur.
Will Murphy. (Up in the bond is William Murphy.) Married
by the Rev. Nathan Anderson. p. 96

19 May 1817. Larkin LEWIS and Nancy Hardy. Sur. James
Hardy. Married 20 May by the Rev. William Blair. p. 63

2 August 1813. Littleberry LEWIS and Sally G. Shelton.
Sur. Henry C. Keatts. p. 54
On the back of the bond: Henry C. Keatts testified there is
no objection on the part of the father of Sally G. Shelton
to this marriage that he knows of.
Married by the Rev. David Nowlin "Since June 1813."

26 March 1815. Nacy LEWIS and Winifred Shelton. Sur.
Nathaniel Gardner. Married 28 March by the Rev. George Dodson. p. 58

31 December 1827. Royal LEWIS and Lucy Lewis, dau. of Sarah
Lewis who consents. Sur. Thomas Madding. Married 3 January
1828 by the Rev. John Leigh. pp. 89, 91.

16 September 1811. Samuel LEWIS and Anney Davis, dau. of
Sarahann Davis. Sur. Joshua Davis. Married 17 Sept. by the
Rev. Thomas Boaz. p. 50

12 February 1814. Spencer LEWIS and Polly Shackleford.
Sur. Garland Shackleford. Nancy Shackleford consents. No
relationship given. Married 12 Feb. by the Rev. William
Blair. p. 56

15 December 1828. Tapley LEWIS and Lily Lewis, who signs
her own consent. Sur. Nasa Lewis. (Daniel Coleman said
Tapley made oath he is 21.) Married by the Rev. John Leigh.
p. 91

30 March 1813. William LEWIS and Fanny Walters, dau. of
Jackson Walters who consents. Sur. William Simpson. Married 2 April by the Rev. William Blair. p. 54

18 October 1824. William LEWIS and Wilmoth Lewis, dau. of
Sarah Lewis who consents. Sur. Thomas Madding. Married 19
Oct. by the Rev. William Blair. p. 81

16 January 1824. Beverly LINDSEY and Martha Stamps, dau. of Timothy Stamps who consents. Sur. John Lindsey. Married by the Rev. William Blair. (Minister says Jan. 15.) p. 81

18 January 1827. Thomas LINN and Frances M. Holt. Married by the Rev. William S. Plummer. Minister's Return. p. 89

27 March 1827. Thomas L. LINTHICUM and Delilah Newton, dau. of William Newton who consents. Sur. Joshua Smith. p. 89

13 April 1814. Amos LIPFORD and Elizabeth Frizzle, dau. of Abraham Frizzle who consents. Sur. William Frizzle. Married 13 April by the Rev. Thomas Boaz. p. 56

20 April 1827. Anthony P. LIPFORD and Elizabeth Ferguson. Sur. William Ferguson. p. 89

14 January 1813. Fielding LIPFORD and Susan Alexander, dau. of William Alexander who consents. Sur. William A. Townes. p. 54

1 February 1814. William LOVE and Mary Railey. Sur. William W. Railey. Married 6 Feb. by the Rev. Thomas Boaz. p. 56

1 August 1822. William LOVE and Polly Witcher. Sur. James Witcher. Married 15 Aug. by the Rev. James Beck. p. 75

29 July 1806. James LOVEENS and Fanny Richardson, dau. of William Richardson who consents. Fanny Richardson also signs the certificate. Sur. Thomas Tulloh. p. 41

27 December 1822. Erasmus LOVELACE and Jane Stimson, dau. of Erasmus Stimson who consents. Sur. Isaac Stimson. p. 75

22 January 1829. Milton T. LOVELL and Paulina V. Lanier. Sur. W. H. Tunstall. Married 22 Jan. by the Rev. John H. Watson. p. 94

3 April 1811. Samuel M. LOVELL and Joanna White, dau. of Raleigh White. Joanna writes her own consent. Sur. William Tunstall. p. 50

23 May 1822. Asa LOVERN and Tabitha Martin, who signs her own certificate. Sur. John Lovern. Married 28 May by the Rev. Ira Ellis. p. 76
(The Register had Asa Sovern and the change to Lovern has been made in pencil.)

12 December 1813. Francis LUCK and Susanna P. Mitchell, dau. of James Mitchell who consents. Sur. James Lovelace. p. 54

31 July 1828. Edmund LUMPKIN and Pary McDaniel. Sur. Paschal W. Ragsdale. Married 21 August by the Rev. Clement McDonald. p. 91

27 May 1816. George LUMPKIN and Nancy Pistole, dau. of Charles Pistole who consents. Sur. Charles Pistole. Married 30 May by the Rev. William Blair. p. 61

15 December 1829. Moore LUMPKIN and Kitty Richardson, dau. of John Richardson who consents. Sur. Charles B. Rodgers. Married by the Rev. Abner Anthony. p. 94

29 January 1828. William LUMPKINS and Martha Dix, dau. of William Dix who requests the license be issued. Sur. James Dix. Married 31 Jan. by the Rev. A. D. Montgomery. p. 91

18 September 1815. Beckwith LYELL and Peggy Owen. Sur. David Owen. Married 21 Sept. by the Rev. Shadrack Mustain. p. 58
Peggy Owens requests the license for "my daughter Peggy Owens...."
Oba. Owen wrote that he was not guardian for Peggy, but was guardian of David and John Owen.

-- ---- 1823. Elijah LYNCH and Fanny Myers. Sur. William Myers. Married January 1823 by the Rev. Ira Ellis. p. 78 (Bond mutilated.)

24 February 1817. Meredith LYNCH and Polly Harvey. Sur. Joseph Lewis. Robert Bullington signs the certificate and says Polly is his ward and step-daughter, and that she is of age. Polly also signs the certificate. Married 25 Feb. by the Rev. James Beck. p. 63
(Robert Bullington married Nancy Harvey in 1815. Register page 57.)

9 February 1819. Robert LYNCH and Polley Myers. Sur. Thomas Chattin. Married 12 Feb. by the Rev. William Blair. p. 69

11 October 1819. William LYONS and Eleanor H. Anderson, dau. of A. Anderson who requests the license be issued. Sur. William Ratliff. p. 69

1 November 1824. John McALLISTER and Martha W. Williams. Sur. James M. Williams, Jr. p. 81

16 September 1822. William McALLISTER and Susanna Dejarnett. Sur. George Dejarnett. p. 75

11 December 1825. James McCARTY and Sarah Seamore. Sur. Parham Seamore. Married 21 Dec. by the Rev. William Blair. p. 84

1 December 1829. Francis McCLANAHAN and Mary Scarce. Sur.
John Green. p. 94

21 February 1825. John McCLANAHAN and Sarah Bailey. Sur.
Christopher Bailey. Married 24 Feb. by the Rev. John W.
Kelly. p. 83

28 December 1815. Robert H. McCOHN and Lucinda W. Goodwin,
who signs her own certificate. Beale Goodwin also signs the
certificate. Sur. William Slayden. Married 4 January 1816
by the Rev. William Blair. p. 59

21 November 1812. James McCOWN and Mourning Lewis, dau. of
James Lewis who consents. Sur. James Lewis. Married 28
Nov. by the Rev. Griffith Dickinson. p. 53

16 January 1826. James C. McCULLOCK and Mary P. Waller,
dau. of Robt. Waller who authorizes the license to be
issued. Sur. Janiel Johns. Married 19 Jan. by the Rev.
Griffith Dickinson. p. 86

3 January 1820. John McCUNE and Lydia Thomas, dau. of Henson Thomas who signs the certificate. Sur. Hiram Elliott.
p. 71

29 April 1817. George McDANIEL and Mary Glascock, who
signs her own certificate. Sur. Elisha Dismukes. p. 64

4 August 1823. Hiram McDANIEL and Elizabeth Dickenson.
Sur. David Dickenson. p. 78

21 May 1825. James McDANIEL and Mary McDaniel, dau. of
Randolph McDaniel who consents. Sur. Aaron McDaniel. Married 26 May by the Rev. Clement McDonald. p. 83

17 March 1823. Matthew McDANIEL and Mildred Thornton. Sur.
Zachariah Thornton. Married 25 March by the Rev. Richard B.
Beck. p. 78

20 August 1821. William McDANIEL and Rachel Daniel. Sur.
Randolph McDaniel. p. 73
Jonah Daniel writes: "Please issue license to William McDan-
iel to marry my Daughter Rebeckah Daniel -----"
                                        Jonah Daniel"
Witnesses: Randolph McDaniel and George Daniel.

8 February 1813. Moses McDONALD and Polly Bates. Sur. Clement McDonald. p. 55

5 January 1811. Nathan McDONALD and Fanny Strange, dau. of
Susanna Strange who consents. Sur. Jesse Strange. Married
by the Rev. William Blair. p. 50

27 November 1820. John McDOWELL and Eunice Weatherford.
Sur. Thomas Cumley. John Weatherford, father of Eunice, and
Eunice, herself, sign the certificate. p. 71

28 August 1827. William McDOWELL and Elizabeth H. Weatherford. Sur. James Johnson. Charles A. Weatherford consents
to this marriage. Relationship not given. p. 89

20 March 1815. Cornelius McGEORGE and Ann Dove, dau. of
William Dove who consents. Sur. Dudley Shelton. Married 25
March by the Rev. Griffith Dickinson. p. 59

25 December 1809. Richard McHANEY and Geriah Davis, dau. of
Thomas Davis. Sur. Thomas Davis. Married 28 Dec. by the
Rev. Griffith Dickinson. p. 47

20 April 1818. William McHANEY and Fanney Templeton, dau.
of Martha Templeton who requests the license be issued. Sur.
Joseph West. Married by the Rev. Griffith Dickinson. p. 66

11 November 1830. Robert McKENDREE and Polley Zena Grubbs.
Sur. John Suttle. Married 12 Nov. by the Rev. Crispin Dickenson. p. 96

27 August 1819. Absolem McKINZIE and Elizabeth Griggory.
Sur. John Astin. Married 12 September by the Rev. James
Beck. p. 69

11 November 1806. Henry McLAUGHLIN and Polley Terry, dau.
of John Terry. Sur. Rawley Madding. Married 14 Nov. by the
Rev. Elias Dodson. p. 41

17 July 1815. John McMILLION and Fanny Burgess. Sur. Pendleton Burgess. John and Fanny sign their own certificates.
p. 58

9 November 1807. William McMILLION and Sally Gravely, dau.
of James Gravilly who consents. Sur. William Graveley.
Married 17 Nov. by the Rev. William Blair. p. 43

14 September 1813. William McMILLION and Susanna Stegall,
who writes her own consent. Sur. John M. Cookey. p. 55

17 April 1821. Jesse McNEALY and Fanny Riddle. Sur. Reubin Riddle. Married -- April by the Rev. Ira Ellis. p. 73

8 January 1824. Jesse McNEALY and Elizabeth Thompson, dau.
of Lary Thompson who requests the license be issued. Sur.
Andrew Thompson. p. 81

27 December 1815. Fryor McNEILY and Sarah Love, who signs
her own certificate. Sur. Daniel Love. Married 31 Dec. by
the Rev. Shadrack Mustain. p. 58

-- January 1823. Jesse McNEILY and Elizabeth Thompson, dau. of Lacy Thompson. Sur. Andrew Thompson. Married Jan. 1823 by the Rev. Ira Ellis. p. 78

18 February 1822. Edward MABES and Elizabeth Travis. Sur. Griffin Dobbin. Request for this license to be issued is signed, "Martha Dabusse." No relationship given. p. 75

27 June 1808. John MADDING and Elizabeth Farguson, dau. of Nathaniel Farguson. Sur. Jonas B. Walker. Joseph Carter, guardian of Elizabeth, consents. Elizabeth also signs the consent. Married by the Rev. George Dodson. p. 45

21 April 1806. Larkin MADDING and Jane Shelton, dau. of Thomas Shelton who consents. Sur. John Shelton. Married 1 May by the Rev. George Dodson. p. 41

8 October 1810. Rawley MADDING and Salley Mayes, dau. of Frances Mayes who consents. Sur. Robert Madding. p. 48

21 November 1825. Scarlet MADDING and Polly Stone. Sur. Richard Stone. Married 24 Nov. by the Rev. John G. Mills. p. 83

13 May 1820. Thomas MADDING and Elizabeth Terry. Sur. Friend Terry. Charles Terry signs the certificate. No relationship stated. p. 71

3 June 1811. Roby MADEN and Juley Mayes. Married by the Rev. Elias Dodson. Minister's Return. p. 50

15 November 1830. Abner MAHAN and Ann Giles. Sur. John Giles. Married 18 Nov. by the Rev. William Blair. p. 96

18 March 1823. David MAHAN and Susanna Giles. Sur. John Giles. p. 78

4 December 1810. Doctor MAHAN and Dolley Lansford, dau. of Isham and Molley Lansford who consent. Sur. Edmund Hodges. p. 48

26 September 1815. John MAHAN and Jane A. Parish, dau. of Peter Parish who consents. Sur. Jonathan Elliott. Married 26 Sept. by the Rev. Thomas Boaz. p. 58

17 January 1814. William MAHAN and Peggy Wright. Sur. Thomas Wright. Married 18 Jan. by the Rev. Thomas Boaz. p. 56

19 February 1830. William Meredith MANLY and Emily Taylor, dau. of John Taylor who consents. Sur. James Taylor. Married 4 March by the Rev. A. D. Montgomery. p. 96

29 October 1812. Harrison MANN and Ann Cook. Sur. Harmon Cook. Married by the Rev. david Nowlin. p. 53

22 July 1823. James MANN and Elizabeth Moss, dau. of William Moss who consents. Sur. Thomas Moss. p. 78

19 February 1823. John MANN and Nancy Kendrick. Sur. Ozburn Kendrick. p. 78

8 December 1825. John MARLER and Mary Stimpson. Sur. Erasmus Stimson. p. 84

22 December 1807. Hezekiah MARLOW and Anne May. Sur. Henry Hall. Married 24 Dec. by the Rev. William Blair. p. 43

19 November 1813. Kinsee MARLOW and Susanna Foust, who writes her own consent. Sur. George Arnn. Married "since June 1813" by the Rev. David Nowlin who says Susanna Forest. p. 54

10 December 1826. Peterson MARLOW and Frances Worsham, dau. of Ludwell Worsham, who requests this license be issued. Sur. Nicholas Lyon. Married 18 Dec. by the Rev. William Blair. p. 86

8 October 1816. William MARRICKS and Maryan Grigg, dau. of Marthy Grigg who authorizes the license be issued and says she is "mother and guardian." Maryan also signs the certificate. Married 10 Oct. by the Rev. James Beck who says, Mary Ann Grigg." p. 61

8 February 1826. David MARSHALL and Salley Sadler, who signs her own certificate. Sur. Thomas Daniel. p. 86

14 December 1824. James MARSHALL and Susan B. Curtis. Sur. Thomas Curtis. James Trotter, guardian of Susan, signs the certificate. p. 81

-- ---- 1809. Thomas MARSHALL and Nancy Brewer, dau. of William Brewer. Sur. Reubin Curtess. p. 47 (Full date not on the bond.)

24 March 1817. Thomas MARSHALL, Jr. and Elizabeth J. Beck. Sur. William Beck. Robert Beck, father of Elizabeth, requests that the license be issued. Married 27 March by the Rev. James Beck. p. 64

3 February 1806. Jesse MARTIN and Betsey Ramsey, dau. of Frances Ramsey who consents. Sur. Henry Atkinson. p. 41

10 December 1815. Joel MARTIN and Frances Roland, dau. of Jesse Roland who is Surety. p. 58

-- ---- 1816. Joel MARTIN and Frances Johnson. Married by the Rev. David Nowlin. Minister's Return. p. 61

28 August 1826. John MARTIN and Susan Goin who writes her own certificate. Sur. Bird I. Yates. Married 28 Aug. by the Rev. Griffith Dickinson who says Susan Going. p. 86

10 November 1828. John W. MARTIN and Elizabeth Hawker, dau. of Ambrose Hawker who consents. Sur. James Hawker. Married 10 Nov. by the Rev. John Leigh. p. 91

20 December 1830. Eliphalet MASTIN and Nancy Russell, dau. of William Russell who consents. Sur. Thomas Turner. Married 22 Dec. by the Rev. John Leigh. p. 96

23 January 1823. Joel MATHERLY and Sally Robertson. Sur. Robert Cook. George Robinson and Saly Robinson sign the certificate. No relationship given. Married 23 Jan. by the Rev. Richard B. Beck. p. 78

1 December 1824. Larkin MATHERLY and Keziah Dunn. Sur. John Dunn. p. 81

17 September 1810. James MATNEY and Polley Mitchell, dau. of Daniel Mitchell. Sur. Littleberry Given. p. 48

1 December 1811. John MATNEY and Nancy Wright, dau. of Thomas Wright who consents. Sur. John Wright. Married 15 Dec. by the Rev. Thomas Sparks. p. 51

28 February 1827. John MATTHEWS and Fanny Biggers. Sur. Matthew Dunn. p. 89

23 December 1808. Thomas MATTHEWS and Sally Dunn, dau. of John Dunn. Sur. Walter Dunn. Married 27 Dec. by the Rev. Thomas Boaz. p. 45

28 December 1825. Samuel B. MATTOX and Nancy Shumate. Sur. Tolison Shumate. Coley and Mary Mattox, parents of Samuel, consent. p. 83

14 January 1817. Gabriel MAY and Elizabeth Still, dau. of John Still who consents. Sur. George May. Married 16 Jan. by the Rev. William Blair. p. 64

20 February 1811. George MAY and Disey Still, dau. of John Still who consents. Sur. James May. Married 21 Feb. by the Rev. Thomas Still. p. 50

31 October 1810. James MAY and Anna Harper, dau. of Nancy Harper. Sur. Nicholas Harper. Married 6 November by the Rev. William Blair. p. 48

3 June 1811. John MAYES and Tabitha Mayes. Sur. Joseph
Mayes. Married 13 June by the Rev. Griffith Dickinson.
p. 50

30 March 1807. Smith MAYES and Winifred Mayes, dau. of
Gardner Mayes who is Surety. Married 5 March by the Rev.
Elias Dodson. p. 43

20 January 1806. William MAYES and Dumey Dodson. Sur.
George Dodson. Married 21 Jan. by the Rev. Elias Dodson,
who says Duna Dodson. p. 41

21 October 1811. Drury MAYHEW and Celia Thacker, dau. of
Benjamin Thacker who is Surety. Married 7 November by the
Rev. Griffith Dickinson. p. 51

13 January 1814. Drewry MAYS and Catharine Holt, dau. of
Lucy Holt who consents. Sur. Matthew H. Holt. Married 15
Jan. by the Rev. William Blair. p. 56

1 February 1830. Drury MAYS and Lena Slayton. Sur. Thomas
Slayton. Married by the Rev. William Blair. (Minister says
29 January.) p. 96

14 November 1816. James MAYS and Sarah Dodson. Sur. George
Dodson. p. 61

28 October 1815. John MAYS and Rachel Sanders. Sur. Jesse
Sanders. Married 7 November by the Rev. Griffith Dickinson. p. 58

18 September 1820. John MAYS and Patsy Douglass, who signs
her own certificate. Sur. Stephen Coleman. p. 71

16 August 1813. Reubin MAYS and Elizabeth Fitzgerald, dau.
of John Fitzgerald who consents. Sur. Sam. Fitzgerald.
Married 2 September by the Rev. William Blair. p. 55

21 December 1825. Tarpley MAYS and Prudence Echols, who
writes her own consent. Sur. Winn Echols. Married 22 Dec.
by the Rev. William Blair. p. 84

6 October 1818. William MAYS and Catharine Roach. Sur.
James Roach. Married 8 Oct. by the Rev. Shadrack Mustain.
p. 66

23 December 1818. William MAYS and Sally Mays, who writes
her own consent. Sur. Flemming Mays. Married by the Rev.
Griffith Dickinson. p. 66

12 March 1823. William MAYS and Sarah Echols. Sur. Wyman
Echols. Married 13 March by the Rev. William Blair. p. 78

19 December 1820. John S. MAYSE and Martha Douglass. Married by the Rev. John Jenkins. Minister's Return. p. 71

13 December 1819. Mayo MEADE and Lucy Mart. Sur. Garrett Davis. Benj. Davis signs the certificate. No relationship given. p. 69

12 July 1806. Meridith MEADE and Rhoda Adams. Sur. William Williams. (William M. Williams on the bond - he signs William Williams.) Married by the Rev. Richard Elliott. p. 41

19 December 1820. Middleton MEADE and Elizabeth Ramsey, dau. of Noton and Rachel Ramsey who consent. Sur. Haley Ramsey. (In bond is Hailey S. Ramsey.) p. 71

8 December 1830. James MEADOWS and Rhoda Ingram, who signs her own consent. Sur. George Mays. Married 9 Dec. by the Rev. William Blair. p. 96

2 November 1829. Joseph MEADOWS and Elizabeth M. Payne. Sur. John Payne. William Payne signs the certificate. No relationship given. Married 5 Nov. by the Rev. Crispin Dickenson. p. 94

26 September 1810. Samuel MEADOWS and Nancey Mart, who writes her own consent. Sur. Thomas Davis, who states that Nancy is 21 years of age. Married 29 Sept. by the Rev. William Blair. p. 48

29 September 1807. William MEADOWS and Jincy Mart, who signs her own consent. Sur. Redmond Adams. p. 43

17 July 1826. Pendleton MEASE and Seeney Thompson. Sur. Caleb Witcher. Marthey Mease (designated as "father" in Register), consents for son. p. 86

5 October 1813. Abraham MEESE and Mildred Hammack, dau. of John Hammack who consents. Sur. Spencer Hammack. p. 54

8 December 1815. Barns MERRICKS and Elizabeth Ingram. Sur. Micajah Dodson. Married 13 Dec. by the Rev. Thomas Boaz. p. 58

28 March 1823. Henry MERRICKS and Mary Smith. Sur. Edward Merricks. Married 30 March by the Rev. William Blair. p. 78

21 December 1806. David MIDKIFF and Elizabeth Nickols, dau. of Charles and Michel Nickles who consent. Sur. Samuel Parsons. p. 41

13 September 1826. Isaiah MIDKIFF and Elizabeth Mottley. Sur. Richard H. Farthing. Margaret Farthing, Grandmother of Elizabeth, requests that the license be issued. p. 86

20 June 1816. John MIDKIFF and Elizabeth Abbott, who signs her own certificate. Sur. Elijah Parsons. Married by the Rev. David Nowlin. p. 61

12 December 1821. Joseph MIDKIFF and Nancy Bradley. Sur. Isham Bradley. Married "since my last return" by the Rev. David Nowlin. p. 73

27 May 1822. Matthew MIDKIFF and Susanna Clever. Sur. John Parsons, Jr. Married -- May 1822 by the Rev. Ira Ellis. p. 75

15 December 1818. Samuel MIDKIFF and Mary Clever. Sur. Richard Midkiff. Married by the Rev. Griffith Dickinson. p. 66

1 July 1809. William MIDKIFF and Susanna Midkiff, dau. of John Midkiff. Sur. John Midkiff. p. 47

30 September 1811. Jacob MILLER and Elizabeth Cox, dau. of George Cox who consents. Sur. Francis Abston. Married 2 October by the Rev. Griffith Dickinson. p. 50

20 October 1817. James MILLER and Nancy Snow. Sur. Daniel Snow. No relationship given. p. 64

30 December 1817. Samuel T. MILLER and Frances E. F. Patrick. Sur. Seth Ward, Jr. Saml. Pannill, guardian of Frances, signs the certificate. Married by the Rev. Griffith Dickinson. p. 64

26 January 1825. Thomas MILLER and Mildred Walrond, who writes her own consent. Sur. Reuben Walrond. p. 83

24 October 1828. George MILLION and Polly Dangerfield, dau. of Henerham Dangerfield who requests that the license be issued. Sur. William Dangerfield. Married 24 Oct. by the Rev. Abner Anthony. p. 91

16 December 1830. William B. MILLNER and Mary H. Keen, dau. of John Keen who consents. Sur. William H. Keen. Married 23 Dec. by the Rev. Nathan Anderson. p. 96

4 February 1823. Daniel MILLS and Catherine Chaney. Sur. Charles Chaney. Married 12 Feb. by the Rev. William Blair. p. 78

12 December 1829. Hezekiah MILLS and Judith Jackson, whose consent says, "I have acted for myself for over twelve months." Sur. Henry Blanks, Jr. Married 12 Dec. by the Rev. Griffith Dickenson, Sr. p. 94

20 March 1820. Joseph W. MILLS and Susanna Berger, dau. of
Jacob Berger who consents. Sur. George Berger. Married --
March by the Rev. Ira Ellis. p. 71

4 March 1820. Anthony MINTER and Jane Bybee, dau. of Joseph
Bybee who consents. Sur. John Bybee. Married 15 March by
the Rev. Shadrack Mustain. p. 71

7 October 1817. Obediah MINTER and Fanny Covington. Sur.
William Austin. Obediah and Fanny sign the certificate -
each is of age. p. 64

20 April 1812. Elisha MITCHELL and Judith Wills. Sur.
Samuel Elliott. p. 53

11 December 1830. Henry MITCHELL and Sarah G. Waller, who
signs her own consent. Sur. William Waller. Married 23 Dec.
by the Rev. William Blair. p. 96

27 November 1826. Isaac MITCHELL and Jane Irby, dau. of
Anna Irby who consents. Sur. Peter Irby. Married 30 Nov.
by the Rev. Shadrack Mustain. p. 86

26 February 1812. James MITCHELL and Lydia Hamrick, dau. of
Sytha Hamrick who consents. Sur. Daniel Jenkins. p. 53

20 December 1824. James A. MITCHELL and Sarah H. Vaden.
Sur. Wilson Vaden. p. 81

19 August 1816. James H. MITCHELL and Polly Tucker. Sur. N.
Tucker. p. 61

29 November 1811. John MITCHELL and Polly Witcher, dau. of
John Witcher, Senr. Sur. James Witcher. p. 51

24 February 1817. Robertson MITCHELL and Polly Chisholm,
dau. of James Chisholm who consents. Sur. Asa Walters.
Married 27 Feb. by the Rev. William Blair. p. 63

5 January 1815. Samuel MITCHELL and Elizabeth Cox. Married
by the Rev. Thomas Boaz. Minister's Return. p. 58
(See Samuel P. Mitchell.)

2 January 1814. Samuel P. MITCHELL and Elizabeth Cox, dau.
of James S. Cox who consents. Sur. Hugh Reynolds. Married
by the Rev. Thomas Boaz. p. 56
(See Samuel Mitchell - 1815.)

21 December 1813. William MITCHELL and Lucinda Gardner,
dau. of Silvany (mother) Gardner who consents. Sur. Daniel
Gardner. Married 23 Dec. by the Rev. William Blair. p. 55

19 December 1825. Josiah C. MONROE and Orfildy Henderson, who writes her own consent. Sur. James Henderson. Married 29 Dec. by the Rev. Shadrack Mustain. p. 84

26 June 1828. Thomas MOODY and Chloe Lewis, dau. of John Lewis, Sr. who consents. Sur. Daniel P. Lewis. p. 91

7 July 1820. Robert L. MOONE and Cynthia A. Sullivan. Sur. Robert Ross. Dan Sullivan signs the certificate. No relationship stated. Married 11 July by the Rev. John Jenkins. p. 71

7 March 1821. Asa MOORE and Mary Moorefield, who signs her own certificate. Sur. John Moore. Married 8 March by the Rev. William Blair. p. 73

27 November 1818. Azariah MOORE and Letitia J. Johnson, dau. of Nancy Johnson who consents. Sur. George W. Johnson. Married by the Rev. David Nowlin. p. 66

17 December 1806. Collins MOORE and Nancey Thacker, dau. of Pleasant Thacker who consents. Sur. Thomas Carey, Jr. p.41

10 January 1814. George MOORE and Salley Hendrick, who writes her own consent. Sur. Alexander Hendrick. Married 13 Jan. by the Rev. William Blair. p. 56

14 September 1813. James MOORE and Elizabeth Wralph, who writes her own consent. Sur. Doctor Peerson. p. 55

2 January 1823. John MOORE and Metildy Vaughan, dau. of William and Presiley Vaughan who consent. Sur. Benjamin Ritcher. p. 78

12 January 1812. Vincent MOORE and Nancy Hatchett, dau. of Edward Hatchett. Sur. Edward Hatchett. Married 12 Jan. by the Rev. Joseph Hatchett. p. 53

23 December 1815. William MOORE and Jincey Minter, dau. of John Minter whose note says Jincey is of age. Sur. George Terrill. p. 58

15 December 1817. William MOORE and Elizabeth McAlaster. Sur. James McAlaster. p. 64

22 December 1818. Joseph MOOREFIELD and Sarah Wade. Sur. Henry W. Stokes. Henry Wade, grandfather of Sarah, signs the certificate. Married by the Rev. David Nowlin. p. 66

19 December 1825. Achilles H. MOORMAN and Eliza S. Calland, dau. of Eliza C. Calland, whose consent says she is "mother and guardian" of Eliza. Sur. Tavner C. Shelton. p. 83

22 May 1822. John MORGAN and Elizabeth Glascock. Sur. William L. Glascock. Geo. McDaniel, guardian of Elizabeth, signs the certificate. p. 75

7 March 1812. Coleman MORRIS and Ony Slate, who signs her own consent. Sur. William Tait. (Up in bond is William Tate.) Married by the Rev. Elisha Dodson. p. 53

2 November 1818. Elijah MORRIS and Jincey Haymore. Sur. William Inman. Married 3 Nov. by the Rev. James Beck. p. 66

4 December 1815. Faris MORRIS and Agness Boaz, dau. of Lydia Boaz who consents. Sur. James Boaz. Married by the Rev. Thomas Boaz. (Minister says Dec. 1) p. 58

12 February 1825. Henry MORRIS and Catharine C. Trotter, dau. of James Trotter who consents. Sur. John M. Inge. p. 83

1 November 1815. Jesse MORRIS and Lidia Inman, dau. of William Inman who consents. Sur. Elijah Morris. Married 2 Nov. by the Rev. Thomas Boaz. p. 58

2 November 1807. Reubin MORRIS and Rhoda Matherley. Sur. Israel Matherley. Married by the Rev. William Blair. (Minister says 1st November.) p. 43

22 June 1817. Richard MORRIS and Patsy Tate, who signs her own certificate. Sur. Holland Hedgpeth. Married by the Rev. George Dodson. p. 64

17 March 1817. Samuel MORRIS and Susan Pierce. Sur. Jeffrey Astin. Married 18 March by the Rev. James Beck. p.64

26 April 1810. John MORRISON and Nancy Thompson, dau. of Elizabeth Thompson. Sur. Caleb Witcher. Married by the Rev. Joseph Hatchett. p. 48

14 December 1813. Wm. John MORRISON and Elizabeth Jones. Sur. Elisha Jones. Married 16 Dec. by the Rev. Joseph Hatchett. p. 54

25 December 1815. David MORTON and Elizabeth Petty. Sur. Levi Garrett. Andrew Petty signs the certificate. No relationship given. p. 59

18 December 1810. Jesse MORTON and Jane Dearing, dau. of John Dearing. Surety: John Dearing. p. 48

-- January 1823. Thomas MOSS and Anna Collie. Sur. Daniel Slayden. p. 78
(There was a consent - half of bond and part of consent are gone.)

26 November 1823. Daniel MOTLEY, Jr. and Jane Shellhorse. Sur. Barnett Shellhorse. Married -- Nov. by the Rev. Ira Ellis. p. 78

4 October 1820. David MOTLEY, Jr. and Giddy Nichols. Sur. Dudley Nichols. Married 4 Oct. by the Rev. Griffith Dickinson. p. 71

17 February 1824. William MOTLEY and Sarah W. Chattin, who writes her own consent. Sur. Ephraim Giles. Married 17 Feb. by the Rev. William Blair. p. 81

9 December 1808. Daniel MOTTLEY, Jr. and Nancy Clopton, dau. of Robert Clopton who consents. Sur. Wesley Shelton. Married by the Rev. David Nowlin. p. 45

29 September 1806. David MOTTLEY and Jencey Wright. Sur. Rice B. Linthicum. Married by the Rev. Willis Hopwood. p. 41

14 January 1812. Henry MOTTLEY and Elizabeth H. Tabb. Sur. Robert Dupey. Married by the Rev. David Nowlin. p. 53

23 January 1826. Horatio MOTTLEY and Nancy Hall. Sur. James Elliott. p. 86

30 December 1807. John MOTTLEY and Giddy Jones. Sur. John Jones. David Mottley, father of John, consents. p. 43

17 January 1807. Joseph MOTTLEY and Polley Jones, dau. of Elisha Jones. Sur. John Jones. David Mottley, father of Joseph, consents. p. 43

29 December 1817. William MOTTLEY and Wilmoth M. Neal, who signs her own certificate. Sur. Thomas Williams. p. 64

17 November 1823. John MOURNING and Elizabeth Irby, dau. of Francis and Martha Irby who consent. Sur. John S. Glenn. Married 27 Nov. by the Rev. Griffith Dickinson. p. 78

5 March 1817. Allen MURPHY and Rebecca Smothers. Sur. John Smothers. Married 6 March by the Rev. Ira Ellis. p. 64

29 November 1806. James MURPHY and Peggy Sands. Sur. Zach. Riddle. p. 41

14 April 1822. John MURPHY and Lucy Tiffin, dau. of Thomas and Elizabeth Tiffin who consent. Sur. Peter L. Tiffin. p. 75

6 March 1823. John MURPHY and Nancy Hagood. Sur. Thomas Moody. Lewis Hagood signs the certificate. No relationship given. Married 13 March by the Rev. Griffith Dickinson. p. 78

110

1 April 1811. Lewis MURPHY and Joanna Deer. Sur. John Morton. Consent of Isiah Morton. No relationship stated. Married 4 April by the Rev. Thomas Still. p. 51

16 November 1818. Pleasant MURPHY and Anna R. Shelton, dau. of William Shelton who signs the certificate. Sur. Vincent H. Shelton. Married by the Rev. Griffith Dickinson. p. 66

3 December 1827. Spencer MURPHY and Martha M. Breedlove. Richard Breedlove consents. No relationship stated. Sur. Pleasant E. Breedlove. p. 89

24 July 1829. Warren D. MURPHY and Elizabeth Dixon, dau. of William Dixon who consents. Sur. Peyton T. Dixon. Married 30 July by the Rev. Richard B. Beck. p. 94

1 November 1824. William MURPHY and Nancy D. Breedlove. Sur. Richard Breedlove. p. 81

8 December 1829. John MURRAY and Sally Holligan. Sur. Fleming B. Bryant. Solomon Hemson, guardian of Salley S. Holigen, consents. p. 94

17 November 1810. James MURRELL and Levina Edds, dau. of John Edds. Sur. Abraham Edds. p. 48

2 December 1816. Henry L. MUSE and Elizabeth Swanson, dau. of William Swanson, Sr., who signs the certificate. Sur. Reubin Hopkins. p. 61

20 February 1809. John MUSE and Nancy Swanson, dau. of William Swanson, Senr. who consents. Sur. Samuel A. Muse. p. 47

3 March 1829. John A. MUSE and Elvira E. Muse. Sur. Robert W. B. Muse. John T. Muse, guardian of Elvira, consents. Married 5 March by the Rev. Orson Martin. p. 94

15 April 1816. John T. MUSE and Nancy Muse, who signs her own certificate. Sur. Jabez Smith. Married by the Rev. David Nowlin. p. 61

23 December 1828. Robert MUSE and Polly Pearson, who signs her own consent. Sur. John T. Muse. Married by the Rev. Orson Martin. (Minister says 22 December.) p. 91

13 March 1861. Thomas MUSE and Elizabeth Bowling, dau. of Joseph Bowling who signs the certificate - says "my daughter." Sur. George Bolling. p. 61

20 October 1829. Avary MUSTAIN and Frances Faris. Sur. Coleman Faris. Married 21 Oct. by the Rev. Griffith Dickenson, Sr. p. 94

6 November 1813. Drury MUSTAIN and Sally Ramsey. Sur.
Noton Ramsey. Noton Ramsey signs the certificate (relationship not given), but he says, "for she is old enough to be
her own guardian." Married "since June 1813" by the Rev.
David Nowlin. p. 54

19 August 1811. Haley MUSTAIN and Elizabeth Butcher, dau.
of Gincy Butcher. Sur. Benjamin Butcher. Married by the
Rev. Griffith Dickinson. (Minister says July 30.) p. 51

16 August 1813. Joel MUSTAIN and Mary Gosney. Sur. Benjamin Gosney. Married 22 Aug. by the Rev. Griffith Dickinson. p. 54

16 August 1813. Shadrack MUSTAIN and Margaret Devin, dau.
of Elizabeth Devin who consents. Sur. William Devin. Married "since June 1813" by the Rev. David Nowlin. p. 55

11 January 1829. Thomas MUSTAIN and Mary Hardy. Sur. Abraham N. Mills. p. 94

2 November 1808. Benjamin MYERS and Elizabeth Corbin. Sur.
Thomas Corbin. Married by the Rev. David Nowlin. p. 45

24 December 1817. Isham MYERS and Patsey Emerson. Sur.
John Myers. p. 64

30 September 1815. Jacob MYERS and Elizabeth Orrender.
Sur. John Myers. Married 1 October by the Rev. Shadrack
Mustain. p. 59

14 February 1816. James MYERS and Fanny Waller. Sur. John
Myers. p. 61

8 November 1808. John MYERS and Rosa Davis, dau. of John
Davis, deceased. Sur. William Davis. p. 45

5 November 1828. Milton MYERS and Sarah G. Hardy. Sur.
Robert G. Hardy. William Myers, father of Milton, consents.
p. 91

10 February 1817. Buckner NANCE and Polley Fisher, dau. of
Bazil Fisher, who signs the certificate and says,"no objection on either side." Sur. Peyton Dickerson. p. 64

15 April 1816. James NANCE and Charlotte Harrison, dau. of
Ro. Harrison whose consent says Capt. James Nance. p. 61

6 July 1807. William NAPIER and Betsey Witcher, dau. of
John Witcher who is Surety. Married 9 July by the Rev.
Joseph Hatchett. p. 43

21 November 1827. William A. NAPIER and Demarius Reynolds. Sur. John Gibson. p. 89

16 November 1807. Arthur NASH and Polley Turley. Sur. Floyd Turley. Married 24 Nov. by the Rev. Joseph Hatchett. p. 43

15 October 1827. William NASH and Catharine Craine. Sur. John Turley. p. 89

16 December 1818. Bolen NEAL and Maryan Flippin, dau. of Joseph Flippin who requests the license be issued. Sur. William Slaydon. Married 19 Dec. by the Rev. William Blair. p. 66

19 August 1806. David NEAL and Neilly Dickinson, dau. of Griffith Dickinson. Sur. Will Tunstall. Married by the Rev. John Jenkins, who says Nelly Dickenson. p. 41

19 January 1817. John NEAL and Lucy Bruce. Sur. Joseph Mays. Married by the Rev. Griffith Dickinson. p. 64

16 January 1826. John NEAL, Jr. and Dinney Dalton. Sur. William Hankins. Married 19 Jan. by the Rev. Shadrack Mustain. p. 86

23 May 1806. Joseph NEAL and Lucey Dalton, dau. of John Dalton who consents. Sur. Ward Bruce. Married by the Rev. Willis Hopwood. p. 41

18 February 1811. Thomas H. NEAL and Wilmoth M. Williams, dau. of James M. Williams. Sur. William Tunstall. Married 21 Feb. by the Rev. Griffith Dickinson. p. 51

20 July 1820. Richd G. NEALE and Tempy C. Shelton. Married by the Rev. Griffith Dickinson. Minister's Return. (Found in Minister's Return - not in the Register.)

27 December 1806. James NELSON and Elizabeth Allen, dau. of Welcome Wm. Allen who consents. Sur. Will P. Harrison. p. 41

4 February 1824. William NELSON and Elizabeth Burch, who signs her own consent. Sur. Peter Holder. Married 5 Feb. by the Rev. William Blair. p. 81

13 September 1830. William NEWBILL and Cynthia Chapman. Sur. Harrison Douglas. Saley Chapman and Cinthy, herself, sign the certificate. Married 15 October by the Rev. John Leigh. p. 96

15 June 1812. Asa NEWBY and Polley Madding, dau. of Rachel Madding who consents. Sur. Robert Mading. p. 53

15 December 1829. Elijah NEWBY and Nancy Hay, dau. of Reubin Hay who consents. Sur. Ambrose Hay. Married 18 Dec. by the Rev. William Blair. p. 94

20 January 1810. Thomas NEWTON and Polly Plexico, dau. of George Plexico who is Surety. Married by the Rev. Joseph Hatchett. p. 48

30 March 1818. Dudley NICHOLAS and Sarah Parsons, who writes her own consent saying she is "over the age of 18." Sur. Samuel Parsons. Married by the Rev. Griffith Dickinson. p. 66

11 January 1817. John NICHOLAS and Lusey Owen. Sur. Christian Slayden. p. 64

24 January 1809. John NICHOLS and Sally Farthing, dau. of William Farthing. Sur. Dudley Farthing. Married 26 Jan. by the Rev. Thomas Payne. p. 47

5 March 1822. Solomon NICHOLS and Susanna Parsons. Sur. Richard Farthing. Married 6 March by the Rev. Ira Ellis. p. 75

-- September 1806. William NICHOLS and Elizabeth Rickey, dau. of James H. Richey who consents. Sur. David Rickee. Married by the Rev. Thomas Sparks. p. 41

13 January 1809. William NICHOLS and Elizabeth Birchey. Married by the Rev. Thomas Sparks. Minister's Return. p.47

24 December 1817. Joseph NOBLE and Martha P. Payne, dau. of William Payne who consents. Sur. William Payne. p. 64

12 July 1828. Chesley M. NOELL and Sarah Gosney. Sur. Lewis Gosney. Married 23 July by the Rev. Griffith Dickinson. p. 91

26 June 1816. Joseph NORCUTT and Sarah M. Hairston, of Pittsylvania County. Sur. David Moore. Janiel Norcutt, of Amherst County, father of Joseph, says Joseph is living in Pittsylvania County. Married by the Rev. David Nowlin. p. 61

2 December 1811. Gideon NORTHCUT and Patsey Pearson, dau. of Richard Pearson who consents. Sur. James Pearson. p. 51

1 September 1820. Henry W. NORTON and Jane Still. Sur. Drury Norton. p. 71

17 October 1814. Jacob NORTON and Nancy Frizzle, dau. of Abraham Frizzell who consents. Sur. Dozier Bradner. Married 9 Novemfer by the Rev. Thomas Boaz. p. 57

114

18 January 1820. Lemuel NORTON and Elender Sparkes, dau.
of Thomas and Elizabeth Sparkes who consent. Sur. Anderson Sparkes. p. 71

2 March 1822. Nehemiah NORTON and Anna Ward, dau. of Elizabeth Ward who consents. Sur. Nathan Ward. p. 75

6 February 1830. Prier F. NORTON and Agness Quinn, dau. of
Margarett Quin who consents. Sur. John Gray. Married 9
Feb. by the Rev. Milton Robertson, who says Prior E. Norton.
p. 96

13 February 1815. Thomas NORTON and Crecinda Wooton, dau.
of Mary Woton,who signs the certificate. Sur. Edmond
Gwinn. p. 59

14 December 1818. Bryan W. NOWLIN and Martha I. Clopton,
dau. of Robert A. Clopton who is Surety. Married by the
Rev. Griffith Dickinson. p. 66

11 June 1829. David NOWLIN and Catharine Martin. Married
by the Rev. Griffith Dickenson, Sr. Minister's Return.
p. 94

25 November 1819. Hopkins NOWLIN and Chloe I. Hall, who
signs her own certificate. Sur. Edward Hall. Married 30
Nov. by the Rev. John Jenkins. p. 69

28 December 1815. John NOWLIN and Nancy Dixon. (By her
name, in parenthesis, is "Halifax") Married by the Rev.
Griffith Dickinson. Minister's Return. p. 59

18 October 1819. Wade NOWLIN and Ann W. Douglass. Sur.
Edward Douglass. Married by the Rev. Griffith Dickinson.
p. 69

10 July 1826. John NUCKOLS and Borintha Grubb. Sur. Jesse
I. Grubb. Married 12 July by the Rev. Richard B. Beck who
says Berintha Grubb. p. 86

27 January 1813. Samuel M. CULLY and Nancy Wright, who
gives her own consent to "Mr. Samuel M. Cully." Sur.
John Walton. p. 55
(Register, now corrected, did have Samuel M. Mully.)

16 September 1811. Absolom NUNNELEE and Patsey Mottley.
Sur. Robert Dupuy. p. 51

12 August 1807. Anthony OAKES and Polley Elliott, dau. of
James Elliott. Sur. William Elliott. Married 18 Aug. by
the Rev. William Blair. p. 43
(Register says Polley's father is Joseph Elliott. Bond says
Jas Elliott, Sent. Also see James Elliott's will 1830.)

19 December 1825. James OAKES and Martha Drain, dau. of William and Nancy Drain who consent. Sur. John Cahall. p. 84

27 September 1828. James OAKES and Evaline Oakes, granddaughter of Elizabeth Oakes who consents. Sur. Richard Coran. p. 91

28 May 1818. Jesse OAKES and Mary Cook. Sur. Harmon Cook. p. 66

2 November 1822. Joab OAKES and Elizabeth Kerby, dau. of Moses Kerby who consents. Sur. William Oakes. p. 75

26 August 1810. John OAKES and Elizabeth Bardin, who signs her own consent. Sur. Will. Oakes. Oath of William Oakes that Elizabeth is 21. p. 48

20 November 1826. John B. OAKES and Elizabeth Thomas, dau. of Henson Thomas who consents. Sur. Samuel Beck. p. 86

2 March 1817. Thomas OAKS and Anna Jones. Sur. Elisha Jones. Married 4 March by the Rev. Shadrack Mustain. p. 64

10 July 1824. William OAKES and Sally Phraley, dau. of John and Teaney Phraley who consent. Sur. Wyatt Adkins. p. 81

22 August 1827. William OAKES and Salley Billings, dau. of Elisha Billins and Patsey Billens who consent. Sur. James Oakes. p. 89

17 January 1825. Frederick OBERTHIER and Sarah Hubbard. Sur. Moses Hubbard. p. 84

7 July 1806. William OLIVER and Betsey Creed Tanner, dau. of Creed Tanner who consents. Sur. John I. Oliver. Married "in 1806" by the Rev. John Atkinson. p. 41

18 July 1808. John ONEAL and Ann Holley. Sur. James Holley. Married 19 July by the Rev. William Blair. p. 45

5 April 1826. John ONEAL, Jr. and Nancy I. Tuggle. Sur. William Tuggle. p. 86

7 January 1826. Pleasant ORRENDER and Nancy Crane. Sur. John T. Crane. Married 12 Jan. by the Rev. Clement McDonald. p. 86

16 September 1822. Robert OVERBY and Elizabeth Pollard, dau. of George Pollard, Sr., who requests the license be issued. Sur. John Pollard. Married 24 Sept. by the Rev. Griffith Dickinson. p. 75

27 December 1817. Wm. H. J. OVERBY and Amanda G. Reagan.
Sur. Danel Reagan. p. 64

20 May 1825. Epaphroditus OWEN and Ludy Irby who signs her
own certificate. Sur. George Irby. Pleasant Owen, father
of Epaphroditus, signs the certificate and says "to Miss
Saluda Irby." Married 25 May by the Rev. Eben Angel. p. 84

26 October 1825. Isaac OWEN and Phebe Hilliard, who gives
her own consent. Sur. David Glenn. Married 27 Oct. by the
Rev. Griffith Dickinson. Thomas Owen, father of Isaac, consents. p. 84

14 September 1818. James OWEN and Polly Holder, dau. of
Delaney Holder who consents. Sur. Isaac Brumfield. p. 66

16 July 1823. James OWEN and Sally Fisher. Sur. William
Fisher and Wm. M. Williams. Married 17 July by the Rev.
Griffith Dickinson. p. 78

4 January 1813. John OWEN and Salley Holder, dau. of Delaney Holder, who consents for his daughter. Sur. Benjamin
Dalton. Married 7 Jan. by the Rev. Griffith Dickinson.
p. 55

11 December 1818. John OWEN and Elizabeth Owen, dau. of
Salley Owen who consents. Sur. William Pigg. p. 66

26 December 1813. Pleasant OWEN and Elizabeth Moore. Sur.
John Shields. p. 55

2 December 1824. Royall OWEN and Letty Woodson, dau. of
Drury Woodson who requests that the license be issued. Sur.
William W. Farmer. p. 81

13 February 1806. Thomas OWEN and Caty Seamorel. Sur.
Zachariah Seamore. p. 41

29 December 1823. Thomas OWEN and Nancy D. Wilson, who signs
her own certificate. Sur. Peyton S. Dixon. p. 78

19 December 1826. Thomas OWEN and Oney Ham, who signs her
own consent. Sur. Henry Blanks, who makes oath Oney is 21.
p. 86

4 November 1822. Thomas OWENS and Martha Citty, dau. of
Jacob Citty, Sr., who requests this license be issued. Sur.
Christopher Citty. Married 7 Nov. by the Rev. Griffith
Dickinson. p. 75

2 December 1824. Wiley OWEN and Polly Woodson, dau. of
Drury Woodson who consents. Sur. William W. Farmer. p. 81

13 February 1821. William OWEN, Jr. and Nancy M. Hailey,
who signs her own certificate. Sur. John Hailey. Married
22 Feb. by the Rev. Griffith Dickinson. p. 73

23 September 1824. William OWEN and Rebecca Haymore, dau.
of John Hamore who consents. Sur. James McDaniel. Married
23 Sept. by the Rev. Clement McDonald. p. 81

1 March 1822. Edward PACE and Ruth Morris. Sur. William
Morris. Married 5 March by the Rev. James Beck. p. 76

17 January 1825. Francis PACE and Lucy Davis, dau. of Joseph and Mercy Davis who consent. Sur. John Davis. Married
by the Rev. Shadrack Mustain. p. 84

4 October 1830. James PACE and Mildred Davis, dau. of Joseph and Mercy Davis who consent. Sur. John Davis. Married
6 Oct. by the Rev. Richard B. Beck. p. 96

17 December 1812. Thomas PARISH and Martha Stone. Sur.
Isaac Stone. No relationship given. Married 24 Dec. by the
Rev. Thomas Boaz. p. 53

20 August 1810. Eli PARKER and Milley Owen, granddaughter
of John Owen who signs the certificate. Sur. Joshua Stone,
Jr. Married by the Rev. Johns Terry. p. 49

22 December 1824. Elias PARKER and Nancy Ham, dau. of Thomas Ham who requests that the license be issued. Sur. Seaton Compton. p. 81

5 June 1819. Elijah PARKER and Elizabeth Bennett. Sur.
Richard Bennett. Married 10 June by the Rev. Shadrack Mustain. p. 69

9 January 1827. George PARKER and Susanna Keesee, dau. of
Richard Keesee, who "authorizes" the license be issued.
Sur. William Keesee. Married 11 Jan. by the Rev. Shadrack
Mustain. p. 89

21 February 1812. John PARKER and Nancy Hundley, dau. of
Joseph Hundley who consents. Sur. John Hundley. p. 53

7 April 1813. Joseph PARKER and Nancy Roach. Sur. Burdill
Roach. Married 15 April by the Rev. Griffith Dickinson.
p. 55

-- ---- 1807. Neley PARKER and Dolly Hay. Married by the
Rev. John Jenkins. Minister's Return. p. 43

12 November 1810. Richard PARKER and Nancy King, who writes
her own consent. Sur. Asa Prewit. Married by the Rev.
George Dodson. p. 49

1 January 1821. Thomas PARKER and Nancy Dalton. Sur.Thomas Dalton. Married 1 Jan. by the Rev. Shadrack Mustain. p. 73

13 July 1820. William PARKER and Lucy W. Terry, who signs her own certificate as Lucy G. Terry. Sur. Robert Terry. Married "since my last return" by the Rev. David Nowlin. This return dated 15 April 1822. pp. 71 &74

19 December 1808. Abraham PARRISH and Susanna Riddle. Sur. Ephraim Giles. Married 20 Dec. by the Rev. William Blair. p. 45

13 January 1811. Abraham C. PARRISH and Mary Devin, dau. of Martha Devin. Sur. Ja^s Devin, who makes oath Mary is of age. Married 17 Jan. by the Rev. Thomas Boaz. p. 51

19 March 1822. Abram C. PARRISH and Anna Parsons. Sur. Elijah Parsons. Married 19 March by the Rev. William Blair. p. 75

15 March 1824. Jesse H. PARRISH and Jane Mitchell. Sur. John R. Parrish. Dorcas Parrish, parent of Jesse, signs the certificate. Married 15 March by the Rev. Richard B. Beck. p. 81

23 November 1822. John R. PARRISH and Nancy Mitchell. Sur. Pleasant Thacker. Married 26 Nov. by the Rev. James Beck. p. 76

11 January 1814. Matthews PARRISH and Elizabeth Bolin, dau. of John Bolin who consents. Sur. Edward Popejoy. Married 11 Jan. by the Rev. Thomas Boaz. p. 57

20 December 1830. Wilson PARRISH and Matilda C. Wells. Sur. James M. Wells. Married 30 Dec. by the Rev. Orson Martin. p. 96

27 February 1821. David PARSONS and Polly Dalton. Sur. John Towler. Married 1 March by the Rev. Shadrack Mustain. p. 73

7 May 1824. Dillard PARSONS and Polly Dalton. Sur. William Dalton. Married -- May by the Rev. Ira Ellis. p. 81

24 December 1823. Elijah PARSONS and Sarah Hagood. Sur. John Murphy. Lewis Hagood signs the certificate. No relationship given. Married 25 Dec. by the Rev. William Blair. p. 78

26 September 1822. James PARSONS and Elizabeth Dalton, dau. of John S. Dalton who consents. Sur. Vincent Parsons. Married -- Sept. by the Rev. Ira Ellis. p. 76

3 February 1824. James PARSONS and Polly Midkiff. Sur. Spencer Midkiff. Married -- Feb. by the Rev. Ira Ellis. p. 81

4 April 1808. Jesse PARSONS and Sally Childress, dau. of Polley Childress who consents. Sur. Nathan Carter. Married 6 April by the Rev. Joseph Hatchett. p. 45

21 July 1806. John PARSONS and Molley Adkins. Sur. Nathaniel Adkins. Married by the Rev. Willis Hopwood. p. 41

24 August 1824. Joseph PARSONS, Sr. and Sally Thompson. Sur. William Holt. Married 24 Aug. by the Rev. Ira Ellis. p. 81

15 December 1830. Levi PARSONS and Elizabeth Midkiff. Sur. Spencer Midkiff. Married 23 Dec. by the Rev. Crispin Dickenson. p. 97

15 March 1813. Meredith PARSONS and Mary Williams. Sur. Nathan Adams. Molley Williams signs the certificate. No relationship given. Married 17 March by the Rev. William Blair. p. 55

15 November 1819. Richard B. PARSONS and Letty Yates. Sur. Richard Farthing. Married 17 Nov. by the Rev. Griffith Dickinson. p. 69

17 January 1814. Samuel PARSONS, Jr. and Hannah J. Hoskins. Sur. Thomas Hoskins. No relationship given. Married 9 February by the Rev. Joseph Hatchett. p. 57

16 July 1810. Stephen PARSONS and Lucy Farthing. Sur. John Farthing. p. 49

29 December 1818. Thomas PARSONS and Frances Clever. Sur. Richard B. Parsons. Elizabeth Clever signs the certificate. No relationship given; but she says, "I have given my consent." Married by the Rev. David Nowlin. p. 66

30 October 1825. Vincent PARSONS and Cenia Bennitt. Sur. John Fralick, who testifies Cenia is of age. p. 84

19 November 1810. Will PARSONS and Salley Bingham, dau. of Edmund Bingham who is Surety. p. 49

23 March 1812. James H. PASS and Polly M. Pistole. Sur. John Pistole. Married 2 April by the Rev. William Blair. p. 53

25 October 1825. John E. F. PATRICK and Nancy F. Patrick. Sur. John F. Patrick. Saml. Pannill, guardian of Nancy, requests the license be issued. Note dated: "Greenhill, Campbell Co." Married 3 Nov. by the Rev. Shadrack Mustain. p.84

23 February 1821. Edward PATTERSON and Polly Mays. Sur.
Joseph Mays. Married 27 Feb. by the Rev. Griffith Dickinson. p. 73

19 November 1821. James M. PATTERSON and Sarah W. Garner.
Sur. James S. Stanley. Married 28 Nov. by the Rev. William
Blair who says <u>Sally W. Gardner</u>. p. 73

6 March 1827. Jarrott PATTERSON and Rhoda Goodwin, who
gives her own consent. Sur. Isham Bradley. p. 89

3 July 1821. John PATTERSON and Polley Chamberlain. Sur.
Britton Chamberlain. p. 73

29 March 1819. Samuel PATTON and Leaner L. Payne. (in pen-
cil is: "Mrs." by Leeanna Lee Fearn.) Sur. Thomas O. Meur.
Leaner signs her own certificate. Married 31 March by the
Rev. William Blair. p. 69
(Charles Payne married Leannah Fearn in 1800. Reg. p. 29.)

-- ---- 1823. Joseph G. PAUL and ---- ----man. Sur. William D. Griggs. Consent, 2 January 18-- "and she is over
15 years old and willing. Signed: Robard Chadman (Seal),
Elisabeth Chadman (Seal). p. 78
(This is a mutilated bond. On the back is December 2 (torn).

9 December 1829. Thomas PAUL and Jane Dalton, dau. of Martin <u>Daulton</u> who consents. Sur. Jesse Garrett. Married 10
Dec. by the Rev. Richard B. Beck. p. 94

20 January 1815. John PAXTON and Sarah Price, dau. of
Daniel Price who consents. Sur. William Price. p. 59

24 August 1827. Baldwin PAYNE and Catharine Coles, who
writes her own consent. Sur. James T. Coles. Married 6
September by the Rev. John W. Kelly. p. 89

18 June 1827. Benjamin PAYNE and Martha L. Shelton. Sur.
Reuben Payne. Married 5 July by the Rev. Griffith Dickinson. p. 89

30 August 1817. Cornelius PAYNE and Louisa Ann Walton.
Sur. Jesse Walton. William Walton, father of Louisa, signs
the certificate. Married 1 September by the Rev. William
Blair. p. 64

29 November 1830. Crispin PAYNE and Susan Shelhorse. Sur.
Henry Shelhorse. Married 2 December by the Rev. Crispin
Dickenson. p. 96

16 January 1826. Frederick N. PAYNE and Mary Mitchell.
Sur. John Mitchell. p. 86

19 November 1827. Henry PAYNE and Catharine Tosh, dau. of George Tosh, who requests this license be issued. Sur. John Tosh. p. 89

19 December 1825. Leroy PAYNE and Rachel Hill, dau. of Joseph Hill who consents. Sur. Tarlton W. Franklin. Married 22 Dec. by the Rev. John Leigh. p. 84

4 April 1829. Reubin PAYNE and Parthena Mitchell. Sur. Frederick A. Payne. Married 9 April by the Rev. Orson Martin. p. 94

16 February 1807. William PAYNE and Sally Garrett, dau. of Thomas Garrett who consents. Sur. Richard Watson. p. 43

20 February 1826. James PEARCE and Lucy Hodges. Consent of Elizabeth Hodges. No relationship given. Sur. David Hodges. p. 86

6 April 1826. Walker PEARCE and Martha Shaw. Sur. Jesse Shaw. Married 9 April by the Rev. Clement McDonald. p. 86

19 August 1822. Jesse PEARMAN and Martha Travis, dau. of John Travis, who requests the license be issued. Sur. John D. Stone. Married 20 Aug. by the Rev. William Blair. p. 75

24 December 1824. Price PEARMAN and Frances Travis, who signs her own certificate. Sur. Richard Travis, who testifies Frances is of age. Married 25 Dec. by the Rev. William Blair. p. 81

17 January 1816. Jesse PEARMON and Mary Reynolds, dau. of Jesse Reynolds who consents. Sur. William Pearman. Married 18 Jan. by the Rev. William Blair. p. 61

22 August 1808. John PEARSON and Lucreasey Taylor, dau. of James Taylor who consents. Sur. William Taylor. Married 23 Aug. by the Rev. Thomas Payne. p. 45

15 December 1809. John M. PEARSON and Jincy Taylor, dau. of James Taylor who is Surety. Married 19 Dec. by the Rev. Thomas Payne. p. 47

1 May 1826. John M. PEARSON and Ann Dunn. Sur. Joseph Fuller. Married 2 May by the Rev. Orson Martin. p. 86

6 March 1821. Jesse PEEK and Jamima Bransome. Sur. Michael Branson. Married 8 March by the Rev. James Beck. p. 73

30 October 1810. Henry PELL and Betsey Jennings, dau. of Robert Jennings whose consent says that he and his wife Susannah consent. Sur. James Collie. Married by the Rev. George Dodson. p. 49

11 July 1818. Joseph PEMBERTON and Frances Goad. Sur. William Parker. Married 16 July by the Rev. Shadrack Mustain. p. 67

22 September 1813. Philip PENN and Louisa Briscoe. Sur. John Briscoe. Davis Rice signs the certificate. No relationship given. p. 55

4 December 1815. Joseph PERKINS and Elizabeth Price, dau. of Daniel Price who consents. Sur. William Price. p. 59

15 December 1806. David PERRY and Oney Witcher, dau. of John Witcher. Sur. John Witcher. Married 1 January by the Rev. Joseph Hatchett. p. 41

24 November 1814. Isham PETTY and Polley Wells. Sur. John Wells. No relationship stated. Married 24 Nov. by the Rev. Thomas Boaz. p. 57

27 December 1825. John W. PHELPS and Dicy Brightwell, whose note says that she is of age. Sur. John Jennings. p. 84

15 May 1828. Richard PHELPS and Bethaney E. Thurmond. Married by the Rev. Abner Anthony. Minister's Return. p. 91

18 January 1819. William PHELPS and Rebeccah C. Davis. Sur. Asa Davis. Married 5 February by the Rev. William Blair. p. 69

21 March 1809. George PHILLIPS and Keziah Scott, dau. of Nimrod Scott who consents. Sur. John Walters. Married by the Rev. George Dodson. p. 47

2 January 1816. William PHILLIPS and Polley Jennings. Sur. Robert Jennings. Married 4 Jan. by the Rev. George Dodson. p. 61

16 September 1822. Henry PICKERAL and Polly Mayhue. Sur. Henry Mayhue. Married 18 Sept. by the Rev. Griffith Dickinson. p. 75

4 April 1818. John PICKERAL and Sarah Arthur. Sur. Lewis Dalton. Married 7 April by the Rev. Shadrack Mustain. p.66

25 September 1826. Thomas PICKERAL and Sally Alvis. Sur. Shadrack Olvis. (Alvis? - he signed with a mark.) p. 86

14 July 1812. William PICKERAL and Martha Gregory. Sur. William Payne. Married 14 July by the Rev. Thomas Payne. p. 53

29 September 1829. Wyatt PICKERAL and Milly Doss. Sur. Stephen Doss. Married 8 October by the Rev. Crispin Dickenson. p. 94

18 July 1808. Richard PICKERALL and Betsy Dalton, dau. of
Milley Slayton. Sur. Elijah Dalton. Married 28 July by the
Rev. Joseph Hatchett. p. 45
(Milly Dalton had married Daniel Slaton in 1805. Reg. p.40)

19 November 1810. Basdell PICKRELL and Lucy Bobbett, dau.
of Randolph Bobbett who consents. Sur. Richard Pickrell.
Married 28 Nov. by the Rev. Joseph Hatchett. p. 49

4 January 1808. Michael PIERCE and Nancy Richards, dau. of
Joseph Richards. Sur. David Richards. Married 7 Jan. by
the Rev. William Blair. p. 45

7 March 1807. Clement PIGG and Nancey Elliott, dau. of
Joseph Elliott. Sur. William Elliott. Married by the Rev.
Thomas Sparks. p. 43

1 November 1824. Peyton PIGG and Susanna Butcher. Sur.
Robert Fendley. p. 81

3 December 1807. William PIKE and Nelly Harvey. Sur. Samuel Harvey. Married 10 Dec. by the Rev. William Blair. p.43

14 August 1815. Charles PISTOLE and Mary Mills. Sur. John
Sutherlin. Charles Pistole, father of Charles, and Anthony
Mills (no relationship given) sign certificates. Married
17 Aug. by the Rev. William Blair. p. 59

11 September 1815. James PITTS and Rebecca Dejarnett, dau.
of George Dejarnett, who requests that the license be granted. Sur. Asa Craddock. Married by the Rev. Nathaniel
Lovelace. p. 59

14 November 1815. Jesse PITTS and Sally Vaughan. Sur.
George Vaughan. George Vaughan signs the certificate. No
relationship stated. p. 59

19 May 1828. Jesse PITTS and Winifred Lovelace. Sur. Thomas Lovelace. p. 91

22 December 1823. William H. PLUNKETT and Mary Stone, dau.
of William H. Stone who says, in his request that the
license be issued, "she is my lawful heir." Sur. Samuel
Stone, Jr. p. 78

27 January 1806. Gabriel POINDEXTER and Micha White, dau.
of Rawley White who consents. Sur. Lawson H. Carter. Married 30 Jan. by the Rev. Richard Dabbs. p. 41

1 April 1813. John POLLARD and Judah Barksdale, dau. of
Molley Barksdale who consents. Sur. Wm. H. Barksdale. p.55

17 December 1818. William POLLARD and Elizabeth Farmer, dau. of Elizabeth Farmer who consents. Sur. John Farmer. p. 66

12 June 1823. Daniel POLLY and Barbara L. Jennings, of Pittsylvania County. Sur. John Jennings. Married 8 July by the Rev. John Leigh, of Halifax County. p. 78

25 October 1825. John B. PONSONBY and Eliza M. Williams. Sur. Nicholas Lewis. Married 2 November by the Rev. A. D. Montgomery. p. 84

19 March 1810. Edward POPEJOY, Jr. and Rachel Bolling, who writes her own consent. Sur. William Prewett. Married by the Rev. Thomas Boaz. (Minister says 13 March.) p. 49

6 January 1824. James PORTICE and Mary Delap, dau. of Martha Delap who consents. Sur. William Oakes. Married 8 Jan. by the Rev. Richard B. Beck. p. 81

20 December 1824. John POWELL and Jane Herndon, dau. of Reuben and Hannah Herndon who consent. Sur. Moses Herndon. p. 81

2 April 1807. Robert POWELL and Sally Davis. Sur. William Davis. Married 4 May by the Rev. Joseph Hatchett. p. 43

7 June 1826. John W. POWER and Elizabeth M. Glass, dau. of Willis Glass who consents. Sur. James A. Luck. p. 86

15 October 1810. John PREWET and Dolley Williams, dau. of Sarah Lovell. Sur. John Lovell. Married by the Rev. Joseph Hatchett. p. 49
(John Lovell was Dolley's step-father. He married Sarah Williams, widow, in 1796. See Register page 22.)

17 June 1829. John PREWETT and Hannah Owen, who writes her own consent. Sur. Joshua B. Swain. p. 94

8 April 1818. Joseph PREWETT and Mary F. Booker, dau. of Richard E. Booker who consents. Sur. John Bolling. Married 9 April by the Rev. James Beck, who says <u>Frances</u> Booker. (She was Mary Frances Booker.) p. 66

18 August 1826. Wiley PREWETT and Nancy Carter. Sur. Ezra Walters. John Walters signs the certificate. No relationship given. He says, "by mutual consent of all parties." Nancy also signs the certificate. Married 22 Aug. by the Rev. William Blair. p. 86

12 November 1810. Abel PRICE and Sarah Hubbard, who signs her own consent. Sur. Hezekiah Hubbard. Married 14 Nov. by the Rev. William Blair. p. 49

17 October 1815. Abel PRICE and Polly Morris, dau. of John Morris who consents. Sur. Hezekiah Hubbard, who made oath that Polly is upwards of 21 years. Married 17 Oct. by the Rev. Thomas Boaz. p. 59

26 November 1814. Booker PRICE and Polley Barker, who writes her own consent. Sur. Thomas Burnett. Married 27 Nov. by the Rev. Thomas Boaz. p. 57

24 October 1807. Fontaine PRICE and Judith Hubbard. Sur. Thomas H. Wooding. Adin Gray writes consent. No relationship given. p. 43

17 December 1830. John P. PRICE and Eliza Hampton, dau. of John Hampton who consents. Sur. Thomas H. Hampton. Married 23 (torn) by the Rev. William Blair. p. 97

15 December 1817. Nathaniel PRICE and Patsey Thacker. Sur. Emanuel E. Thacker. p. 64

3 February 1810. Philip B. PRICE and Rachel Crain, dau. of Susanna Crain who consents. Sur. Thomas Crain. Married 6 Feb. by the Rev. William Blair. p. 49

13 January 1812. Philip B. PRICE and Polly Bolling. Sur. John Bolling. Married 14 Jan. by the Rev. William Blair. p.53

27 March 1820. Philip B. PRICE and Polly Blades. Sur. Micajah Willis. p. 71

29 September 1813. Samuel PRICE and Sally Jenkins, dau. of John Jenkins who consents. Sur. Daniel Jenkins. Married "since June 1813" by the Rev. David Nowlin. p. 55

20 September 1819. Stephen PRICE and Rebecca Parrish. Sur. Allen Chandler. Married 23 Sept. by the Rev. James Beck. p. 69

22 May 1815. Thomas PRICE and Nancy Chessher, dau. of William Chessher who signs the certificate. Sur. Daniel Chessher. Married 24 May by the Rev. Thomas Boaz. p. 59

21 September 1819. Thompson PRICE and Lucy Coleman, dau. of Choloe Coleman who consents. Sur. Johnson Coleman. p. 69

20 March 1826. William PRICE and Ann S. Coleman, who gives her own consent. Chloe Coleman signs the certificate saying that Ann is of age. Sur. Spilsby Coleman. p. 86

126

14 September 1817. John L. PRIDDY and Martha H. Tucker. Sur. Nelson Tucker. p. 64

20 October 1813. John PRITCHETT and Sarah Inge, dau. of John Inge wno consents. Sur. Stephen Dance. p. 55

8 November 1817. Joshua PRITCHETT and Elisa Inge, dau. of John Inge who consents. Sur. John Pritchett. p. 64

21 January 1828. Robert PRITCHETT and Sarah Fitzgerald, dau. of Walter Fitzgerald who authorizes the license be issued. Sur. Samuel S. Gilmore. p. 91

22 August 1810. Thomas PROSIZE and Susanna --------. Sur. Spencer Medkiff. p. 49
(The bride's last name is not on the bond.)

14 March 1809. Asa PRUITT and Tabitha Farguson, who writes her own consent. Robert Farguson says daughter is 21. Sur. Charles Seal. Married by the Rev. George Dodson. p.47

14 January 1829. Joseph PRUITT and Sarah Thomas who gives her own consent. Sur. John Merrick. Married by the Rev. Clement McDonald. (Minister says 15 December 1829.) p.94

11 March 1816. William PRUNALS and Elizabeth Pearman. Sur. William Pearman. Nathan and Frances Pearman consent. No relationship stated. p. 61

3 March 1820. John PUCKETT and Dicy Chainey, dau. of Abraham Chainey who says Dicy is of age. John Puckett also signs the certificate. Sur. Samuel Milium. Married 4 March by the Rev. William Blair. p. 71

26 May 1828. Stephen C. PUCKETT and Susannah Weldon. Sur. Jonathan Weldon. Married 5 June by the Rev. William Blair. p. 91

28 September 1830. James PUGH and Sarah Bruce. Sur. Overton Pugh. Thomas Bruce signs the certificate. No relationship given. Married by the Rev. Eben Angel. p. 97

11 April 1826. Overton PUGH and Matilda Bruce. Thomas Bruce requests the license be issued. Sur. Meredith Bruce. Married 16 April by the Rev. Eben Angel. p. 86

8 July 1830. Tilghmon A. PULLIN and Montilda A. Muse. Sur. John A. Muse. John T. Muse consents. Married 15 July by the Rev. Orson Martin. p. 97

20 February 1809. William QUINN and Nancy Wright, dau. of Thomas Wright who is Surety. Married 20 Feb. by the Rev. Thomas Sparks. p. 47

7 November 1808. Lewis RAFE and Lucy Kidd, dau. of Samuel
Kidd who consents. Sur. Moses Kidd. Married 7 Nov. by the
Rev. Thomas Boaz. p. 45

4 August 1821. Daniel RAGAN and Elizabeth Griggs, who
signs her own certificate. Sur. John H. Overby. p. 73

3 May 1828. George RAGLAND and Elizabeth J. Terry, dau. of
Champness Terry who consents. Sur. George Townes. Married
14 May by the Rev. John G. Mills. p. 91

29 September 1806. Gideon RAGLAND and Artemisia Wilson,
dau. of John Wilson, Sr. who consents. Sur. Thomas Wilson.
Married by the Rev. John Atkinson. Return dated 5 March
1808. pp. 41 & 45

8 December 1818. Hezekiah RAGSDALE and Elizabeth Hays, dau.
of Reubin Hay who consents. Sur. John Ragsdale. p. 67

31 October 1815. John RAGSDALE and Polly Watts. Sur.
Joshua Watts. Married 2 November by the Rev. Thomas Sparks.
p. 59

24 September 1827. Paschal W. RAGSDALE and Elizabeth M.
Fallen, dau. of Redmund Falling, whose consent says daughter Elizabeth M. Falling. Sur. Littleberry Fallin. p.89

26 June 1821. Thomas RAGSDALE and Lucy B. Carter. Sur.
Charles Carter. Married 28 June by the Rev. William Blair.
p. 73

25 March 1812. Watson RAGSDALE and Nancy Wright. Married
by the Rev. Thomas Sparks. Minister's Return. p. 53

24 March 1812. Wilson RAGSDALE and Elizabeth Wright, dau.
of James Wright who consents. Sur. Thomas Elliott. p. 53

6 January 1806. Vincent RALEY and Judah Robertson, dau. of
Joseph Robertson who consents. Sur. William Robertson.
Married by the Rev. Willis Hopwood. p. 41

18 January 1808. Noton RAMSEY and Rachel Witcher, dau. of
William Witcher. Sur. Vincent Witcher. Married 11 February by the Rev. Joseph Hatchett. p. 45

12 February 1811. Theoderick RAMSY and Patsey Thompson.
Married by the Rev. David Nowlin. Minister's Return. p. 51

17 December 1825. James RATLIFF and Elizabeth V. Anderson,
dau. of C. Anderson who consents. Sur. William Ratliff.
p. 84

1 February 1810. Newbill RATLIFF and Edy Covington. Sur. John Farguson. Married by the Rev. George Dodson. p. 49

8 October 1821. Pendleton RATLIFF and Elizabeth Anderson, dau. of William Anderson who consents. Sur. William Ratliff. p. 73

2 April 1821. William RATLIFF and Martha Anderson, dau. of Chas. Anderson who consents. Sur. Pendleton Ratliff. Married 3 April by the Rev. William Blair. p. 73

16 November 1811. George REED and Salley Phillips, dau. of Sally Phillips who consents. Sur. George Phillips. p. 51

12 February 1811. Walter REED and Salley Philips. Married by the Rev. George Dodson. Minister's Return. p. 51

24 November 1825. William REESE and Sarah Bryant, who writes her own certificate. Sur. Wiley Prewett. Married 24 Nov. by the Rev. John Leigh. p. 84

16 November 1829. Berryman REYNOLDS and Nancy Adkins, who signs her own consent. Sur. Noton Jefferson. p. 94

17 November 1817. Bowen REYNOLDS and Sarah Mues. Sur. Thos. O. Muse. p. 64

17 August 1825. Burton REYNOLDS and Polley Durham. Sur. John Reynolds. Ste. Turner signs the certificate saying that Polley is a girl of color he raised, that she is now 18 and has consented to marry Burton Reynolds. p. 84

16 October 1822. Daniel REYNOLDS and Polly Bradley. Sur. Isham Bradley. Married -- Oct. by the Rev. Ira Ellis. p.76

11 February 1828. Featherston F. REYNOLDS and Susan F. Napier. Sur. William A. Napier. Anthony Epperson and Elizabeth Epperson sign the certificate saying that Susan F. Napier is "at liberty to marry -----." p. 91

3 May 1826. James M. REYNOLDS and Rebecca Giles. Sur. John Giles. Married 18 May by the Rev. William Blair. p. 87

20 February 1815. Joseph REYNOLDS, Jr. and Manerva Collins, dau. of Kizia Collins who consents. Sur. Jesse Oakes. Married 21 Feb. by the Rev. James Beck. p. 59

11 August 1825. Joseph REYNOLDS and Mary Seymore. Married Aug. 1825 by the Rev. William Blair. Minister's Return. p. 84

19 December 1825. Joseph D. REYNOLDS and Elizabeth Mahan.
Sur. David Mahan. p. 84

21 February 1820. Robert REYNOLDS and Susanna Carter. Sur.
Nathan Carter. p. 71

17 December 1827. Samuel REYNOLDS and Judith P. Hubbard.
Sur. Moses Hubbard. p. 89

12 February 1811. Thomas REYNOLDS and Nelley Boaz, dau. of
Shadrack Boaz, whose consent was sent by the Surety, James
Still. Married 5 March by the Rev. Thomas Boaz. p. 51

21 March 1814. William REYNOLDS and Nancy Blair. Sur.
James Blair. Married 29 March by the Rev. William Blair.
No relationship given. p. 57

14 March 1816. William REYNOLDS and Elizabeth Pearman.
Married by the Rev. William Blair. Minister's Return. p.61

12 October 1826. Benjamin RICE and Matilda Goad, dau. of
Sarah Goad who requests that the license be issued. Sur.
William Bobbitt. Married 14 Oct. by the Rev. Shadrack Mus-
tain. p. 86

20 December 1824. James B. RICE and Elizabeth Richardson,
Elizabeth and her mother, Frances Richardson, sign the cer-
tificate. Sur. Charles Lucas. Married 23 Dec. by the Rev.
William Blair. p. 81

23 October 1828. Joseph RICE and Catharine Towler, dau. of
William Toler. Sur. Christopher Toler, who testifies that
Catharine is "upwards of 21." p. 91

-- March 1827. William RICE and Lucy W. Russell, who writes
her own consent, dated 24 March 1827. Sur. Robert Walters.
p. 89

28 April 1817. David RICHARDS and Patsy Smith. Sur. John
Hutchings. Randolph Smith signs the certificate. No relationship given. Married 1 May by the Rev. James Beck. p.64

13 August 1823. James C. RICHARDS and Martha Allen, dau. of
Welcome W. Allen who consents. Sur. Pinkney Scott. p. 78

13 January 1828. David RICHARDSON and Patsey Warfe. Sur.
Elisha Lewis. Thomas Richardson, father of David, requests
this license be issued. p. 92

21 October 1811. Edmund RICHARDSON and Polley D. Harrison,
who writes her own consent. Sur. Nathaniel Harrison. Married 29 Oct. by the Rev. Thomas Sparks. p. 51

8 October 1823. Elijah RICHARDSON and Lucy Colley, dau. of
James and Nancy Colley who consent. Sur. Joseph Jennings.
Married 8 Oct. by the Rev. John Leigh, M.G., Halifax County,
Virginia. p. 78

27 January 1809. Henry RICHARDSON and Sally Waddill, dau.
of Charles Waddill who is Surety. Married by the Rev.
George Dodson. p. 47

31 January 1818. Henry RICHARDSON and Betsey Waddill, dau.
of Charles Waddill who consents. Sur. Marshall Waddill.
p. 67

10 November 1811. James RICHARDSON and Ann Ware. Sur.
William Ware. No relationship given. Married 3 December
by the Rev. Thomas Sparks. p. 51

15 August 1814. John RICHARDSON and Rebecca Jennings. Sur.
Robert Jennings. Married by the Rev. George Dodson. p. 57

15 November 1806. William RICHARDSON and Ailcey Thurman,
dau. of John and Nancy Thurman who consent. Sur. James
Thurman. Married 17 Nov. by the Rev. William Blair. p.41

30 December 1822. Nathaniel RICKETTS and Sarah Dodson.
Sur. Ralph Dodson. Married 2 January 1823 by the Rev. William Blair. p. 76

15 October 1813. Bassel RIDDLE and Milly Hill, (widow),
whose consent says, "to Basel Riddel." (Bassel Riddle
signs with a mark.) Sur. Zachariah Riddle. Married by
the Rev. George Dodson. p. 55

5 April 1814. Burgess RIDDLE and Elizabeth Easley. Sur.
Thomas Easley. No relationship given. Married 5 April by
the Rev. Thomas Boaz. p. 57

26 July 1813. Jacob RIDDLE and Polly Butt. Sur. Basdel
Riddle. Ambrose Hawker signs the certificate. He says,
"She being a child left to me from her infancy by her par-
ents which is not in this part of the cuntry."
Married by the Rev. George Dodson. p. 55

14 April 1823. James RIDDLE and Nancy Eanes, who writes
her own consent. Sur. William Eanes. p. 78

19 January 1829. James RIDDLE and Mary C. Yates. Sur.
John Yates. Married 3 February by the Rev. Crispin Dickinson. p. 94

24 October 1826. John RIDDLE and Martha Eanes. Sur.
Arthur W. Eanes. p. 87

18 December 1822. Thomas F. RIDDLE and Sarah Blanks, dau. of Jos. Blanks who consents. Sur. William Farthing. Married 19 Dec. by the Rev. Griffith Dickinson. p. 76

25 August 1820. William RIDDLE and Patsy Giles. Sur. Daniel Dunbar. Married -- Aug. by the Rev. Ira Ellis. p. 71

20 May 1826. William RIDDLE and Mildred Parsons, who writes her own consent. Sur. John G. Parsons. p. 87

7 December 1813. Zachariah RIDDLE and Eddy Hill. Sur. Basel Riddle, who certifies he is guardian of Eddy Hill. (He signs with a mark.) Married by the Rev. George Dodson. p. 55

10 July 1811. Henry RIENARD and Frances Mart, dau. of Fanney Mart whose consent says daughter Fanney. Sur. William Meadow. p. 51

5 January 1811. John RIGGIN and Nancy Taylor, dau. of Mary Taylor. Sur. Jeffrey Austin. p. 50
(The Register has this name Kiggon - the bond has Riggin.)

5 April 1808. John RIGNEY and Anna Atkins, dau. of William and Polley Atkins who consent. Sur. James Peake. p. 45

19 April 1813. Jacob RINER and Sarah Haymore. Sur. Daniel Haymore. Married 14 May by the Rev. Thomas Boaz. p. 55

1 November 1825. John RITCHIE and Caseyann Williams, dau. of Charles Williams who consents. Sur. Charles D. Williams. p. 84

27 December 1817. Robert RITCHEY and Jane Murphy. Sur. Robert Ritchey. Thomas and Anna Murphy consent. No relationship given. p. 64

18 November 1822. Jesse RIVES and Betsey Chainey. Sur. Abraham Chainey. Married 28 Nov. by the Rev. John Leigh, of Halifax County, Virginia. p. 76

31 August 1830. Elijah ROACH and Wilmoth Owen, dau. of Pleasant B. Owen who consents. Sur. John B. Barrett. p. 97

20 November 1820. John ROACH and Sarah Cox, who signs her own certificate. Sur. George Cox. Married 22 Nov. by the Rev. Shadrack Mustain. p. 71

22 December 1818. Thomas ROACH and Nancy Mattox. Sur. Littleberry Dalton. Request that the license be issued signed by Polly Mattox, mother of Nancy, and Burditt Roach, father of Thomas. Married 24 Dec. by the Rev. Shadrack Mustain. p. 67

22 January 1813. William ROACH and Peggy Dove. Sur. George Dove. Married 28 Jan. by the Rev. Griffith Dickinson. p. 55

26 April 1821. Abraham ROARER and Polly Wright. Sur. Thomas Wright. Married by the Rev. David Nowlin. p. 73

3 March 1823. Rudolph ROARER and Millicent Lamb. Sur. William A. Townes. Catharine Lamb authorized the license be issued. No relationship stated. Married 6 March by the Rev. Ira Ellis who says Rudolph Rorer. p. 79

30 December 1806. Christopher ROBERTSON and Mourning Towler, dau. of Joseph Towler who consents. Sur. Henry Jacobs. p. 42

25 February 1807. Christopher ROBERTSON and Salley Pettey, dau. of Davis Pettey who consents. Sur. Ellis Wilson. Married 5 March by the Rev. William Blair. p. 43

27 November 1813. Christopher ROBERTSON, Jr. and Mary Ragsdale. Sur. Thomas Ragsdale. Married 1 December by the Rev. William Blair. p. 55

29 September 1812. Edward ROBERTSON, Jr. and Anne R. W. F. Shepherd. Sur. Christopher Robertson. Married 30 Sept. by the Rev. Griffith Dickinson. p. 53

9 December 1816. Edward ROBERTSON, Jr. and Nancy Thompson. Sur. Rawley Thompson. Nancy gives her own consent. She is daughter of Washington Thompson who says his daughter is of age. p. 61

16 April 1821. Edward ROBERTSON and Polley Wilson, dau. of Ignˢ Wilson. Sur. Clement Wilson. Married 26 April by the Rev. James Beck. p. 73

17 December 1810. George ROBERTSON and Elizabeth Coleman, dau. of Cloe Coleman. Sur. Daniel Coleman. Married 25 Dec. by the Rev. William Blair. p. 49

21 January 1811. James ROBERTSON and Patsey S. Coleman, dau. of Cloe Coleman. Patsey writes her own consent. Sur. Joseph Carter. Married 24 Jan. by the Rev. William Blair. p. 51

27 June 1820. John ROBERTSON and Louisa Wooding, who writes her own certificate. Sur. Robert T. Wooding. Married 29 June by the Rev. William Blair. p. 71

24 November 1828. Milton ROBERTSON and Isabel W. Shelton, who signs her own consent. Sur. Robertson Shelton. p. 94

2 March 1830. Milton ROBERTSON and Mary West. Married by
the Rev. Thomas Sparks. Minister's Return. p. 97

15 July 1822. Nathaniel ROBERTSON and Prucilla Stokes.
Sur. Allen Stokes, Jr. Married 18 July by the Rev. James
Beck. p. 76

20 December 1824. Peter ROBERTSON and Nancy Price, dau. of
Cutty Price, who signs the certificate. Sur. William I.
Shelton. p. 81

14 December 1818. Samuel ROBERTSON and Elizabeth Shelton,
dau. of Leroy Shelton, who requests the license be issued.
Sur. Thompson Price. Married 17 Dec. by the Rev. James
Beck. p. 67

12 December 1812. Thompson ROBERTSON and Chloe R. Shelton.
Sur. Abraham C. Shelton. Married 15 Dec. by the Rev. Griffith Dickinson. p. 53

11 September 1826. William ROBERTSON and Martha Owen.
Sur. Joshua Smith. p. 87

17 November 1823. Elijah ROBINSON and Elizabeth Murphy,
dau. of Thomas Murphy who consents. Sur. Richard B. Beck.
Married 27 Nov. by the Rev. Richard B. Beck. p. 78

5 November 1821. Munford B. ROBINSON and Mary P. Matherly,
dau. of Joel Matherly who consents. Sur. Shadrack Matherly.
Married 6 Nov. by the Rev. James Beck. p. 73

25 December 1813. Benjamin B. ROGERS and Oney Stokes. Sur.
Allen Stokes, Jr. p. 55

31 October 1812. Joseph ROGERS and Lucy Woodson, dau. of
Allen Woodson who consents. Sur. Joseph Woodson. Married
by the Rev. David Nowlin. p. 53

1 November 1828. Turner H. ROGERS and Mary Kelly, dau. of
James E. Kelly, who requests that this license be issued.
Sur. Thomas Dejarnett. p. 92

20 March 1826. William B. ROGERS and Sarah Stone. Sur.
Isaac Stone. p. 87

17 March 1807. Simon ROLAND and Polley Robertson. Married
by the Rev. Griffith Dickinson. Minister's Return. p. 43

21 February 1814. David RORER and Ann M. Brown. Sur.
James Custard, who testifies that Ann M. Brown is of age.
Married 3 March by the Rev. Joseph Hatchett. p. 57

134

28 March 1811. George RORER and Nancy Nowlin, dau. of
James Nowlin who consents. Abraham Rorer, father of George,
consents. Sur. John Rorer and Sherod Newlin. Married by
the Rev. David Nowlin. p. 51

6 January 1814. John RORER and Sally Bennett. Sur. Richard Bennett. Married 13 Jan. by the Rev. Joseph Hatchett.
p. 57

2 May 1816. George ROSS and Patsy Ragsdale. Sur. Levi
Watts. p. 61

6 March 1818. John ROSS and Mary M. Allen, dau. of Apphia
Allen who consents. Sur. Lewis B. Allen. p. 67

19 December 1808. Jerome ROSSON and Effey Davis, dau. of
Frances Davis. Sur. Robert Powell. Married by the Rev.
David Nowlin. p. 45

25 November 1815. Henry ROWLAND and Anna Shelton. Sur.
William Denning. p. 59

23 December 1816. Henry ROWLAND and Patsy Bradley. Sur.
William Bradley. p. 61

25 December 1813. Jesse ROWLAND and Mary Mitchell. Sur.
Reubin Mitchell. Mary Mitchell signs the certificate. No
relationship stated. Married 30 Dec. by the Rev. Griffith
Dickinson. p. 55

1 November 1808. John ROWLAND and Nancy Tucker. Married
by the Rev. Griffith Dickinson. Minister's Return. p. 45

27 November 1822. Nathaniel R. ROYALL and Frances A. Carter. Sur. John R. Carter. Elizabeth Royall and John Carter sign the certificates. No relationship shown. p. 76

4 March 1816. David ROYSTER and Nancy Echols. Sur. William Echols. Married 7 March by the Rev. John Jenkins.
p. 61

23 February 1820. Henry P. RUCKER and Judith Glascock.
Sur. William S. Glascock. George McDaniel signs the certi-
ficate. No relationship given. Married 24 Feb. by the
Rev. John Jenkins. p. 71

21 December 1819. Reuben D. RUCKER and Mary Glascock. Sur.
William S. Glascock. George McDaniel, guardian of Mary,
signs the certificate. Married 23 Dec. by the Rev. John
Jenkins. p. 69

27 December 1811. Cannon RUMLEY and Patsey Dabney. Sur.
Richard Farthing. Married 28 Dec. by the Rev. Thomas
Payne. p. 51

21 December 1830. Jamerson C. RUSSELL and Catharine Adams. dau. of Joseph Adams who consents. Sur. Stephen Dodson. Married 22 Dec. by the Rev. John Leigh, Halifax Co. p. 97

16 February 1807. John RUSSELL and Elizabeth Nash. Sur. Samuel Guy. p. 43

19 January 1814. James RYBURN and Nancy Echols, dau. of Obediah Echols. Sur. Obediah P. Terry. Married "since June 1813" by the Rev. David Nowlin. p. 57

31 December 1816. Benjamin SADLER and Sally Hendrick, who gives her own consent. Sur. Creed Sadler. Married 31 Dec. by the Rev. William Blair. p. 61

18 December 1818. Creed SADLER and Catharine Fitzgerald. Sur. Asa Fitzgerald. Matthew Fitzgerald signs the certificate and says, "both are of age and the proceedings meet my entire approbation." p. 67

12 April 1813. Thomas SADLER and Mary Nancy Clark, dau. of John and Jean Clark who consent. Sur. George Cook. Married 13 April by the Rev. William Blair. p. 55

3 March 1816. Isaac SANDERS and Mary Chisenhall, dau. of John Chisenhall who consents. Sur. William Dove. p. 61

2 November 1827. Jesse SANDERS and Nancy Coe, dau. of Jemima Coe who consents. Sur. Nathaniel B. Sanders. Married 8 Nov. by the Rev. Griffith Dickinson. p. 89

21 October 1817. Joshua SANDERS and Letty Arnold. Sur. George Arnold. Married by the Rev. Griffith Dickinson. p.64

20 December 1812. William SANDERS and Polley Hundley, dau. of Joseph Hundley who consents. Sur. John Hundley. p. 53

7 August 1828. Abner SAUNDERS and Polly Gilbert. Married by the Rev. Abner Anthony. Minister's Return. p. 92

21 December 1829. Amos SAUNDERS and Margaret Dove. Sur. William Dove. Married 22 Dec. by the Rev. Griffith Dickinson. p. 94

27 November 1823. Booker SAUNDERS and Lettice Mayes, dau. of Elizabeth Mays whose consent says both are of age. Sur. George Saunders. Married 27 Nov. by the Rev. Griffith Dickinson. p. 79

4 January 1812. Daniel SAUNDERS and Sally Dove, dau. of Leonard Dove who is Surety. Married 9 Jan. by the Rev. Griffith Dickinson. p. 53

5 January 1812. Francis SAUNDERS and Stacia Mays. Sur.
Joseph Mays. Married 7 Jan. by the Rev. Griffith Dickinson. p. 53

18 September 1820. George SAUNDERS and Levina Mays, dau.
of Elizabeth Mays, who signs the certificate. Sur. William Mays. Married 21 Sept. by the Rev. Griffith Dickinson. p. 71

10 January 1826. Jeremiah SAUNDERS and Fanney Bailess.
Sur. Arthur Farmer. Elisha Bayles' consent says Fanna
Bayles. p. 87

12 December 1811. John SAUNDERS and Nancy McCraw, who
writes her own consent. Sur. James Mustain. p. 51

31 August 1816. Leonard SAUNDERS and Celina Simpson. Sur.
Thomas Simpson. Married 5 September by the Rev. Shadrack
Mustain. p. 61

15 January 1827. Nathan SAUNDERS and Rebecca Parsons.
Sur. John Parsons. Married 15 Jan. by the Rev. Shadrack
Mustain. p. 89

10 September 1816. Nathaniel B. SAUNDERS and Elizabeth
Coe, dau. of Jemima Coe, who gives "full and free consent."
Sur. Robert Waller. Married 12 Sept. by the Rev. Shadrack
Mustain. p. 62

8 October 1818. William SAUNDERS and Sarah Coe, dau. of
Jemima Coe who consents. Sur. Nathaniel B. Saunders. Married by the Rev. Griffith Dickinson. p. 67

12 September 1810. David SCARCE and Elvi Oteneal. Sur.
George Scarce. p. 49
On the back of bond is written: "Geo. Scarce made oath before the Deputy Clerk (name not given) - Elvi is over 21
and her father, John Oteneal, has no objection to the marriage."

16 April 1821. George SCARCE and Nancy Gammon, dau. of William Gammon who consents. Sur. Thomas Scarce. p. 73

18 November 1822. James SCARCE and Polly Ritcher. Sur.
Benjamin Ritcher. p. 76

15 December 1829. James SCARCE and Tabitha Mullins, who
writes her own consent. Sur. Joel C. Harvill. p. 94

23 February 1825. Leonard SCARCE and Sally Ritchie, who
gives her own consent as Sally Ritchey. Sur. John H. Callahan. Married (Minister says September 24, 1824) by the
Rev. Clement McDonald. p. 82 & p. 84
(Return made in 1827 - had marriages for years 1824, 25&26)

17 May 1819. Joseph SCATES and Betsey T. Hart. Sur. James Hart. Married 18 May by the Rev. Ira Ellis. p. 69

23 October 1823. Starling SCOTT and Bethenia Durham. Sur. George Harper. p. 79

12 April 1830. Allen SCRUGGS and Elizabeth Faris. Danl. Johns, guardian of Elizabeth, consents. Sur. James B. Faris. Married 15 April by the Rev. Griffith Dickenson, Sr. p. 97

-- ---- 1807. Drury SCRUGGS and Milley Dejarnett. Married by the Rev. Johns Terry. Minister's Return. p. 43

3 March 1807. Charles SEAL and Sally Prewitt, who signs her own consent. Sur. Soloman Seal. p. 44

22 December 1813. Joel SEAL and Sally Earp, dau. of Samuel Earp who says, "she being of age." Sur. William Seal. Married by the Rev. George Dodson. p. 55

4 March 1816. William SEALE and Sarah Owen. Her consent says, "being of lawful age and fatherless." It is signed: Sarah (mark) Owen. Sur. Joel Seal. Married 17 March by the Rev. William Blair. p. 61

9 September 1830. William B. SEAMORE and Elizabeth E. Terry, granddaughter of Francis Haley who consents. Sur. John Douglas. Married 16 Sept. by the Rev. Griffith Dickenson, Sr. p. 97

10 January 1828. Abner SEAY and Susan W. Bass, dau. of Susan Bass who consents for her daughter. Sur. Anthony Blanks. Married 11 Jan. by the Rev. Griffith Dickinson who says Susannah W. Bass. p. 92

21 October 1822. Thornton SEE (or Lee) and Sarah Norton, who signs her own certificate. Sur. Drury Norton. p. 76

20 May 1811. Burwell SELF and Elizabeth Hay, dau. of Thomas Hay who consents. Sur. Obadiah Ham. p. 51

15 January 1821. Henry SERGEANT and Elizabeth Ware, dau. of William Ware, who requests that the license be issued. Sur. William H. Dupuy. p. 73

7 August 1821. William SETTLE and Polly Grubb. Sur. Jesse Grubb. Married 8 Aug. by the Rev. James Beck. p. 73

20 March 1830. Garland SHACKLEFORD and Isabella M. Shelton. Margaret Shelton consents. Sur. John Shackleford. Married 28 March by the Rev. Nathan Anderson. p. 97

16 April 1828. Henry SHACKLEFORD and Matilda Watson. Sur. Levi Watson. Married 17 April by the Rev. Clement McDonald. p. 92
(The Register has Minister, Clement Dickenson. This marriage is reported by the Rev. Clement McDonald - returned 1 September 1829.)

19 December 1816. John SHACKLEFORD and Sarah Chesenhall. Sur. John Chesenhall. p. 62

12 December 1820. John SHACKELFORD and Malinda H. Witcher. Sur. James Woodall. Caleb Witcher signs the certificate. No relationship given. Married 14 Dec. by the Rev. Shadrack Mustain. p. 71

12 January 1830. John SHACKLEFORD and Nancy Shelton, dau. of Margaret Shelton who consents. Sur. Jesse Drain. p.97

27 December 1814. Richard D. SHACKLEFORD and Susan H. Medlock. Sur. William H. Glascock. p. 57

16 March 1812. William SHACKLEFORD and Anne Reynolds. Sur. Jesse Reynolds. p. 53

16 February 1807. William SHANKS and Judith Callaway, who writes her own consent. Sur. Francis Callaway. p. 44

26 June 1818. Edward SHARP and Lydia Neal. Sur. (not given on bond.) Married by the Rev. Griffith Dickinson. p. 67

7 November 1810. Angish SHAW and Milly Free, dau. of Nicholas Free who consents and is Surety. Married 8 Nov. by the Rev. William Blair. p. 49

22 November 1826. Charles SHAW and Prisilla Stanley. Sur. Ezra Walters. Luke Stanley requests this license be issued. No relationship given. p. 87

2 February 1807. Jesse SHAW and Lucinda Lang. Sur. Jeffrey Astin. p. 44

28 December 1830. Anderson P. SHEALS and Barbary Hill, dau. of Ann Hill who consents. Sur. Isham Bradley. Married 29 Dec. by the Rev. William Blair, who says Anderson P. Shields. p. 97

20 December 1830. Henry SHELHORSE and Elizabeth Bates. Sur. Isaac Bates. Married 23 Dec. by the Rev. Crispin Dickenson. p. 97

14 August 1812. Jacob SHELHORSE and Polly Woodson, dau. of Murry Woodson. Sur. John Woodson. Married by the Rev. David Nowlin. p. 53

22 September 1817. Jacob SHELHORSE and Polley Haynes. Sur.
James Bailey. Married 24 Sept. by the Rev. Shadrack Mustain. p. 64

24 February 1808. Abraham SHELTON and Peggy Gibson, dau.
of Joel Gibson who consents. Sur. Bailer Gibson. p. 45

17 June 1823. Abraham SHELTON and Anna Robertson, who
writes her own consent. Sur. Presley Oakes. p. 79

-- ---- 1817. Abraham C. SHELTON and Mary L. Claiborne.
Married by the Rev. Griffith Dickinson. Minister's Return.
p. 64

1 February 1819. Bennett SHELTON and Sarah Hill, dau. of
Joseph Hill, who requests this license be issued. Sur. William Shelton. Married 4 Feb. by the Rev. William Blair.
p. 69

-- March 1817. Beverly S. SHELTON and Sibby B. Tucker.
Married by the Rev. Ira Ellis. Minister's Return. p. 64

15 March 1819. Beverly S. SHELTON and Sibby B. Tucker, who
signs her own certificate and says she is daughter of Elizabeth Tucker "in the County of Pittsylvania." Sur. Daniel
Tucker. Married March --, 1819 by the Rev. Ira Ellis. p.69
(See Beverly S. Shelton - 1817. There are two reports.)

16 October 1827. Creed T. SHELTON and Lina Holland. Joseph
Holland consents. Sur. Levi Abbott. Married 18 Oct. by the
Rev. Griffith Dickinson. p. 89

26 October 1807. Crispin SHELTON and Polley Waller, dau. of
John Waller, Sr. Sur. John Waller, Jr. Married by the Rev.
Griffith Dickinson. (Minister says 19 Oct. 1807.) p. 44

20 April 1829. Crispin SHELTON and Jane D. Walden, who writes her own consent. Sur. John Mustain. Married 20 April
by the Rev. Crispin Dickenson. p. 94

22 July 1809. Daniel SHELTON and Nelly Parsons. Sur. Merridith Parsons. p. 47

24 April 1816. Dudley SHELTON and Polly Haden. Sur. John
Haden, Sr. Married by the Rev. Griffith Dickinson. (Minister says 19 April.) p. 62

17 May 1824. Frederick L. SHELTON and Marinda W. Shelton,
dau. of Washington Shelton who, in his consent, says
<u>Miranda</u>. Sur. Leroy Payne. p. 81

140

27 November 1826. Gabriel SHELTON and Rebecca Johnson, dau. of William Johnson who consents. Sur. James Hall. Married 14 December by the Rev. William Blair. p. 87

2 February 1809. Geter SHELTON and Rachel Hatchett, who writes her own consent. Sur. John Cameron. Benjamin Shelton signs the certificate. p. 47

26 December 1808. Henry SHELTON and Polly Madding, dau. of Sarah Madding who consents. Sur. John Madding. Married by the Rev. George Dodson. p. 45

7 November 1812. Hundley SHELTON and Elizabeth Bruce. Sur. Thomas Bruce. p. 53

10 August 1807. James SHELTON and Anne Shelton, dau. of George Shelton. Sur. Spencer Shelton. Married by the Rev. George Dodson. p. 44

23 September 1807. Joel SHELTON and Anna Coe. Married by the Rev. Griffith Dickinson. Minister's Return. p. 43

29 April 1810. Joel SHELTON and Emily Smith. Married by the Rev. Griffith Dickinson. Minister's Return. p. 49

1 August 1825. John SHELTON and Nancy Irby, who gives her own consent. Sur. David Glenn, who testifies Nancy is 21. Married 2 Aug. by the Rev. Griffith Dickinson. p. 84

15 December 1828. John SHELTON and Elizabeth Orander, who gives her own consent. Sur. Pleasant Orander. Married 17 Dec. by the Rev. Clement McDonald. p. 92

15 December 1823. John G. SHELTON and Milly Payne. Sur. John L. Payne. Married -- Dec. by the Rev. Ira Ellis. p. 79

29 November 1828. Landford SHELTON and Mary R. Williams. Sur. William Williams. p. 92

31 January 1829. Lemuel SHELTON and Mary S. Gosney, who signs her own consent. Sur. Coleman Shelton. Married 12 February by the Rev. Crispin Dickenson. p. 94

2 December 1828. Leroy G. SHELTON and Sally Woodard, who gives her own consent. Sur. Mecajah Willis. p. 92

15 December 1823. Lewis C. SHELTON and Jane B. Payne. Sur. John L. Payne. Married -- Dec. by the Rev. Ira Ellis. p. 79

17 August 1818. Littleberry SHELTON and Betsey Mustaine. Sur. Avery Mustain. Married 27 Aug. by the Rev. Shadrack Mustain who says Elizabeth Mustain. p. 67

2 August 1821. Mark SHELTON and Gillian Hall, dau. of John Hall who consents. Sur. William H. Hall. Married 15 Aug. by the Rev. William Blair. p. 73

17 September 1827. Mastin M. SHELTON and Polley L. Shelton, who gives her own consent. Sur. Reuben B. Payne. p. 89

21 September 1824. Meacon SHELTON and Jane Tucker. Sur. Reuben B. Payne. Susanna Tucker gives consent. No relationship given. p. 81

16 December 1824. Meacon A. SHELTON and Ann R. Evans. Married by the Rev. Griffith Dickinson. Minister's Return. p. 82

30 May 1828. Meacon A. SHELTON and Anna Berger, dau. of Jacob Berger, Jr. who consents. Sur. William A. Anthony. Married 3 June by the Rev. Griffith Dickinson. p. 92

15 January 1816. Merritt SHELTON and Sally Bradley, dau. of Daniel Bradley who requests that this license be issued. Sur. Samuel Bradley. Married 18 Jan. by the Rev. William Blair. p. 62

20 October 1828. Moses H. SHELTON and Nancy C. Shelton. Sur. Crispen Shelton. Married 23 Oct. by the Rev. Clement McDonald. p. 92

21 January 1820. Noah SHELTON and Lydia Hill, dau. of Joseph Hill who says his daughter is of age and he has no objection. Sur. Bennett Shelton. Married 21 Jan. by the Rev. William Blair. p. 71

5 November 1827. Peter SHELTON and Pamelia Shelton, dau. of Crispen Shelton who consents. Sur. Moses Shelton. Married 6 Nov. by the Rev. Crispen Dickenson. p. 89

14 September 1825. Peter R. SHELTON and Eleasure P. Shelton, dau. of Richard Shelton who consents. Sur. Lewis Shelton. p. 84

8 April 1814. Richard P. SHELTON and Martha D. Keatts, dau. of Charles Keatts who consents. Sur. Henry C. Keatts. Married 9 April by the Rev. Joseph Hatchett. p. 57

2 January 1811. Robert SHELTON and Patsey Donaldson, dau. of John Donaldson who consents. Sur. James Donaldson. Married by the Rev. Elias Dodson. p. 51

3 May 1819. Robert SHELTON and Mary S. Davis. Sur. Thomas G. Tunstall. Married 4 May by the Rev. William Blair
who says Mary M. Davis. p. 69
(The Register has "Mary M. Davis" and does not give her
parents' names. Written in pencil : Mary S. Davis, dau. of
Thomas and Sarah (Meadow) Davis. The bond has Mary S.
Davis.)

21 November 1828. Robertson SHELTON and Elizabeth Thornton,
22, who writes her own consent. Sur. William Oakes. p. 92

5 February 1809. Spencer SHELTON and Margaret Ingram, dau.
of William and Elizabeth Ingram, whose consent says Margaret is of lawful age. Sur. George Ingram. Married by the
Rev. George Dodson. p. 47

5 November 1824. Taviner C. SHELTON and Leatitia Calland,
dau. of Eliza C. Callands whose consent says that she is
mother and guardian of Letitia. She also says, Doct<u>r</u>
Taviner C. Shelton. Sur. Willis G. Cousins. p. 81

22 October 1827. Theophilus Q. SHELTON and Elizabeth P.
Dunn. Sur. William Dunn. Thomas Shelton, Sr., father of
Theophilus, consents. p. 89

5 June 1824. Thomas L. SHELTON and Mary M. Shelton, dau.
of Willis Shelton who consents. Sur. Tarlton W. Franklin.
Married 11 June by the Rev. Ira Ellis. p. 81

17 May 1813. Vincent SHELTON, Jr. and Nancy Waller. Sur.
William Waller. Married 21 May by the Rev. Griffith Dickinson. p. 55

22 June 1814. Vincent H. SHELTON and Letty S. Shelton,
dau. of William Shelton who consents. Sur. Wesley Shelton. Married 28 June by the Rev. Griffith Dickinson. p.57

17 August 1829. Will H. SHELTON and Elizabeth A. Williams,
dau. of W. M. Williams, whose consent says <u>William</u> H. Shelton. Sur. Frs. L. Royall. Married 18 Aug. by the Rev.
William Blair. p. 94

24 June 1806. William SHELTON and Mary Ann Campbell, dau.
of John Campbell who consents. Sur. Sherwood Nowlin. Married 26 June by the Rev. Joseph Hatchett. p. 42

16 December 1816. William SHELTON and Anna Hall. Sur.
John Hall. Married 19 Dec. by the Rev. William Blair.
p. 62

17 May 1824. William I. SHELTON and Elizabeth Robertson,
dau. of George Robertson who consents. Sur. George B.
Sutherlin. p. 81

3 January 1827. William S. SHELTON and Patsy M. Blackburn, who writes her own consent. Sur. Littleberry Lewis. Married 4 Jan. by the Rev. Griffith Dickinson. p. 89

23 January 1807. James SHIELDS and Nancy Garner, dau. of William Garner who consents and is Surety. p. 44

25 December 1821. James SHIELDS and Sarah C. Adams. Sur. James Adams. p. 74

24 December 1823. James SHIELDS and Sarah Neal. Sur. Abraham Neal. Married 25 Dec. by the Rev. Griffith Dickinson. p. 79

21 October 1816. Josiah SHIELDS and Patsey Bingum. Sur. Edmund Bingum. Married 23 Oct. by the Rev. John Jenkins, who says Patsey Bingham. p. 62

19 November 1810. Pleasant SHIELDS and Unity Marshall, who gives her own consent. (Written in pencil is "widow." Sur. Thomas Shelton. Married by the Rev. John Atkinson. p. 49

26 December 1813. Pleasant SHIELDS and Elizabeth Moore. Married by the Rev. William Blair. Minister's Return. p.55

4 August 1808. John SHOCKLEY and Elizabeth Towler, dau. of Joseph Towler who consents. Sur. Elijah Towler. p. 45

17 December 1828. Shadrack SHOCKLEY and Elizabeth Towler. Sur. John Towler. p. 92

26 October 1818. Enoch SHOEMAKE and Susanna Boaz, dau. of Lydia Boaz who consents. Sur. John Nelson. Married 29 Oct. by the Rev. James Beck. p. 67

10 April 1829. Booker SHORTER and Tabitha Hubbard. Sur. George Terrell. Benjamin Terrell signs the certificate saying Tabitha is a woman that he has raised and "if she has any Parents I don't know where they are." John Shorter (on above paper) says his son, Booker, is of age. Married by the Rev. Eben Angel. p. 94

21 February 1814. William SHUMATE and Anney McMillion. Sur. John McMillion. Both parties sign the certificate. p. 57

19 November 1810. Asail SIKES and Anny Newby. Sur. Asa Newby. Married by the Rev. George Dodson. p. 49

2 December 1809. William SILCOCK and Elizabeth Massie. License by Will Tunstall, Clerk, "to any Minister of the Gospel in Virginia" for the above marriage." Married by the Rev. John Terry. p. 47

29 October 1810. Jeremiah SIMPSON and Elizabeth Alderson, who signs her own consent. Sur. John Bennett, who says Elizabeth is 21 and over. Married by the Rev. George Dodson. p. 49

23 December 1830. Jeremiah SIMPSON and Alsey Lindsey, dau. of William Lindsey who consents. Sur. John R. Anderson. Married 30 Dec. by the Rev. William Blair. p. 97

22 December 1819. Presley SIMPSON and Fanney Dalton. Sur. William Mays. William Simpson, father of Presley, signs the certificate saying his son is not of age. Married 22 Dec. by the Rev. Griffith Dickinson. p. 69

24 December 1829. William SIMPSON and Martha Mayhue. Sur. Bluford E. Bennett. Married 24 Dec. by the Rev. Crispen Dickenson. p. 94

4 September 1812. Doct. Robert W. SLAUGHTER and Nancy W. Anderson, dau. of Thomas Anderson who consents. Sur. Edmond Fitzgerald. p. 53

17 November 1828. Abel SLAYDEN and Artemisia Dodson. Sur. Abner C. Shelton. W. H. Shelton, guardian of <u>Artemesia</u>, consents. p. 92

11 March 1808. Daniel SLAYDEN and Dotia Dodson. Sur. William Dodson. Married by the Rev. George Dodson. p. 45

18 December 1809. Benjamin SLAYDON and Polley Pistole, dau. of Charles Pistole. Sur. David Pistole. Married 22 Dec. by the Rev. William Blair. p. 47

16 December 1822. James SLAYDON and Eleanor L. Blair, dau. of William Blair who consents. Sur. Johnson E. Atkins. Married 19 Dec. by the Rev. James Beck. p. 76

15 December 1823. Patrick SLAYDON and Margaret Slaydon, who signs her own certificate. Sur. William Simpson. Married 16 Dec. by the Rev. William Blair. p. 79

17 February 1817. William SLAYDON and Susanna Flippin, dau. of Joseph Flippin who signs the certificate. Sur. Meredith Jennings. Married 23 Feb. by the Rev. William Blair. p. 64

28 November 1816. James SLAYTON and Polley R. Winfield Wilkinson. Sur. John P. Wilkinson. Thomas Wilkinson, guardian of <u>Polly</u> R. Winfield Wilkinson, signs the certificate. Married 29 Nov. by the Rev. William Blair. p. 62

15 November 1825. Sanders SLAYTON and Selety Simpson, dau.
of William Simpson who consents. Sur. Lewis Simpson. Married 17 Nov. by the Rev. William Blair. p. 84

20 October 1817. Allen SMITH and Elizabeth Mitchell, dau.
of Michael Mitchell who consents. Sur. Thompson Pell. p. 64

25 September 1820. Charles SMITH and Elizabeth Dangerfield.
Sur. John Watson, Sr. Married 5 October by the Rev. Shadrack Mustain. p. 71

18 August 1806. George SMITH and Lucky Adkins. Sur. William Adkins. p. 42

8 June 1825. Henry SMITH and Sarah Brightwell, who gives
her own consent. Sur. John Richardson. Married -- June by
the Rev. William Blair. p. 84

7 September 1818. Hezekiah SMITH, Jr. and Susanna Price.
Sur. Thompson Price. Cutbird Price consents. No relationship stated. Married by the Rev. David Nowlin. p. 67

31 October 1827. Jabez SMITH and Susan Royster, dau. of
William Royster who consents. Sur. Thomas S. Jones. p. 89

17 July 1809. James SMITH and Lucy Hix Bates. Sur. Ayres
Hodnett. David Nowlin, Guardian, signs the certificate.
p. 47

9 November 1818. Joel S. SMITH and Sally Smith. Sur. William Smith. Randolph Smith signs the certificate - "by the
consent of their parents." No relationship given. Married
9 Nov. by the Rev. James Beck. p. 67

2 March 1825. John SMITH, Jr. and Matilda Ann Callaway.
Sur. John W. Bagwell. Eliza Calland signs the certificate.
No relationship given. Married 2 March by the Rev. John W.
Kelly. p. 84

12 September 1829. John H. SMITH and Rebecca M. White, who
signs her own consent. Sur. Abram Clement. Married 17
Sept. by the Rev. Griffith Dickenson. p. 94

3 August 1816. Joshua SMITH and Martitia Stokes. Sur.
Allen Stokes, Jun. Married 8 Aug. by the Rev. James Beck.
p. 62

25 April 1825. Sexton W. SMITH and Mary Wilson, dau. of
John Wilson who consents. Sur. Thomas Moody. Married May
--, 1825 by the Rev. William Blair. p. 84

18 December 1815. Stephen SMITH and Rebecca Boaz. Sur.
David R. Boaz. p. 59

146

2 November 1822. Thomas SMITH and Martha Hawker, dau. of
Philip Hawker who consents. Sur. Tunstall Ferguson. Married 5 Nov. by the Rev. William Blair. p. 76

16 June 1808. Thomas L. SMITH and Sally Clay, dau. of Matthew Clay, Esq. Sur. John Waller, Jr. Married by the Rev.
John Jenkins. p. 45

15 March 1807. William SMITH and Polley Anglin, dau. of
Elizabeth Anglin who consents. Sur. Henry Inman. Married
16 March by the Rev. William Blair. p. 43

9 May 1816. William SMITH and Sarah B. M. F. Patrick.
Sur. Thomas H. Read. Married by the Rev. Nathan Lovelace.
p. 62

5 February 1821. William SMITH and Elizabeth Robertson,
dau. of Christopher Robertson who consents. Sur. Nathaniel Robertson. Married 8 Feb. by the Rev. James Beck. p.73

26 September 1812. Campbell SMITHSON and Sarah Terrill,
dau. of Benjamin Terrell who writes Sarah is "with age."
Sur. John Murrell. p. 53

22 August 1810. Hezekiah P. SMITHSON and Henrietta Carter,
dau. of Presley Carter who consents. Sur. Thornton Carter.
p. 49

20 June 1817. Benjamin SNEAD and Priscilla Dews. Sur.
Samuel Birthwright. p. 64

9 November. 1818. John SNEED and Sarah Hill. Sur. Julius
Allen. James D. Patton, guardian of Sarah Hill, consents.
Consent dated: Danville, Virginia, Nov. 7, 1818. p. 67

6 June 1825. Edmund SNOW and Nancy Lawless, dau. of Sary
Lawless who consents. Sur. Orlando Smith. Married 7 June
by the Rev. William Blair. p. 84

10 March 1817. Jabez SNOW and Fanny Parker. Sur. David
Parker. Married 13 March by the Rev. Shadrack Mustain.
p. 64

26 January 1828. Richard D. SNOW and Mary Parker. Sur.
Alexander O. Parker. Married 26 Jan. by the Rev. Joel T.
Adams. p. 92

29 September 1830. Alexander B. SOYARS and Sarah Fontaine.
Sur. John H. Smith. Thomas B. Fontaine, father of Sarah,
consents. Thomas P. Soyars signs the certificate. Married
by the Rev. William Blair. (Minister says 22 Sept.) p.97

3 October 1820. James SOYARS, Jr. and Elizabeth Fowlkes. Sur. Anderson Fowlkes. p. 71

9 January 1811. Joseph SOYARS and Patsey Price, dau. of William Price who consents. Sur. William Crain. Married 2 Jan. by the Rev. William Blair. p. 51

15 October 1822. Pleasant SOYARS and Polly Coleman. Sur. Spilsby Coleman. Chloe T. Coleman, mother of Polly, says Polly is of age. Both she and Polly sign the certificate. Married 17 Oct. by the Rev. William Blair. p. 76

15 November 1819. John SPARKES and Abigal Sparkes. Sur. Henry Beggerly. Caty Sparks gives consent. No relationship given. Married 18 Nov. by the Rev. Thomas Sparks. p.69

29 August 1816. Addison SPARKS and Polly Watts. Sur. Levi Watts. p. 62

-- ---- 1807. John SPARKS and Judah Dodson. Married by the Rev. Thomas Sparks. Minister's Return. p. 43

26 December 1818. Matthew SPARKS and Mary Vaughn, dau. of William Vaughn who consents. Sur. Pleasant Vaughn. p. 67

16 November 1829. Thomas SPARKS and Mary Ann Booth. Nancy Booth consents. Sur. Thomas S. Drain. p. 94

22 September 1827. Hudson SPARROW and Sarah Posey, dau. of Robert Posey. Sur. Joseph H. Turner. Married 27 Sept. by the Rev. John Leigh, Halifax County, Virginia. p. 89

19 October 1819. James SPENCER and Sally Murphey. Sur. William Ware. William Murphy signs the certificate. No relationship given. Married 22 Oct. by the Rev. Thomas Sparks. p. 69

10 August 1807. William SPENCER and Joyce Dodson. Sur. George Dodson. Married by the Rev. George Dodson. p. 43

19 May 1826. James S. SPRATTEN and Sarah Hardy. Sur. Thomas Smith. Geo. Spratten, father of James, and Thomas Hardy, father of Sarah, consent. Married 23 May by the Rev. William Blair. p. 87

30 August 1827. Gilliam STACY and Jane Ritchie. Sur. Benjamin Ritchie. p. 89

21 November 1814. Bird STAMPS and Elizabeth Tanner, dau. of Thomas Tanner who is Surety. Married 24 Nov. by the Rev. Thomas Boaz. p. 57

12 March 1821. Richard STANLEY and Lucy Wilson, dau. of Thomas Wilson who consents. Sur. James Conner. Married 13 March by the Rev. William Blair. p. 73

20 November 1815. Samuel STEELE and Sarah H. Glascock, dau. of Mary Glascock who consents. Sur. Elisha Dismukes. Married by the Rev. John Jenkins. (Minister says 19 November.) p. 59

21 March 1825. Thomas I. STEPHENS and Elizabeth Meade. Sur. William A. Stephens. Ramsy Meade signs the certificate saying both are of age. p. 84

1 March 1828. William G. STEPHENS and Eliza George. Married by the Rev. Griffith Dickenson. Minister's Return. p. 92

16 April 1810. Josiah STILL and Anne Still, dau. of John Still who is Surety. Married 26 April by the Rev. William Blair. p. 49

27 February 1810. Baggle STIMSON and Rachel Stimson, dau. of Erasmus Stimson who consents. Sur. Solomon Stimson. Married by the Rev. George Dodson. p. 49

7 November 1825. Erasmus STIMPSON, Senor. and Elizabeth Irby, who gives her own consent. Sur. John Marler. p. 84

21 April 1817. Allen STOKES, Jr. and Mary Robertson. Sur. William Robertson. Married 8 May by the Rev. James Beck. p. 64

17 March 1807. John STOKES and Elizabeth Johnson. Married by the Rev. Griffith Dickinson. Minister's Return. p. 43

4 December 1820. Thomas STOKES and Sarah Dews, dau. of William Dews who consents. Sur. Henry Stokes. Married 7 Dec. by the Rev. Griffith Dickinson. p. 71

31 October 1827. Asher STONE and Judith Royall. Sur. Peter G. Cousins. Isaac Stone, father of Asher, and Elizabeth Royall, mother of Judith, consent. p. 89

6 October 1808. Clack STONE and Elizabeth Mottley, dau. of Samuel Motley whose consent says Elizabeth F. Motley. Sur. Thos. B. Tunstall and John Shelton. p. 45

25 November 1807. Coleman STONE and Caty F. Patrick, dau. of Birthland Patrick who consents. Sur. Clack Stone. Married by the Rev. John Jenkins. p. 44

29 January 1827. Edmund STONE and Nancy C. Dickenson, dau. of Crispen Dickenson who consents. Sur. Samuel Berger. Married by the Rev. John W. Kelly. p. 89

4 February 1816. James STONE and Amey Morton, who signs her own certificate. Sur. John Morton. Married 6 February 1817 by the Rev. James Beck. p. 61
(This bond is dated as stated. On the back is 4 Feb. 1817, written by some Court Official.)

20 May 1822. Joel STONE and Polly Myres. Sur. Stephen Myers. Married 20 May by the Rev. Richard B. Beck. p. 76

21 ---- 1812. John STONE and Mary Keesee, who writes her own consent, dated 21 October 1812. Sur. Charles Keesee. p. 53

19 August 1822. John D. STONE and Elender Travis, dau. of John Travis who requests that this license be issued. Sur. Jesse Pearman. Married 20 Aug. by the Rev. William Blair. p. 76

11 December 1824. John H. STONE and Elizabeth J. Womack. Sur. Charles W. Womack. Married 15 Dec. by the Rev. William Blair who says Elizabeth I. Womack. p. 81

23 September 1817. Ludwell STONE and Mariah Morton, who signs her own certificate. Sur. John Morton. Married 6 November by the Rev. James Beck. p. 64

27 December 1825. Peter STONE and Martha Thomas. Sur. Green Barker. Martha writes her own consent. China Thomas says daughter, Patsy, is "a single woman, free, disengaged and has my full consent." p. 84

10 August 1814. Samuel STONE and Phoebe H. Clark, dau. of William Clark who consents. Sur. Will L. Clark. Married 11 Aug. by the Rev. Griffith Dickinson. p. 57

15 December 1823. John STOW and Susan Thomas, dau. of Henson Thomas who consents. Sur. Samuel Beck. p. 79

27 December 1826. Henry STREET and Sarah Tribble, who gives her own consent. Sur. David Echols. p. 87

20 January 1806. Paul STREET and Rhoda Echols, who signs her own consent. Sur. David Echols. p. 42

16 June 1817. Archibald STUART and Elizabeth Pannill. Sur. Thos. G. Tunstall. p. 64

23 September 1816. Grief STUART and Polly Cahall, dau. of Peter Cahall who consents. Sur. James Cahall. p. 62

21 January 1811. John STUART and Betsy Walker, dau. of Samuel Walker who is Surety. p. 51

150

21 December 1822. Nevin STUART and Rachel Doss, who signs
her own certificate. Sur. Lewis Dalton. Married 24 Dec.
by the Rev. Griffith Dickinson. p. 76

30 March 1816. Peter B. STUBBLEFIELD and Sally Worsham,
dau. of Thomas Worsham who consents. Sur. George Wilson.
p. 61

19 September 1815. Wiatt STUBBLEFIELD and Mary Worsham.
Sur. Thomas Whitworth. p. 59

5 July 1829. Absolem STULTZ and Belinda Norman. Sur.
Marshall Norman. Married 1 September by the Rev. A. D.
Montgomery. p. 94

6 January 1816. Daniel SULLIVAN and Sarah G. Barnett, who
signs her own certificate. Sur. Nathaniel Wilson. p. 61

18 February 1830. James M. SUTHERLAND and Martha Willis.
Married by the Rev. A. D. Montgomery. Minister's Return.
p. 97

17 April 1815. Philimon SUTHERLAND and Polly Berger, dau.
of Jacob Berger. Sur. George Berger. Married 25 April by
the Rev. Joseph Hatchett. p. 59
(See Jacob Berger's Will - 1837.)

16 February 1824. George R. SUTHERLIN and Elizabeth Thompson, dau. of Samuel Thompson whose request that this
license be issued, says George Robertson Sutherlin. p. 81

12 May 1818. John SUTHERLIN and Sally E. Conway. Sur.
Thomas Barnett. Christopher Conway signs the certificate.
No relationship given. Married 14 May by the Rev. William
Blair. p. 67

13 December 1824. Thomas SUTHERLIN and Frances Sutherlin.
Sur. Nicholas Lyon. Walter Fitzgerald, guardian of Thomas,
consents. Mary Sutherlin consents for Frances. Married
16 Dec. by the Rev. William Blair. p. 81

25 January 1813. John SWEPSON and Winny Bruce, dau. of
James Bruce who consents. Sur. Thomas Bruce. Married 4
February by the Rev. Griffith Dickinson. p. 55

20 June 1827. George W. SWEPSTON and Polly Elliott. Sur.
William Elliott. p. 89

29 October 1807. Thomas SWEPSTON and Elizabeth Atkinson.
Sur. Leonard Dove. In requesting the license, William Tun-
stall's note says, "She has been a free agent for Ten years."
Married 31 Oct. by the Rev. Griffith Dickinson. p. 43

15 March 1828. William SWEPSTON and Martha May. Sur. John Elliott. p. 92

18 February 1822. William SWINNEY and Sarah Hobson, who signs her own certificate. Sur. John Waldrond. Married 21 March by the Rev. Griffith Dickinson. p. 76

17 February 1817. Powel SYKES and Elizabeth Plumly. Sur. Pleasant Phears. p. 64

5 December 1806. Williston TALBOTT and Nancy Keesee, dau. of John Keesee who consents. Sur. John Keesee. Married by the Rev. John Jenkins. p. 42

16 November 1818. Daniel TALLEY and Lucy Moorefield, dau. of More Morefield who consents. Sur. Joseph Moorefield. Married by the Rev. David Nowlin. p. 67

7 September 1824. Lodwick TALLEY and Elizabeth Hill, dau. of Joseph Hill who consents. Sur. Peyton Talley. p. 81 (Register has Sodwick Talley - both bond and consent have Lodwick.)

12 July 1817. Allen C. TANNER and Mathew Bates. Sur. Joel H. Tanner. Thomas B. Jones, guardian of Mathew Bates, signs the certificate. Married 14 July by the Rev. William Blair. p. 64

9 March 1814. Floyd TANNER and Elizabeth Terry, dau. of Benjamin Terry who signs the certificate. Elizabeth also signs the certificate. Sur. Asa Tanner. Married 10 March by the Rev. William Blair. p. 57

19 December 1808. Peterson R. TARPLEY and Catherine Jones, who writes her own consent to marry Mr. Peterson R. Tarpley. (The Register has Tapley.) Sur. James Yancey. p. 45

7 July 1830. Champness TATE and Polly Dodson, (widow of Jos. Dodson, deceased), who writes her own consent. Sur. Hugh H. Dodson. p. 97

16 March 1813. Henry TATE and Lucy Johnson, dau. of Thomas Johnson who is Surety. p. 55

20 November 1827. Jesse N. TATE and Julianna Hiptinchall. Married by the Rev. Abner Anthony. Minister's Return. p.89

13 March 1819. William I. TATE and Nancy Law. Sur. David Law. Married 15 March by the Rev. Joel Ashworth who says, "within a few days after this date." p. 69

22 March 1821. Daniel TAYLOR and Elizabeth McDonald, dau. of Randolph McDonald who consents. Sur. Aaron McDonald. p. 73

4 December 1822. Daniel TAYLOR and Lucinda Shackleford.
Sur. James Woodall. Married 12 Dec. by the Rev. Richard B.
Beck. p. 76

15 March 1830. George TAYLOR and Martha Harrison. Sur.
Washington M. Harrison. Married 25 March by the Rev. Griffith Dickenson, Sr. p. 97

-- February 1817. John TAYLOR and Jane Shackleford. Married by the Rev. Ira Ellis. Minister's Return. p. 64
(See John Taylor - 1819.)

17 February 1819. John TAYLOR and Jane Shackleford. Sur.
James Woodall. Jonathan Stone, of Henry County, guardian
of Jane, and Jane, herself, sign the certificate. Married
Feb. 1819 by the Rev. Ira Ellis. p. 69

8 May 1826. John TAYLOR and Zerishe McDonald, dau. of Randolph McDonald who consents. Sur. Aaron McDonald. Married
11 May by the Rev. Clement McDonald. p. 87

18 December 1829. John TAYLOR and Nancy Warf, dau. of Ann
Warf who consents. Sur. David Ritcherson. John Tallor
signs the certificate. p. 95

15 November 1819. Munford TAYLOR and Milley Shackleford.
Sur. James Woodall. Married 18 Nov. by the Rev. Ira Ellis.
p. 69

18 August 1817. Temple B. TAYLOR and Polly Butcher. Sur.
James Murphy. Married by the Rev. Griffith Dickinson. p.64

7 December 1822. Thomas TAYLOR and Melinda Abston, dau.
of Francis Abston who signs the certificate. Sur. John A.
Swepston. Married 8 Dec. by the Rev. Griffith Dickinson
who says Malinda. p. 76

31 December 1824. Edmund TEMPLETON and Elizabeth King.
Sur. James King. James King, father of Elizabeth, and
Elizabeth, herself, sign the certificate. Married 31 Dec.
by the Rev. Shadrack Mustain. p. 81

7 December 1814. James TEMPLETON and Patsey Faris, dau.of
Juriah Faris who consents. Sur. Joseph West. Married by
the Rev. Nathaniel Lovelace. p. 57

21 February 1820. Charles R. TERRELL and Peggy Williams.
Sur. James Galarby. Married 24 Feb. by the Rev. William
Blair. p. 71

27 December 1811. George TERRELL and Patsey Wayne, dau.
of Joseph Wayne who consents. Sur. Joseph Wayne. p. 51

21 January 1822. Jesse TERRELL and Nancy Hill, dau. of Joseph Hill who says his daughter, Nancy, is of age. Sur. Noah Shelton. Married 24 Jan. by the Rev. William Blair. p. 76

15 May 1826. Champness TERRY and Jane Stamps, dau. of Timothy Stamps who consents. Sur. Alexander I. Walters. p. 87

17 March 1828. Champness TERRY and Rhody Thompson, dau. of David Thompson who consents. Sur. Thomas Williams. Married 20 March by the Rev. John Leigh, of Halifax County. p. 92

17 September 1810. Daniel TERRY and Polley Clopton, dau. of Robert Clopton who consents. Sur. George Townes. Married by the Rev. David Nowlin. p. 49

24 June 1820. David C. TERRY and Elizabeth Madding, dau. of Rachel Madding who consents. Sur. Thomas Madding. p. 72

9 November 1824. Friend S. TERRY and Nancy Corder. Sur. Shadrack Corder. p. 81

30 September 1811. George TERRY and Elizabeth Grigsby, dau. of Moses Grigsby. Married by the Rev. William Blair. Minister's Return. p. 51

6 November 1809. James TERRY and Elizabeth Terry, dau. of John Terry who consents. Sur. Samuel Guy. Married by the Rev. Elias Dodson. p. 47

14 December 1820. John TERRY and Herrietta Hobson. Married by the Rev. Griffith Dickinson. Minister's Return. p.71

18 November 1822. Joseph B. TERRY and Elizabeth Woodson. Sur. Allen Woodson, Jr. p. 76

14 November 1808. Moses TERRY and Polley Nash, dau. of John Nash who is Surety. Married by the Rev. Elias Dodson, "since my last return." p. 45

6 June 1808. Nathaniel TERRY and Polly Stone, dau. of Joshua Stone. Sur. Clack Stone. p. 45

16 January 1809. Nathaniel TERRY and Elizabeth C. Haley, dau. of Joseph E. Haley who consents. Sur. Temple Haley. Married 18 Jan. by the Rev. Griffith Dickinson. p. 47

25 May 1812. Nathaniel TERRY and Penelope Adams, dau. of Elizabeth Adams who consents. Sur. Chas. L. Adams. Married 29 May by the Rev. Griffith Dickinson. p. 53

19 June 1815. Obediah P. TERRY and Patsy Mottley. Sur.
Daniel Mottley. Married by the Rev. David Nowlin. p. 59

11 November 1828. Stephen TERRY and Lucinda Leftwich.
Married by the Rev. Griffith Dickenson. Minister's Return.
p. 92

17 March 1809. Walker TERRY and Polley Rosson, dau. of
Joseph Rosson who consents and is Surety. p. 47

20 March 1810. William TERRY, Jr. and Lettice S. Johnson,
dau. of Richard Johnson who consents. Sur. James Garland.
p. 49

20 June 1808. William S. TERRY and Elizabeth W. Williams,
dau. of James Williams. Sur. Js. M. Williams. Married 14
July by the Rev. Robert Hurt. p. 45

29 September 1823. William L. TERRY and Sally C. Terry,
who signs her own consent. Sur. Robert Terry. Married by
the Rev. David Nowlin. p. 79

3 May 1808. Absolom THACKER and Sally Atkins, dau. of
Nathaniel Atkins who is Surety. p. 45

4 September 1816. Amos THACKER and Rebeccah Thacker. Sur.
Anderson Thacker. Married 8 Sept. by the Rev. Shadrack
Mustain. p. 62

25 February 1819. Emanuel THACKER and Milley Hodges. Sur.
Pleasant Thacker. Moses Hodges signs the certificate. No
relationship given. Married 4 March by the Rev. James Beck.
p. 69

1 December 1815. Humphrey THACKER and Darkey Keesee. Sur.
John Keesee. Married 7 Dec. by the Rev. Shadrack Mustain.
p. 59

15 December 1823. Jesse THACKER and Polly Goodwin. Sur.
Walker Goodwin. Married 18 Dec. by the Rev. William Blair.
p. 79

2 May 1820. Pleasant THACKER and Patsy Walker. Sur. Benjamin Walker. Married 2 May by the Rev. James Beck. p. 71

21 September 1818. Benjamin THOMAS and Susan Aron. Sur.
Jacob Aron. p. 67   (He signs with a mark.)

10 December 1821. Haston THOMAS and Jane Dangerfield, dau.
of Herinham Dangerfield who requests that yhis license be
issued. Sur. John T. Hammock. p. 74

5 November 1821. Henry THOMAS and Levina Thacker, who
signs her own consent. Sur. Allen Parrish. Married by the
Rev. Ira Ellis. p. 74

6 May 1817. Ichabod THOMAS and Sally Astin. Sur. Samuel
Calland. William Astin consents. Relationship not given.
Married 8 May by the Rev. James Beck. p. 64

17 November 1817. James THOMAS, Jr. and Elizabeth W. Meadows. Sur. John Nowlin. Jonas and Lucy Meadows, parents
of Elizabeth, sign the certificate. p. 64

16 November 1820. Jesse THOMAS and Nancy Dickerson. Sur.
Walter Fitzgerald. Married 28 Nov. by the Rev. William
Blair. p. 72

28 January 1806. John THOMAS and Delila Turner. Sur. Jesse
Turner. Married by the Rev. William Blair who says, "in
January 1806." p. 42

16 October 1815. John W. THOMAS and Nancy Watkins. Sur.
James Watkins. Married 31 Oct. by the Rev. Thomas Boaz.
p. 59

1 October 1806. Jonathan THOMAS, Junr. and Judith Walker.
Sur. David Walker. Married 7 Oct. by the Rev. William
Blair. p. 42

2 June 1828. Jonathan K. THOMAS and Polly Williams. Sur.
James Williams. p. 92

16 April 1821. Nathaniel THOMAS and Rebecca E. Walters,
dau. of Arch. Walters who requests that this license be issued. Sur. Joel Dodson. Married 19 April by the Rev. William Blair. p. 73

5 December 1829. Philip THOMAS and Eady Meed, who signs
her own consent. Sur. William H. Tunstall. Married 10 Dec.
by the Rev. Orson Martin. p. 95

16 November 1829. William A. THOMAS and Elizabeth Payne.
Sur. William B. Giles. Giles Payne signs the certificate.
No relationship given. Married 19 Nov. by the Rev. Crispin
Dickenson. p. 95

29 October 1825. William P. THOMAS and Araminta Motley,
dau. of Joseph Motley who consents. Sur. Allen Motley.
Married November 1825 by the Rev. William Blair. p. 84

21 November 1812. David THOMPSON and Polly Anderson, dau.
of Jacob Anderson who consents. Sur. Meriweather Anderson
and Jacob Anderson. John Thompson, father of David, consents. p. 53

7 December 1818. James S. THOMPSON and Tabitha M. Fontaine.
Sur. Peter Fontaine. Elizabeth Fontaine, mother of Tabitha,
consents. Tabitha also signs the certificate. p. 67

20 December 1824. Jeremiah THOMPSON and Milly High. Sur.
David High. Married 22 Dec. by the Rev. William Blair.
p. 81

28 February 1810. Horatio THOMPSON and Lucinda Thompson,
dau. of Samuel Thompson who consents. Sur. Lewis Thompson.
Married 1 March by the Rev. William Blair. p. 49

1 September 1814. John THOMPSON, Jr. and Mary Edwards.
Sur. William Thompson. William Tunstall certifies Mary is
of age. Married 2 Sept. by the Rev. Joseph Hatchett. p.57

10 February 1820. John THOMPSON and Mary Anderson. Sur.
Richard Thompson. Polley Anderson signs the certificate.
No relationship given. Married 17 Feb. by the Rev. Wil-
liam Blair. p. 71

15 April 1816. Nathan THOMPSON and Susanna Fralick. Sur.
Abisha Watson. Married "in 1816" by the Rev. Shadrack
Mustain. p. 62

5 September 1826. Nathan THOMPSON and Willey Martin, dau.
of Robert Martin and "wife" who consent. Sur. John Fralick. p. 87

25 May 1818. Rawley THOMPSON and Jane F. Anderson. Sur.
Robert H. Slaughter. Mary Anderson, guardian of Jane, consents. p. 67

15 January 1827. Rawley THOMPSON and Ann D. Clement.
Stephen Clement consents. Sur. Abraham Clement. Married
24 Jan. by the Rev. Griffith Dickenson, Sr. p. 90

20 June 1807. Richard THOMPSON and Betsey Hight. Sur.
Edward Hight. Married by the Rev. John Jenkins. p. 44

31 July 1821. Samuel THOMPSON and Patsy Terry, who signs
her own certificate. Sur. Rawley Thompson. Married 1
August by the Rev. Griffith Dickinson. p. 73

28 October 1822. Samuel THOMPSON, Jr. and Nancy Davis.
Sur. Garrett Davis. Married Oct. 1822 by the Rev. Ira
Ellis. p. 76

26 April 1815. Thomas THOMPSON and Jane Towler, dau. of
Joseph Towler who consents. Sur. William Towler. Married
27 April by the Rev. Joseph Hatchett. p. 59

25 September 1806. William THOMPSON and Frances A. Muse, dau. of John Muse, Sr. who consents. Sur. David Thompson. Married by the Rev. Willis Hopwood. p. 42

15 January 1815. William THOMPSON and Nancy Mullings. Each signs the certificate. Sur. Abraham Rorer. Married by the Rev. David Nowlin who says Nancy Mullins. p. 59

2 October 1826. John THORNTON and Mary Thornton, dau. of Moses Thornton who consents. Sur. James Wilson. p. 87

10 December 1819. Reuben THORNTON and Mary Tiffin, dau. of Thomas and Elizabeth Tiffin who sign the certificate. Sur. William Oakes. p. 69

21 May 1827. Rowland THORNTON and Sarah Bennett, dau. of Travis and Jane Bennett who consent. Sur. Lewis B. Bennett. p. 89

11 February 1830. Wiley THORNTON and Mary Wilson, dau. of William Wilson who consents. Sur. Thomas Wilson. Married 16 Feb. by the Rev. Richard B. Beck. p. 97

17 March 1806. Nathan THURMAN and Martha Mitchell, dau. of Mary Mitchell who consents. Sur. Elisha Barber. Married by the Rev. Willis Hopwood. p. 42

7 October 1816. Nathan THURMAN and Polley Angel. Sur. Eben Angel. p. 62

30 December 1816. Robert THURMAN and Camilla Smith, dau. of Jno. Smith, who requests that this license be issued. Sur. John Smith, "Minor". Married by the Rev. John C. Taylor. p. 62
"10 Feb. 1817. Henry Cty.
This is to certify I solemnized Matrimony between Robert Thurman of Lynchburg and Camilia Smith of Pittsylvania.
John C. Taylor."

-- November 1811. McDaniel TINSLEY and Anny Millner, dau. of Wmfon. Millner who consents. Sur. Joshua Bright. p. 51

22 March 1821. Daniel TOLER and Elizabeth McDaniel. Married by the Rev. William Davis. Minister's Return. p. 74.

24 February 1821. William B. TOLER and Tabitha Carroll, dau. of Ethredel Carroll. (This in the bond.) Sur. Etheldred Carroll. p. 73

1 October 1813. Jonathan TOLLE and Elizabeth Arrington, dau. of Samuel Arrington who consents. Sur. William Tolle. p.55

1 October 1807. Lacy TOMBLIN and Selah Davis. Sur. William Rodgers. Married by the Rev. John Jenkins, who says Lacy Tomlin and Celia Davis. p. 44
(A note from Ben Brawner, which Selah also signs, says, "She being an orphan that I have raised from an infant.")

12 August 1818. James T. TOMPKINS and Susan Pigg. Sur. Clement Pigg. E. Tompkins, father of James, signs the certificate. Married 13 Aug. by the Rev. James Beck. p. 67

6 November 1815. John TOMPKINS and Nelly Giles. Sur. Stephen Giles. Edward Tompkins, father of John, and George Giles, father of Nelly (says she is under age), sign the certificate. Married 9 Nov. by the Rev. William Blair. p. 59

12 June 1820. Samuel TOMPKINS and Margarett Hutchings, dau. of M. Hutchings, who authorizes the license be issued. Sur. Stokley Hutchings. Married 15 June by the Rev. William Blair. p. 72

26 September 1823. William TOSH and Nancy Crider. Sur. Andrew Crider. Married October 1823 by the Rev. Ira Ellis. p. 79

15 March 1819. Cornelius TOWLER and Catharine Goad, dau. of Jemimah Goad who consents. Sur. William B. Arthur. Married 25 March by the Rev. Shadrack Mustain. p. 69

12 September 1807. Elijah TOWLER and Polley Rorer, dau. of Betsey Rorer who consents. Sur. Henry Jacobs. Married 13 October by the Rev. Joseph Hatchett. p. 44

18 January 1808. John TOWLER and Sarah Dalton, dau. of John S. Dalton who consents. Sur. Peter Clark. Married 22 Jan. by the Rev. Joseph Hatchett. p. 45

3 August 1825. Peyton TOWLER and Elizabeth Towler, dau. of Elijah Towler who authorizes the license be issued. Sur. Jesse Minter. Married 6 Aug. by the Rev. Griffith Dickinson. p. 84

10 August 1819. George TOWNES and Eliza. B. Tunstall. Married by the Rev. Ira Ellis. Minister's Return. p. 69

2 April 1828. Robert TOWNES and Salley Lipscomb, who signs her own consent. Sur. George P. Keesee. Married 24 April by the Rev. A. D. Montgomery. p. 92

31 January 1815. Stephen C. TOWNES and Catharine H. Williams, dau. of J. M. Williams who signs the certificate. Sur. Stephen Coleman. p. 59

29 December 1810. William A. TOWNES and Margaret Lamb, dau.
of Catherine Lamb. Sur. Julias Allen. Married 1 January by
the Rev. William Blair. p. 49

22 September 1806. James TRAVIS and Patsey Kidd, dau. of
Samuel Kidd who consents. Sur. Moses Kidd. Married 30
Sept. by the Rev. William Blair. p. 42

21 February 1829. Richard TRAVIS and Mary Parson. Sur.
Bailey Parsons. Elizabeth Parsons signs the certificate.
No relationship given. p. 95

29 March 1830. Wm. M. TREADWAY and Nancy I. Millner, dau.
of Williamson Millner who consents. Sur. A. B. Johns. (In
top of bond is Anthony B. Johns.) Married 1 April by the
Rev. William Davis. p. 97

17 November 1827. Michael P. TRIBBLE and Mary McHaney.
Sur. William McHaney. John McHaney consents. No relationship given. p. 89

20 January 1817. James TROTTER and Ann W. Pritchett, who
signs her own certificate. Sur. William Pritchett. William
and John Pritchett certify Ann is of age. Married 22 Jan.
by the Rev. James Beck. p. 64

4 April 1818. George TUCK and Betsy Holder. Sur. Delany
Holder. p. 67

24 January 1827. Thomas B. TUCK and Jane Hendrick, dau. of
Jane Hendrick who consents. Sur. John W. Dillard. Married
30 Jan. by the Rev. Eben Angel. p. 89

16 September 1817. Coulson TUCKER and Judith Warren, who
gives her own consent as Judah Warren. Sur. Saunders Warren. Married by the Rev. James Beck. (Minister says 15
September.) p. 64

13 October 1823. David TUCKER and Christiana Berger. Sur.
Daniel Berger. Jacob Berger, Sr. signs the certificate. No
relationship stated. p. 79

21 November 1825. William TUCKER and Nancy Faris. Sur.
Daniel Johns. p. 84

16 November 1829. William A. TUCKER and Eliz[a] J. Whitehead,
dau. of Richard Whitehead who consents. Sur. John H. Smith.
Married 25 Nov. by the Rev. Griffith Dickenson, Sr. p. 95

18 February 1826. William C. TUCKER and Mildred H. Gilbert,
dau. of George Gilbert who authorizes the license be issued.
Sur. Cornelius Gilbert. Married 21 Feb. by the Rev. Shadrack Mustain. p. 87

22 February 1827. Samuel TUNSTALL and Ann Tunstall. Married by the Rev. William Blair. Minister's Return. p. 89

11 July 1820. Thos. G. TUNSTALL and Sarah L. Sullivan. Married by the Rev. John Jenkins. Minister's Return. p. 71

4 March 1808. Christian TURK and Caty Groff. Sur. William Shelton. Married 6 March by the Rev. Joseph Hatchett. p.45

23 November 1807. Floyd TURLEY and Patsey Turley, dau. of James Turley, Jr. and "wife" who consent. Sur. John Turley. p. 44

7 May 1818. John TURLEY ahd Peggy Craine. Sur. Jacob Craine. Married 7 May by the Rev. Shadrack Mustain. p. 67

17 June 1823. Sanford M. TURLEY and Polly Crayne. Sur. John Turley. James Turley, father of Sanford, consents. Married June 1823 by the Rev. Ira Ellis. p. 79

19 December 1808. Admire TURNER and Peggy Garrett, dau. of Thomas Garrett. Sur. Thomas Garrett. p. 45

15 January 1810. Anthony I. TURNER and Kerren C. Yancey, dau. of William Yancey who consents. Sur. Thos. B. Tunstall. p. 49

15 April 1811. Cornelius TURNER and Locky Gilbert, dau. of Jeremiah Gilbert. Sur. John Gilbert. Married 2 May by the Rev. Griffith Dickinson. p. 51

2 October 1828. Henry H. TURNER and Mourning Pitts, dau. of Lucy Pitts who requests that this license be issued. Sur. Thomas Dejarnett. p. 92

9 March 1813. John TURNER and Nancy Gilbert. Sur. George Gilbert. Married 11 March by the Rev. Griffith Dickinson. p. 55

22 December 1829. Joseph H. TURNER and Sarah Slayton, dau. of Daniel Slayton who consents. Sur. William Slayton. Married 23 Dec. by the Rev. William Blair. p. 94

11 October 1812. Robert TURNER and Polly Couch, dau. of Elisha Couch who authorizes the license be granted. Sur. John Johns. Married 11 Oct. by the Rev. Griffith Dickinson. p. 53

4 November 1818. William TURNER and Susanna Black, Sur. Nathaniel Black. Married by the Rev. David Nowlin. p.67 (Thomas Black, will 1814, names, among others, wife Susanna and daughter Susanna. Consent signed: Susannah Black. Wits. to consent: Thos., Margaret S., Eleanor S. Black.)

30 September 1811. George TYREE and Elizabeth Grigsby, dau.
of Moses Grigsby who consents. Sur. Redmond Adams. Married
10 October by the Rev. William Blair. p. 51

31 August 1827. John TYLER and Elizabeth Holt, dau. of
Miles and Sally Holt who consent. Sur. James Holt. p. 89

4 January 1825. John UHLES and Nancy Bray. Sur. Christopher Bray. Married 4 Jan. by the Rev. Richard B. Beck.
p. 84

15 September 1829. Samuel UHLES and Willy Deer, who writes
her own consent. Sur. George Elliott. p. 95

20 July 1829. Braddock G. VADEN and Nancy Slayton, dau. of
Daniel Slayton who consents. Sur. James W. Conway. Married
23 July by the Rev. William Blair. p. 95

4 December 1826. Giles H. VADEN and Dolley H. Easley, dau.
of Robert Easley who requests that this license be issued.
Sur. Peter Barksdale. p. 87

21 January 1828. Wilson VADEN and Elizabeth Terry. Sur.
William L. Terry. Married 24 Jan. by the Rev. Griffith
Dickenson. p. 92

15 November 1822. George VAUGHAN and Henritta Turner, who
signs her own certificate. Sur. Thomas T. Vaughan. Married 15 Nov. by the Rev. Shadrack Mustain. p. 76

7 September 1827. John VAUGHAN and Martha Lane, who signs
her own consent. Sur. John W. Walker. Married 8 Sept. by
the Rev. Griffith Dickinson. p. 90

4 August 1818. William VAUGHAN and Sally East. Sur.
Ezekiel East. p. 67

24 December 1817. Perry VAUGHN and Kiziah Hay, dau. of
Reubin Hay who consents. Sur. Woodson Hay. p. 64

7 December 1813. Josiah VERMILLION and Anna Semones, dau.
of John Semones who consents. Sur. John B. Howard. p. 55

17 January 1806. Robert VERMILLION and Nancey McGlasson,
dau. of Matthew McGlasson who consents. Sur. Arthur Robertson. p. 42

6 March 1806. John VIRGILS and Elizabeth Barker, dau. of
Stephen Barker who is Surety. Married 13 March by the Rev.
James Nelson, Baptist. p. 42

13 November 1817. Noel WADDELL and Selety Walters, dau. of
Robert Walters who signs the certificate. Sur. William
Simpson. p. 65

27 December 1826. Hampton WADE and Mary King. Sur. Munford King. Tabitha and Elijah King sign the certificate and Mary, also, signs it. Married 28 Dec. by the Rev. Clement McDonald. p. 87

27 March 1806. Henry WADE and Polley Stone. Married by the Rev. Griffith Dickinson. Minister's Return. p. 42

6 January 1812. Christopher WAGGONER and Sally Hughey, dau. of Robert Hughey. Sur. Allen Hughey. Married 9 Jan. by the Rev. Joseph Hatchett. p. 53

14 April 1824. Henry B. WALDEN and Phebe Farthing. Sur. Shimei Watson. Married 15 April by the Rev. Griffith Dickinson. p. 82

19 October 1812. Richard WALDEN and Polley Walden. Sur. Chas. Walden. Married 31 Oct. by the Rev. Griffith Dickinson. p. 53

29 October 1827. Armisted WALKER and Kesiar Barret. Sur. John Barret. Married 29 Oct. by the Rev. Griffith Dickinson. p. 90

11 December 1810. David WALKER and Elizabeth Dickenson. Married by the Rev. William Blair. Minister's Return. p.49

29 December 1825. Elijah WALKER and Martha Carpotts. Sur. Vincent Walker. Ephraim C. Potts' consent says "Martha Potts." (Was her name Martha Carr Potts?) Married 5 January 1826 by the Rev. Griffith Dickinson. p. 84

18 January 1813. Jeremiah W. WALKER and Lucy M. Hart. Sur. James Hart. Married by the Rev. Joseph Hatchett. (Minister says 9 January.) p. 55

13 March 1827. John WALKER and Judith Vaughan, who signs her own consent. Sur. John Worsham. Married 20 March by the Rev. Eben Angel. p. 90

9 September 1829. John WALKER and Susannah Uhles. Sur. John Elliott. Pegy Gaulden, guardian of John Walker, and Eve Uhles, mother of Susanna, write consents. Married 8 Sept. by the Rev. Richard B. Beck. p. 95

5 December 1815. John WALKER and Milly Covington. Sur. William Austin. John Walker, Mille(y), herself, and Fanny Covington sign the certificate and say both parties are of age. Married 6 Dec. by the Rev. James Beck. p. 59

3 March 1820. Joseph WALKER and Susannah M. Muse. Sur.
John Hundley. Thomas Muse signs the certificate. No relationship given. Wording is: ------"at liberty to take out
a license to marry Susannah Mariah Muse." p. 72

15 February 1809. Robert WALKER and Nancy Colbert, dau. of
Lemuel Colbert who consents. Sur. Champness Mays. Married
18 Feb. by the Rev. Griffith Dickinson. p. 47

21 September 1816. Stephen WALKER and Elizabeth Tiffin,
dau. of Thomas Tiffin who consents. Sur. Joseph Hyler. p.62

18 March 1816. William WALKER and Patsy Wells. Sur. John
Wells. p. 62

29 December 1830. William C. WALKER and Lucy Coe, dau. of
Jemima Coe whose consent says Lucy is under age. Lucy also
signs the certificate. Sur. John C. Waller. Married 30
Dec. by the Rev. Griffith Dickenson, Sr. p. 97

30 December 1822. William P. WALKER and Nancy Woodall.
Sur. James Woodall. Married 2 January 1822 by the Rev.
James Beck. p. 76

22 February 1821. Miles WALL and Rebecca Dishman, dau. of
John Dishman who signs the certificate. Sur. Joel C. Harvill. p. 74

16 December 1822. David WALLACE and Judith Eades, dau. of
Alfred Edds whose consent says David Wallace. Sur. Edward
Doss. Married 21 Dec. by the Rev. Shadrack Mustain. p. 76
(The Register has "David Wallce" and correction in pencil
says "Wallace.")

27 December 1823. Wyatt WALLACE and Elizabeth Crider. Sur.
Reuben Bennett. p. 79

4 April 1825. David WALLIS and Nancy Goad, dau. of Sarah
Goad who consents. Sur. Jesse Minter. Married 9 April by
the Rev. John W. Kelly. p. 84
(The Register has David Wallace - the bond, he signs and the
consent have Wallis.)

24 January 1815. Abner WALLER and Sarah Hall, dau. of John
Hall who consents. Sur. Thomas Watson. Married 27 Jan. by
the Rev. William Blair. p. 59

18 September 1826. David WALLER and Mildred Slayton. Sur.
Thomas Slayton. Married 25 November by the Rev. William
Blair. p. 87

21 December 1826. John WALLER and Elsey Dews. Married by
the Rev. Griffith Dickinson. Minister's Return. p. 87

9 December 1816. Robert WALLER and Patsey Johns, dau. of Mary Johns who signs the certificate. Sur. Daniel Johns. Married 10 Dec. by the Rev. Shadrack Mustain. p. 62

21 February 1820. Thomas WALLER and Nancy Jennings. Sur. Johnson Glass. Married 24 Feb. by the Rev. Griffith Dickinson. p. 72

15 December 1825. Peter WALLS and Elizabeth Dailey, who gives her own consent. Sur. Miles Walls. p. 84

4 February 1828. Richard WALNE and Louisa Gilbert, dau. of George Gilbert who requests that this license be issued. Sur. William Stone. p. 92

15 December 1817. Asa WALROND and Nancey Motley, who signs her own certificate. Sur. Charles Irby. p. 65

15 May 1826. Alexander WALTERS and Louisa Wilson, dau. of John Wilson who requests that this license be issued. Sur. Champness Terry. Married 25 May by the Rev. William Blair. p. 87

12 November 1815. Ezra WALTERS and Lydia Nelson. Sur. Evan Shaw. Married 15 Nov. by the Rev. William Blair. p.59

29 December 1807. Lemuel WALTERS and Elizabeth Dodson, dau. of Joshua Dodson. Sur. Laban Walters. Married by the Rev. Elias Dodson. p. 44

-- January 1813. Robert WALTERS and Elizabeth Atkinson. Sur. John Dodson. Consent of Josiah Atkinson for daughter Elizabeth. She also signs the certificate. Married 21 January by the Rev. William Blair. p. 55

29 December 1812. Spicer WALTERS and Lydia Stamps, dau. of Leyanner Stamps who consents. Sur. William Burgiss. Married 12 January 1813 by the Rev. William Blair. p. 53

2 December 1811. Abel WALTON and Polley Wood, dau. of Joseph Wood who consents. Polly also signs the consent. Sur. Jeremiah Wood. p. 51

7 July 1806. Jesse WALTON and Polley Hutchings, dau. of Moses Hutchings who consents. Sur. John Hutchings. Married by the Rev. Richard Elliott. p. 42

27 September 1827. Jesse S. WALTON and Eliza G. Lanier, dau. of J. A. Lanier who consents. Sur. Edward Lanier. p. 90

1 March 1830. John WALTON and Mary Swanson, dau. of William
Swanson who consents. Sur. William G. Swanson. Married 4
March by the Rev. Orson Martin. p. 97

15 November 1824. Robert N. WALTON and Frances Soyars, dau.
of James Soyars who authorizes the license be granted. Sur.
John Soyars. Married 18 Nov. by the Rev. William Blair.
p. 82

15 October 1828. Thomas W. WALTON and Nancy W. Shelton,
dau. of Leroy Shelton who consents. Sur. Alexander B.
Soyars. Married 16 Oct. by the Rev. William Blair. p. 92

2 September 1811. Francis WARD and Polley Coleman, who
writes her own consent. Sur. Daniel Coleman. p. 51

17 October 1815. Robert WARE and Sally W. Coleman. Sur.
Stephen Coleman. p. 59

14 May 1830. William WARE and Catharine Daniel. Sur. Martin Daniel. Married 15 May by the Rev. M. Robertson. p. 97

21 December 1829. William WARF and Sarah Dameron, who gives
her own consent. Sur. William Hudson. Roger Warf consents
for William. p. 95

26 September 1814. Jesse WARREN and Sarah Muck, who writes
her own consent. Sur. Samuel Craddock. p. 57

20 October 1806. John WARREN and Judah Parmer. Sur.
Samuel Craddock. Cloe Parmer writes a consent. No rela-
tionship given. Consent dated Oct. 20, 1806. Married 2
November by the Rev. William Blair. p. 42

29 January 1807. Morton WARREN and Priscilla Craddock, dau.
of Samuel Craddock who, and "his wife", consent. Sur.
George Arnn. Married 3 February by the Rev. William Blair.
p. 44

19 January 1807. Saunders WARREN and Susanna Craddock, dau.
of Samuel Craddock, Sr. who, with his wife, consent. Sur.
Samuel Craddock. Married Jan. 1807 by the Rev. William
Blair. p. 44

14 March 1807. John WATKINS and Nancy Wilson, who writes
her own consent. Sur. P. Astin. p. 44
(The Surety so signs - up in the bond is Peter Astin.)

9 January 1829. Edward H. WATSON and Catharine Nichols.
Sur. John Nichols. Married 13 Jan. by the Rev. Crispin
Dickenson. p. 95

17 May 1821. John WATSON and Elizabeth Dangerfield. Sur. John Dangerfield. Married May 1821 by the Rev. Ira Ellis who says: John Watson, Sr., H. C. p. 74

17 June 1822. John WATSON and Martha D. Echols, dau. of Obediah Echols who requests that this license be issued. Sur. James Conner. Married 17 June by the Rev. Griffith Dickinson. p. 76

3 February 1823. Shimei WATSON and Mary Farthing. Sur. Stokely Farthing. W. Farthing signs the certificate. No relationship given. Married 6 Feb. by the Rev. Griffith Dickinson. p. 79

16 January 1809. William WATSON and Rodah Midkiff, dau. of John Midkiff. Sur. David Midkiff. p. 47

22 January 1810. William WATSON and Jane A. Shelton. Married by the Rev. Thomas Sparks. Minister's Return. p. 49

23 January 1822. Edmund WAWL and Ritty Dismung, who signs her own certificate. Sur. Joel C. Harvill. p. 76

17 February 1821. Emanuel WAYNE and Nancy Angel. Sur. Edward Doss. Eben Angel's consent says Nancy is 21. No relationship stated. Married 19 Feb. by the Rev. Shadrack Mustain. p. 74

23 February 1824. Hugh WEIR and Elizabeth R. Smith, dau. of William Smith who authorizes the license be issued. Sur. William Holt. Married 25 Feb. by the Rev. Griffith Dickinson. p. 82

4 January 1821. Jonathan WELDON and Nancy Burch, who signs her own certificate. Sur. Robert Burch. p. 74

8 June 1825. Joel WELLS and Sarah E. M. Tarpley, dau. of William M. Tarpley who consents. Sur. Solomon Fuller. p. 84

21 January 1828. John WELLS and Nancy Hardy. Sur. William Hardy. William Hardy requests that this license be issued. Married 5 February (Minister says 1826) by the Rev. William Blair. p. 92

19 December 1808. Joseph WELLS and Sally Fuller, dau. of Zachariah and Letty Fuller who consent. Sur. Leonard Brooks. Married 21 or 22 of Dec. by the Rev. William Blair. (He reported this marriage twice.) p. 45

15 April 1811. John WERE and Nancy Sparks. Sur. Edward Murphy. (John signs with a mark.) p. 51

22 April 1816. Charles WEST and Rhoda Watson, dau. of
John Watson who requests this license be issued. Sur.
William Watson, who says Rhoda is upwards of 21 years.
Married by the Rev. David Nowlin. p. 62

23 September 1817. Cornelius WEST and Rachel Lonarde.
Sur. Jacob Saunders. Married 2 October by the Rev. Shadrack Mustain who says Rachel Leonard. p. 65

2 December 1811. Geoege WEST and Polley Clark, dau. of
William Clark who is Surety. p. 51

18 August 1817. Robert WEST and Peggy Saunders. Sur.
Jacob Saunders. Married by the Rev. Griffith Dickinson.
p. 65

10 January 1811. William WEST and Salley Hamrick, dau. of
David Hamrick who consents. Sur. George West, Jr. p. 51

22 March 1821. William WEST and Nancy King, dau. of James
King who consents. Sur. John B. King. p. 74

10 January 1811. James WESTBROOK and Patsey Thompson.
Married by the Rev. David Nowlin. Minister's Return. p.51

19 February 1823. Thomas WESTBROOK and Nancy Covington,
dau. of John Covington who consents. Sur. Asa Scott. Married 27 Feb. by the Rev. William Blair. p. 79

15 October 1824. Tilghman WESTBROOKS and Lucy Davis,
whose certificate says she is of age. Sur. Thomas Smith.
Married 16 Oct. by the Rev. William Blair. p. 82

10 December 1819. Abraham WHITE and Patsey Hardey, dau.
of John Hardey who requests that this license be issued.
Sur. Wesley Hardy. Married 15 Dec. by the Rev. William
Blair. p. 70

27 March 1807. Benjamin WHITE and Rebeckah Zachary. Sur.
Talliaferro Carter. p. 44

30 March 1826. Henry WHITE and Elizabeth A. Garland. Sur.
Nicholas A. Garland. p. 87.

30 July 1827. James B. WHITE and Harriet Mottley. Sur.
James Johnson. Daniel Terry consents. Doesn't say for
which one. p. 90

21 December 1829. James D. WHITE and Elizabeth H. Roberts,
dau. of Michael Roberts who consents. Sur. Martin Mason.
Married 23 Dec. by the Rev. Joel T. Adams. p. 95

16 August 1824. Jeremiah M. WHITE and Lettice Hodnett.
Sur. Daniel Hodnett. p. 82

22 December 1812. Joseph WHITE and Clary Harvey, dau. of
Samuel Harvey who consents. Sur. Lewis Morgan. p. 53

26 February 1822. Macon WHITE and Nancy Tanner, dau. of
Thomas Tanner who requests that this license be issued.
Sur. James G. Davis. p. 76

-- ---- 1821. Meacon WHITE and Nancy Tanner. Married by
the Rev. David Nowlin. Minister's Return. p. 74
(See Macon White - 1822.)

19 March 1808. William WHITE and Polley Twedwell. Sur.
Silas Twedwell. Married by the Rev. George Dodson. p. 45

6 November 1830. William WHITE and Nancy Hart. Married by
the Rev. Griffith Dickenson, Sr. Minister's Return. p. 97

18 July 1820. James WHITEHEAD and Martha Coats, who signs
her own certificate. Sur. Marbell C. Whitehead. p. 72

4 February 1828. Marbell C. WHITEHEAD and Dolley C. Stone,
dau. of Benjamin Stone who requests that this license be
issued. Sur. Abraham Lewis. Married 7 Feb. by the Rev.
Griffith Dickenson. p. 92

6 April 1827. William WHITEHURST and Mary Ferguson, who
writes her own consent. Sur. John Ratliff. Married 11
June by the Rev. John W. Kelly. p. 90

15 November 1824. Henry WHITEMORE and Jane Compton, dau.
of Jeremiah Compton whose consent says Jane is of age, and
Henry Whitemore is of Halifax County. Sur. Micajah Compton. Married 16 Nov. by the Rev. Griffith Dickinson. p.82

29 July 1817. William WHITLOCK and Anna Faris, who signs
her own certificate. Sur. Peyton W. Faris. p. 65

27 November 1816. Bezaleel WIER, Sen. and Elizabeth Harris,
who signs her own consent. Sur. John Sutherlin. Married
3 December by the Rev. William Blair. p. 62

5 October 1807. Thomas WIER and Agness Slayton, dau. of
Joseph and Milley Slayton who consent. Sur. Daniel E.
Slayton. Married by the Rev. George Dodson. p. 44

12 July 1819. Gunny L. WILBORN and Sarah M. Stone, dau. of
William H. Stone who requests this license be issued. Re-
quest dated 12 July 1819. Sur. Griffith Dickenson, Jr.
Married by the Rev. Griffith Dickenson. p. 65
(The Register has 1817 - bond and father's note are 1819.)

-- ---- 1817. Gunney L. WILBURNE and Sarah M. Stone. Married by the Rev. Griffith Dickinson. Minister's Return. p. 65   (See Gunny L. Wilborn - 1819.)

30 January 1827. Erasmus D. WILCOX and Jane C. Stamps. Sur. Joshua Howerton. Elizabeth Wilcox, grandmother of Jane, consents. Married 1 February by the Rev. William S. Plummer. p. 90

12 December 1816. John C. WILCOX and Polly Pierce. Sur. Robert Pierce. p. 62

30 November 1811. James WILKINS and Susanna Dix. Sur. Robert Ferguson. Married 3 December by the Rev. William Blair. p. 51

10 November 1823. Frederick WILKINSON and Martha Jane Terry, dau. of Benj. Terry who requests this license be issued. Sur. William Fontaine. Married by the Rev. David Nowlin. p. 79

9 February 1818. John P. WILKINSON and Elizabeth Neal, dau. of Simon Neal who consents. Sur. Boling Neal. Married 12 Feb. by the Rev. William Blair. p. 67

3 December 1818. Otway WILKINSON and Fanny M. Ellis. Sur. Nicholas M. Ellis. p. 67

16 December 1822. Pendleton R. WILKINSON and Jane Harris Wier, dau. of Elizabeth and Bezaleel Wier, Sr., who sign the certificate. Sur. James Yarbrough. Married 17 Dec. by the Rev. William Blair. p. 76

11 February 1818. Cornelius WILLIAMS and Nancy Shelton. Sur. Noah Shelton. Married 13 Feb. by the Rev. William Blair. p. 67

16 November 1818. Edward P. WILLIAMS and Phebe H. White. Sur. John White. Married by the Rev. David Nowlin. p. 67 (Doctor Edward Pierpont Williams and Phebe Howson (White) Williams had their home in Halifax County, Virginia. K.B.W.)

24 December 1812. Fontaine WILLIAMS and Nancy Hamrick. Sur. Elisha Barbour, who says Nancy is of age. Fontaine Williams signs the certificate. p. 53

22 February 1819. Francis W. WILLIAMS and Sally Lansdown, who gives her own consent. Sur. Obediah P. Terry. Married by the Rev. David Nowlin. p. 70

12 February 1806. James WILLIAMS and Elizabeth Morrice. Sur. William Morrice. p. 42

3 May 1820. James M. WILLIAMS, Jr. and Elsa B. Motley. Sur. William Mottley. J. M. Williams, father of James, consents. Henry Mottley, guardian and brother of Elsa, consents. p. 72

13 November 1827. James M. WILLIAMS and Sarah G. Davis. Sur. William Evins. Samuel Williams, father of James, signs the certificate. Married 13 Nov. by the Rev. John W. Kelly. p. 90

16 January 1806. John WILLIAMS and Elizabeth Lewis. Married by the Rev. Griffith Dickinson. Minister's Return. p. 42

13 November 1815. John WILLIAMS and Elizabeth Wooding, dau. of Thomas H. Wooding who is Surety. p. 59

5 April 1822. John WILLIAMS and Sally Haynes. Sur. James Witcher. Married April 1822 by the Rev. Ira Ellis. p. 76

28 January 1830. Mastin WILLIAMS and Nancy Pass. Married by the Rev. A. D. Montgomery who says Martin Williams. Ministers Return. p. 97   (Register has Mastin.)

6 February 1807. Nathan WILLIAMS and Mary Morris. Sur. William Morris. No relationship given. Married 17 Feb. by the Rev. William Blair. p. 44

21 February 1814. Philip D. WILLIAMS and Jane Bryant. Sur. Elisha Bryant. No relationship given. Married 24 Feb. by the Rev. William Blair. p. 57

24 April 1820. Philip G. WILLIAMS and Nancy Chaney, dau. of Thomas Chaney who consents. Sur. Frederick Wilkinson. p. 72

15 December 1817. Robertson WILLIAMS and Sally Craine. Sur. Samuel Price. William Price, grandfather of Sally, consents. p. 65

6 December 1819. Thomas WILLIAMS and Harriett Boyd. Sur. Thomas G. Tunstall. George Boyd requests that this license be issued saying, "because he is about to Marry into my family." p. 70

11 January 1808. William WILLIAMS and Ann Bailey, dau. of Charles Bailey who consents. Sur. Washington Shelton. Married 12 Jan. by the Rev. Thomas Payne. p. 46

-- ---- 1817. William M. WILLIAMS and Martha Douglass. Married by the Rev. Griffith Dickinson. Minister's Return. p. 65

29 September 1814. John WILLIAMSON and Susanna Barnitt.
Sur. Geo. S. Sutherlin. p. 57

3 March 1816. James M. WILLIS and Sarah Martin. Sur.
Bailey Martin. Robert Willis, father of James, and Salley
Martin (no relationship given) sign the certificates. p. 62

15 December 1828. Joel WILLIS and Judith Chaney, dau. of
William Chaney who authorizes this license be issued. Sur.
Joshua D. Chaney. Married 31 Dec. by the Rev. John G.
Mills. p. 92

2 July 1821. Micajah WILLIS and Siller Jones. Sur. John
Bollin. p. 74

15 October 1807. Richard WILLIS and Nancy Wier, dau. of
John Wier. Sur. Bozaleel Wier. Married by the Rev. George
Dodson. p. 44

16 December 1816. Samuel WILLIS and Polley Farmer. Sur.
Martin Farmer. p. 62

7 March 1814. William WILLIS and Rhoda Farmer, dau. of Marlin Farmer who consents. Sur. John Easley, Jr. Married
"since June 1813" by the Rev. David Nowlin. p. 57

15 March 1813. Jesse WILLS and Parthena Perkins, dau. of
Mary Perkins who consents. Sur. Benjamin Watkins. Married
19 March by the Rev. William Davis. p. 55

5 November 1806. Ellis WILSON and Elizabeth Pettey, dau.
of Davis Pettey who consents. Sur. John Wilson. Married by
the Rev. Thomas Sparks. p. 42

13 October 1806. Hardin WILSON and Nancy Fitzgerald, dau.
of Edmond Fitzgerald who consents. Sur. Asa Wilson. p. 42

22 February 1819. John WILSON and Jincy Hillard, who signs
her own certificate. Sur. David Glenn. Married by the Rev.
Griffith Dickinson. p. 69

17 February 1829. John WILSON and Elizabeth Rowland, dau.
of John Rowland who consents. Sur. Roial Walker. (Signs
with a mark.) Married 18 Feb. by the Rev. Griffith Dickinson. p. 95

14 January 1828. Nathan D. WILSON and Roselanard Robertson,
dau. of George Robertson whose consent says Rosillamond.
She signs same on the certificate. Sur. George Fowlkes.
p. 92

18 December 1826. Peter WILSON and Sarah Voss, dau. of
Greenbury Voss who consents. Sur. Okelly Voss. Married
10 April 1827 by the Rev. M. Robertson. p. 87

-- ---- 1817. Robert WILSON and Catharine A. Pannill.
Married by the Rev. Griffith Dickinson. Minister's Return.
p. 65

15 November 1819. William W. WILSON and Sally Price. Sur.
Samuel Price. Married 15 Nov. by the Rev. James Beck. p.70

15 January 1827. E. Y. WIMBISH and Eliza H. Terry, dau. of
Jeremiah Terry who consents. Sur. William L. Terry. Married 17 Jan. by the Rev. John W. Kelly who says Epaphroditus Y. Wimbish. p. 90

20 December 1819. Thomas WINGFIELD and Betsey Witcher.
Sur. Vincent Witcher. p. 70

4 October 1821. Matthew WINFREE and Sarah I. Hall, who
signs her own certificate. Sur. Franklin S. Johnson. p.74

13 January 1826. German I. WINGO and Ann Y. Beadles. Sur.
Lewis Y. Beadles. Married 17 Jan. by the Rev. William
Blair. p. 87

18 February 1824. William WINN and Lucy Whitehurst. Sur.
William C. Franklin. Wm. Whitehurst gives consent. No
relationship stated. p. 82

11 May 1816. Caleb WITCHER and Fanny James, who writes her
own consent. Sur. Reubin Witcher. Married by the Rev.
Joel Ashworth. p. 62

27 October 1820. Caleb WITCHER, Junor. and Polly Dangerfield. Sur. Ephriam Witcher. p. 72

20 March 1819. Ephraim WITCHER and Winifred Hailey. Sur.
Lovelace Haly. Married by the Rev. David Nowlin. p. 69

28 December 1811. James WITCHER and Tempy Witcher, dau. of
John Witcher. Sur. James Witcher, Sr. Married 31 Dec. by
the Rev. Joseph Hatchett. p. 51

13 September 1813. James WITCHER and Gilly Edwards. Sur.
George A. Edwards, who testifies Gilly is of age. Married
"since June 1813" by the Rev. David Nowlin. p. 55

2 June 1821. James WITCHER and Elizabeth Beavers, dau. of
Joseph Beavers who requests that this license be issued.
Sur. Isham Griffin. Married June 1821 by the Rev. Ira
Ellis. p. 74

22 November 1823. James WITCHER and Nancy Swanson, dau. of William Swanson, Jr. who consents. Sur. Joseph Fuller. Married 25 Nov. by the Rev. Orson Martin. p. 79

13 February 1816. Joab WITCHER and Janey McNealy. Sur. William Love. William McNealy signs the certificate - says Jeney. No relationship given. James Witcher signs request that the license be issued. Married 15 Feb. by the Rev. Shadrack Mustain. p. 62

3 December 1811. John WITCHER and Polley Witcher. Married by the Rev. Joseph Hatchett. Minister's Return. p. 51

16 June 1806. Reuben WITCHER and Judah Edwards. Sur. Daniel C. Edwards. Married 17 July by the Rev. Joseph Hatchett. p. 42

18 September 1816. Samuel WITTEN and Ellender White. Sur. Rawley White. Married by the Rev. David Nowlin who says Samuel Whitten. p. 62

4 April 1824. Charles W. WOMACK and Martha Glascock. Sur. Elisha Dismarks. (Dismukes?) George McDaniel, (no relationship given), requests that this license be issued and says Wm. W. Womack, of Halifax County, is father of Charles. p. 81

15 December 1828. John D. WOMACK and Chrischania D. Motley. Sur. Henry Mottley. Married 18 Dec. by the Rev. Griffith Dickenson. p. 92

11 July 1825. William WOMACK and Martha Thompson. Sur. George W. Thompson. Married 16 July by the Rev. William Blair who says Martha J.Thompson. p. 84

7 November 1808. Layton WOOD and Susanna Owen, dau. of John Owing who consents. Sur. Ambrose Haley, Jr. p. 45

14 March 1817. Samuel WOOD and Sarah Wood. Sur. Gerald Ford, who says both are of age. Joseph Wood, father of Samuel, "has no objection." Married 15 March by the Rev. William Blair. p. 65

29 November 1821. Anderson WOODALL and Maria Jones, who signs her own certificate. Sur. James S. Woodall. Married "since my last return" by the Rev. David Nowlin. p. 74

21 August 1815. Daniel H. WOODALL and Sally Woodall, whose consent says she is over 21. Sur. George Hall. Married 15 September by the Rev. James Beck. p. 59

19 July 1825. James S. WOODALL and Ellender Deboe, dau. of Philip Deboe who consents. Sur. Abraham Deboe. Married 21 July by the Rev. Griffith Dickinson. p. 84

29 January 1817. John WOODALL and Elizabeth Gauldin. Sur. Auda Gauldin, who makes oath before WM. Holt, D.C., that he believes that his father, Wm. Gauldin, has no objection to the above marriage. Married 30 Jan. by the Rev. James Beck. p. 65

17 December 1827. Thomas W. WOODING and Elizabeth A. Crews, dau. of Chrischana Crews who consents. Sur. Richard I. (or J.?) Shelton. Married 20 Dec. by the Rev. Griffith Dickinson. p. 90

10 December 1815. Allen WOODSON and Nancy Farmer, dau. of Marlin Farmer who requests that this license be issued. Sur. Samuel Willis. Married by the Rev. David Nowlin. p.59

-- ---- 1809. Jesse WOODSON and Lucy Hodnett. Married by the Rev. David Nowlin. Minister's Return. p. 47

30 September 1817. John C. WOODSON and Sally Russell. Married by the Rev. William Blair. Minister's Return. p. 65

15 December 1806. Joseph WOODSON and Sally Allen, dau. of David Allen, deceased. Sur. James D. Patton. p. 42

13 October 1812. Joseph WOODSON and Elizabeth Hodnett. Sur. Jesse Woodson. Married by the Rev. David Nowlin. p.53

19 January 1824. Stephen WOODSON and Selina Woodson. Sur. Robert Posey. Married by the Rev. David Nowlin. p. 81

21 March 1826. Pleasant WOODY and Permelia Walters, dau. of Archibald Walters who consents. Sur. John Shields. Married 17 April by the Rev. William Blair. p. 87

22 December 1824. Willis WOODY and Avey R. Law, dau. of David Law who requests that this license be issued. Sur. Adam Law. Married 30 Dec. by the Rev. Orson Martin. p.82

28 October 1812. William WOOLSEY and Anna Betterton. Consent of Wm. Betterton, Senr.
NOTE: This is consent only - and NOT in the Register.

8 August 1817. William WOOTEN and Sarah Ragan. Sur. Daniel Ragan. Married "the 20th 1812" by the Rev. Thomas Sparks. p. 65

1 September 1828. Archibald D. WORSHAM and Dolley M. Bruce. John Bruce requests this license be issued. No relationship given. Sur. George Bruce. Married 10 December by the Rev. Eben Angel. p. 92

14 December 1824. George WORSHAM and Susanna Prewitt.
Sur. Hugh Darby. p. 82

20 December 1810. Harold WORSHAM and Nancy Duly. Married
by the Rev. William Blair. Minister's Return. p. 49

19 March 1821. Thomas WORSHAM and Louisa Ragsdale. Sur.
Thomas Ragsdale. p. 74

17 April 1818. William WORSHAM and Elizabeth Ragsdale,
dau. of Thomas Ragsdale who signs the certificate and says
Elizabeth M. Ragsdale. Sur. Pyrant Thompson. p. 67

13 January 1826. William WORSHAM and Frances Giles. Sur.
Smith Giles. Married 19 Jan. by the Rev. William Blair.
p. 87

19 December 1808. Robert WORTHAM and Anne Briscoe. Sur.
David Rice. Married by the Rev. Thomas Sparks. p. 45

9 August 1820. Nathaniel WRAY and Nancy Hundley, who
signs her own certificate. Sur. Mastin Pearson. Married
10 Aug. by the Rev. Richard B. Beck. p. 72

3 December 1822. Christopher WRIGHT and Betsy Debo. Sur.
Abraham Debo. Married Dec. 1822 by the Rev. Ira Ellis.
p. 76

8 May 1818. George WRIGHT and Eleanor Thomas. Sur. John
Ragsdale. p. 67

5 November 1806. James WRIGHT and Patsy Watts. Sur. Levi
Watts. Married by the Rev. Thomas Sparks. p. 42

20 December 1819. John P. WRIGHT and Polley Witcher. Sur.
William Witcher. Married "since my last return" by the
Rev. David Nowlin. (Return dated 15 April 1822.) p. 69

5 March 1828. Larkin WRIGHT and Louisa Myers. Sur.
George Myers. p. 92

5 January 1829. Shadrack WRIGHT and Sarah Myers. Sur.
George Myers. p. 95

17 February 1823. William WRIGHT and Phitney Slayden.
Sur. John Slayden. Richard P. Wright, father of William,
consents, says Phitney is a daughter of Mr. John Slayden.
p. 79

8 February 1819. James YARBROUGH and Margaret Harris. Sur.
Bezaleel Wier, Jr. Bezaleel Wier, and Elizabeth Weir,
sign the certificate. Married 9 Feb. by the Rev. William
Blair. p. 70
Bezaleel Wier, Sr. married Elizabeth Harris in 1816. p.62

29 July 1822. Byrd S. YATES and Hilly Walrond. Sur. Francis C. Walrond. John Walrond signs the certificate. No relationship given. Married 1 August by the Rev. Griffith Dickinson. p. 76

15 February 1809. Charles YATES and Elizabeth Groff, dau. of Henry Groff, Senr. Sur. Henry Groff, Junr. Married by the Rev. Joseph Hatchett. p. 47

1 January 1828. Collin W. YATES and Martha Mottley. Sur. John Mottley. Married 22 Jan. by the Rev. Crispen Dickenson. p. 92

7 December 1829. William R. YATES and Elizabeth McLaughlan, dau. of Henry McLaughlan who consents. Sur. George W. Turner. Married 10 Dec. by the Rev. John Leigh. p. 95

15 February 1808. John YATES and Nancy Taylor, dau. of Obediah Taylor. Sur. Joseph Yates. Stephen Yates, father of John, says his son is of age. p. 46

15 April 1822. Thomas YEATES and Polley Boswell. Sur. Charles Boswell. Married 19 April by the Rev. Griffith Dickinson. p. 76

30 November 1812. William YEATES and Polly Shelhorse, dau. of Barnett Shelhorse who consents. Sur. Jacob Shelhorse. Married 3 December by the Rev. Joseph Hatchett. p. 53

8 April 1819. Stephen YEATTS and Polley Terry. Sur. David Terry. Married by the Rev. William Blair. p. 70

23 October 1822. Joseph YEAMAN and Patsy Shelton. Sur. William Shelton. Married 26 Oct. by the Rev. William Blair who says Martha Shelton. p. 76

27 December 1827. William T. YEARBREY and Polley Drain, dau. of William and Nancy Drain who consent. Sur. James Oakes. Married 10 January 1828 by the Rev. Richard B. Beck. p. 90

13 September 1823. Chesley D. YOUNG and Daphney Haraway. Sur. Robt. Burd. James Haraway signs the certificate and says, "Daphney, a woman of color and now under my care." p. 79

17 November 1806. George YOUNG and Dicie James. Sur. John Travis. p. 42

3 January 1822. George W. YOUNG and Agness Witcher. Sur. James Witcher. Vincent Witcher, guardian of Agness, signs the certificate. p. 76

18 November 1828. John YOUNG and Elizabeth Crump. Married by the Rev. Abner Anthony. Minister's Return. p. 92

29 September 1826. Oglesby YOUNG and Jane Debo. Sur. William Love. p. 87

9 December 1828. William H. YOUNG and Lucinda Mann. Sur. Harrison Mann. p. 92

15 December 1829. John YOUNGER and Elizabeth Jones. Sur. Thomas B. Jones. Married 17 Dec. by the Rev. Griffith Dickenson, Sr. p. 95

18 August 1811. Thomas YOUNGER and Martha Crowder, who writes her own consent. Sur. Jesse Walton, Jr. p. 51

1 February 1817. Thomas ZACHERY and Sally Matteny. Sur. John Matney. p. 65

20 March 1811. Jacob ZEEGLER and Rachel Rosson, dau. of Joseph Rosson who is Surety. Married 20 March by the Rev. Joseph Hatchett. P. 51

14 October 1824. Jacob ZINK and Nancy Campbell, who signs her own certificate. Sur. Samuell Campbell. Married 14 Oct. by the Rev. Joseph Hatchett. p. 82

PITTSYLVANIA COUNTY, VIRGINIA

NOTE: The following Pittsylvania County Marriage Bonds were
recently found at the Virginia State Libraryin a box marked
"unidentified papers."

Of the fifteen found, nine of them are in Mrs. Williams book of
Pittsylvania Marriages 1806-1830, however the information under-
lined on this sheet was not given in the bookand will be a wel-
comed addition. Six of the Bonds do not appear in the book.

Jan. 15, 1810   Selby Benson & Nancy Worsham (shown as Nancy Osborn
                in the book), daughter of Thomas Worsham.

Jan. 15, 1810   William Burgess & Nancy Lewis, dau. of William Lewi

March 15, 1810 Nathaniel Barnett & Betsey Sutherlin, daughter of
                Thomas Sutherlin.

April 10, 1810 Rowley M. Curtis & Anne Robertson, dau.of Edward
                Robertson.

May 8, 1810   Isaac Apsher & Polly Taylor, dau. of James Taylor.

July 16, 1810   Samuel Blair & Polly Raynolds (SIC).

Aug. 14, 1810   John Blair & Sally Wade.

Aug. 8, 1810   Eppa Booth & Dicey Wall, Dicey above age 21.

Oct. 9, 1810   John Anderson, Jr. & Lucy Waldin, daughter of John
                Waldin.

Oct. 9, 1810   Vincent Brown & Mildred Reynolds, daughter of Jesse
                Reynolds.

Oct. 15, 1810   James W. Brookes & Patsey Thompson, daughter of
                Elizabeth. (NOTE: Consent dated Nov.15, 1810).

Oct. 15, 1810   Daniel Burchfield & Sally Chumbly, daughter of
                Francis Chumbly.

Dec. 11, 1810   Thomas Burnett & Thomas Still, dau. of Thomas Still

Dec. 17, 1810   William Burgess & Rhoday Chaney, dau. of Tech[e].

Dec. 17, 1810   Abraham Chaney & Nancy Donnelson, daughter of
                James and Elizabeth Donnelson.

Sent to me, Kathleen Booth Williams, by Mrs. Emma Robertson Mathen
                                      1718 Glenview Road
                                      Richmond, Virginia 23222

      Received November 21, 1969,
      with permission to use them.

INDEX TO BRIDES

184

DAVIS, Martha 43
    Mary 44
    Mary M. 142
    Mary S. 142
    Mildred 73, 117
    Nancy 71, 156
    Rebecca C. 122
    Rosa 111
    Sally 124
    Sarah 31
    Sarah G. 170
    Selah 158
DAWSON, Jane F. 76
DEARING, Jane 108
    Margaret 13
DEBO, Betsy 175
    Catharine 76
    Jane 177
    Nancy 33
    Polley 34
    Sally 81
DEBOE, Elender 174
DEER, Joanna 110
    Willy 161
DEJARNETT, Milley 137
    Polly 31
    Rebecca 123
    Susanna 97
DELAP, Mary 124
DENNISON, Elizabeth 13
    Nancy 33
DENT, Ruth Ann 57
DEVIN, Elizabeth 82, 111
    Lucea 39
    Lucy 11
    Margaret 111
    Mary 118
    Sarah Smith 82
DEWS, Elsey 163
    Mary 58
    Priscilla 146
    Sarah 148
    Susanna 20
    Susannah 40
DICKENSON, Elizabeth 98, 162
    Judith 74
    Nancy C. 148
    Nelly 112
    Lucy H. 11
DICKERSON, Nancy 155
DICKINSON, Neilly 112
    Sarah 58
DICKSON, Judith 43

DISHMAN, Rebecca 163
DISMONG, Nancy 66
DIX, Martha 97
    Tamson A. 2
    Susanna 169
DIXON, Elizabeth 110
    Nancy 114
DISMUNG, Ritty 166
DODSON, Artemesia 144
    Artemisia 144
    Caron 76
    Dotia 144
    Dumey 103
    Duna 103
    Elizabeth 43, 79, 83
        87, 164
    Joyce 147
    Judah 147
    Karen 76
    Lydia 41
    Peggy 30
    Polley M. 42
    Polly 151
    Rhoda 30
    Sarah 103, 130
    Susannah 75
DONALDSON, Frances 5
    Patsey 141
DONALSON, Nancy 26
DONNELSON, Rebecca 19
DOSS, Martha 41
    Mary Ann 45
    Milly 122
    Rachel 150
    Susanna 77
DOUGLAS, Rebecca 23
DOUGLASS, Ann W. 114
    Martha 104, 170
    Martha G. 29
    Patsy 103
    Sarah 82
DOVE, Ann 99
    Fanny 36
    Jane 89
    Margaret 135
    Peggy 132
    Sally 135
    Sarah 1
    Tabitha 12
DRAIN, Martha 115
    Polley 176
DRANE, Sally 18
DUDLEY, Fanny 84

DULY, Nancy 175
DUNBAR, Louisa 63
  Nancy 82
  Rose Ann 55
DUNCAN, Fanny 14
DUNN, Ann 121
  Elizabeth P. 142
  Keziah 102
  Mary M. 86
  Sally 102
DUPUY, Polley I. 90
DURHAM, Bethenia 137
  Polley 128
DURRATT, Mary 45
DURRETT, Elizabeth 24
DYER, Elizabeth 73
  Frankey 17
  Nancy 3
  Seludy 90

E

EADES, Judith 163
EADS, Polly 20
EANES, Martha 130
  Nancy 130
  Polley 16
  Rebecca 87
EARLS, Judea 22
EARP, Elizabeth 31
  Lucy 48
  Precilla 31
  Sally 137
EASLEY, Dolley H. 161
  Elizabeth 130
  Lucy 63
  Sarah M. 9
  Sarah W. 79
EAST, Obedience 91
  Philidia 30
  Sally 161
ECHOLS, Elizabeth W. 64
  Martha D. 166
  Nancy 134, 135
  Prudence 103
  Rhoda 149
  Sarah 5, 103
  Susan 3
EDDES, Anna 7
EDDS, Jane 93
  Levinia 110
  Sarah 8
EDWARDS, Elizabeth 89

EDWARDS, Gilly 172
  Jean 61
  Judah 173
  Mary 156
  Nancy 12
ELIOT, Jane 46
ELLIOTT, Jane 46
  Nancey 123
  Polley 114
  Polly 2, 150
ELLIS, Fanny M. 169
EMERSON, Patsey 111
EMMERSON, Anna 84
  Judith 84
  Sally 84
ENGLISH, Polly 45
EPPERSON, Elizabeth 27, 30
  Mary 54
EUDALEY, Elizabeth 76
EVANS, Ann R. 141
  Elizabeth 72

F

FACKLER, Lettice R. 27
FALLEN, Elizabeth M. 127
  Nancey 51
FALLING, Elizabeth M. 126
FARGUSON, Elizabeth 100
  Molley 48
  Tabitha 126
FARIS, Anna 168
  Christina W. 9
  Elizabeth 137
  Frances 110
  Jane 52
  Martha 86
  Nancy 89, 159
  Patsey 152
  Polley B. 92
FARLEY, Ann M. 52
FARMER, Alcey 70
  Elizabeth 124
  Frances 74
  Lucy 32, 86
  Nancy 174
  Polley 171
  Polly 8
  Rhoda 171
  Sarah 84
  Susan 80
FARRIS, Polley 2

FARTHING, Ann 17
   Dorothy 54
   Elizabeth 53
   Lucy 119
   Mary 166
   Phebe 162
   Rebecca 53, 54
   Sally 113
   Susan 53
FEARN, Mary 43
FERGUSON, Elizabeth 96
   Mary 168
   Nancy S. 60
   Patsy 41
   Rebecca 68
FISHER, Elizabeth 26
   Polley 111
   Sally 116
FITZGERALD, Catharine 60, 135
   Elizabeth 90, 103
   Nancy 171
   Sarah 126
FLIPPIN, Maryan 112
   Susanna 144
FONTAINE, Polley 19
   Sarah 146
   Tabitha M. 156
FORD, Mary 26
FOREST, Susanna 101
FOSTER, Sally 6
FOUST, Caty 33
   Maryan 68
   Susanna 33, 101
FOWLKES, Elizabeth 147
FRALICK, Susanna 156
FRANCIS, Nancy 41
FRANKLIN, Martha A. 39
FREE, Milly 138
FRIZZLE, Elizabeth 96
   Nancy 113
   Rebecca 28
   Tabitha 81
FULLER, Anna 47
   Anney 47
   Martha 46
   Polley 18
   Sally 166
   Susannah 80
FUQUA, Amy 93

G

GALDING, Nancy 49
GALLOWAY, Nancy 56
GAMMON, Nancy 136
   Visey 7
GARDNER, Anna 60
   Catharine 42
   Lucinda 106
   Polly 41
   Sally W. 120
GARLAND, Elizabeth A. 167
GARNER, Nancy 143
   Sarah W. 120
GARRETT, Ann 75
   Elizabeth 52
   Peggy 160
   Rebecca 88
   Sally 121
GAULDIN, Elizabeth 174
GEESLING, Elizabeth K. 16
GEORGE, Dolley 75
   Eliza 148
   Elizabeth 46
   Maria 23
   Mildred 66
   Peggy 139
GILBERT, Catharine 37
   Locky 160
   Louisa 164
   Martha 49
   Mildred H. 159
   Nancy 160
   Polly 135
   Wilmuth 62
GILES, Ann 100
   Elizabeth 46, 63
   Frances 175
   Martha 87
   Nelly 158
   Patsy 131
   Rebecca 128
   Sarah H. 25
   Susanna 100
GIPSON, Elmyry 9
GLASCO, Elizabeth 35
GLASCOCK, Chloe 4
   Elizabeth 108
   Judith 134
   Martha 173
   Mary 98, 134
   Sarah H. 148
GLASGOW, Elizabeth 51

LOVE, Mary Ann 46
  Nancy 72
  Sarah 99
LOVELACE, Betsey Ann 20
  Winifred 123
LUMPKIN, Martha R. 51
LUCAS, Mary 41
LYON, Mary 63

Mc

McALASTER, Elizabeth 107
McBRIDE, Nancy 8
McCRAW, Nancy 136
McCULLOCK, Phebe 8
McDANIEL, Anna 79
  Chloe 61
  Elizabeth 157
  Isbell 61
  Kezia 68
  Maro 42
  Martha 44
  Mary 98
  Pary 97
  Zeria 68
McDONALD, Elizabeth 151
  Zerishe 152
McGLASSON, Nancey 161
McGRIGOR, Clarissa Ruffin 44
McHANEY, Juriah 64
  Mary 159
McLAUGHLAN, Elizabeth 176
McMILLION, Anney 143
  Dorcas 31
McNEALY, Janey 173
McNEELEY, Elizabeth 33

M

MADDING, Elizabeth 153
  Polley 112
  Polly 140
  Willey 72
MAHAN, Elizabeth 129
  Martha 52
  Marthey 52
  Nancy 61
  Polly 85
  Rebecca 18
MAHON, Sarah 21
  Susanna 65
MALLICOTT, Frankey 91

MANN, Lucinda 177
MARKHAM, Catharine M. 23
  Rebecka 8
  Rebecker J. 8
MARSHALL, Maria 42, 61
  Unity 143
MART, Fanney 131
  Frances 131
  Jincy 104
  Lucy 104
  Nancey 104
MARTIN, Bathena 3
  Catharine 114
  Elizabeth 12
  Polley 62
  Sarah 171
  Tabitha 96
  Willey 156
  Winnifred 6
MASON, Maria 79
  Temperance 44
  Tempitha 44
MASSIE, Elizabeth 143
MATHERLEY, Rhoda 108
MATHERLY, Mary P. 133
MATTENY, Sally 177
MATTHEWS, Jane 14
MATTOX, Coley V. 36
  Elizabeth 27
  Nancy 131
MAXY, Susannah 33
MAY, Anne 101
  Jane 50
  Martha 151
  Susanna 50
MAYES, Juley 100
  Lettice 11, 135
  Mary 83
  Salley 100
  Tabitha 103
  Winifred 103
MAYHEW, Ludey 20
  Nancy 35
MAYHUE, Catharine 43
  Letty 20
  Martha 144
  Polly 122
MAYS, Levina 136
  Polly 120
  Rhoda 13
  Rody 13
  Sally 103
  Stacia 136

MEADE, Sally 1
MEADOWS, Elizabeth W. 155
   Nancy 57
   MEAS, Milley 84
MEDLOCK, Susan H. 138
MEED, Eady 155
MEES, Sarah 71
MERRITT, Mary 37
MICHAUX, Rebecca 78
   Sarah W. 60
MICKLEBERRY, Jane 41
MIDKIFF, Betsey 87
   Elizabeth 119
   Phebe 27
   Polly 119
   Rodah 166
   Susan 76
   Susanna 105
MILLER, Rachel 28
MILLNER, Anny 157
   Elizabeth 54
   Julia Ann 71
   Margaret 6
   Nancy I. 159
MILLS, Lucy 52
   Martha 71
   Mary 123
MINTER, Anna 94
   Jincey 107
   Susanna 3
MITCHELL, Elizabeth 59, 93,
  145
   Jane 8, 118
   Martha 157
   Mary 120, 134
   Nancy 44, 118
   Parthena 121
   Polley 102
   Sally 68
   Susanna P. 96
MOON, Elizabeth 70
MOORE, Elizabeth 116, 143
   Elizabeth W. 43
   Rhody A. 32
   Sally 75
MOOREFIELD, Francis 1
   Lucy 151
   Mary 107
MORGAN, Elizabeth 66
MORRICE, Elizabeth 169
MORRIS, Dorcas 83
   Mary 170
   Nancy 24

MORRIS, Polly 125
   Ruth 117
MORTON, Amey 149
   Mariah 149
   Nancy 3
MOSS, Elizabeth 101
MOTLEY, Araminta 155
   Chrischania D. 173
   Elizabeth F. 148
   Elsa B. 170
   Mary J. 77
   Nancey 164
   Nancy 31
   Sarah 53
MOTTLEY, Elizabeth 5, 26,
  104, 148
   Harriet 167
   Martha 176
   Patsey 114
   Patsy 154
   Sally 93
MUCK, Sarah 165
MUES, Sarah 128
MULLINGS, Nancy 157
MULLINS, Nancy 157
   Tabitha 136
MURPHEY, Sally 147
MURPHY, Eleanor 16
   Elenor 16
   Elizabeth 133
   Jane 131
   Sally 2
MUSE, Elizabeth T. 71
   Elvira E. 110
   Frances A. 157
   Montilda A. 126
   Nancy 110
   Sally W. 24
   Susannah M. 163
   Susannah Mariah 163
MUSTAIN, Elizabeth 141
   Mary Polley 45
   Sudy 36
   Tabitha 86
MUSTAINE, Betsey 141
MYERS, Elizabeth 43
   Fanny 97
   Jincey 27
   Louisa 175
   Nancy 41
   Polley 97
   Sarah 175
MYRES, Polly 149

N

NANCE, Martha M. 94
NAPIER, Elizabeth 34, 51,
  68
  Susan F. 128
NAPPER, Elizabeth 51
NASH, Elizabeth 135
  Polley 153
NEAL, Elizabeth 169
  Frances 11
  Lucy 34
  Lydda 35
  Lydia 138
  Polly 55
  Sarah 143
  Susanna 7
  Wilmoth M. 109
NEEL, Mary 43
NELSON, Betsy 86
  Elizabeth 86
  Lydia 164
  Nancy 15
  Polly 71
NEWBELL, Bartia 55
NEWBILL, Polly 10
NEWBY, Anny 143
NEWMAN, Polley 11
NEWTON, Delilah 96
  Minta C. 68
NICHOLAS, Rebecca 22
NICHOLS, Catharine 165
  Elizabeth 104
  Giddy 109
NOBLE, Ann Marie 63
NORMAN, Belinda 150
NORTON, Sarah 137
NOWLIN, Ann 88
  Ann Bibb 40
  Catharine 44
  Nancy 134
  Rebecca J. 52
NUCHOLS, Martha 59
NUCKOLS, Betsy 59
  Mourning 59

O

OAKES, Evaline 115
  Margarett 90
  Phebe 3
  Sabra 82
  Sally 17

OAKES, Susanna 20
OAKS, Polly 31
ODENEAL, Mary 16
OLIVER, Polly 27
  Rhoda B. 83
O'NEAL, Sally 48
ORANDER, Elizabeth 140
ORRENDER, Elizabeth 111
  Nancy 20
  Sally 72
OSBORN, Nancy 12
OSBOURN, Anna 32
OTENEAL, Elvi 136
OWEN, Elizabeth 31, 116
  Hannah 124
  Lucinda 11
  Lusey 113
  Martha 133
  Milley 117
  Nancy 36
  Peggy 97
  Sally 1, 62
  Sarah 93, 137
  Susanna 173
  Tempy 1
  Wilmoth 131
OWENS, Peggy 97
OZBURN, Mary 80

P

PACE, Lucy 15
PANNILL, Catharine A. 172
  Elizabeth 149
PARISH, Ann 67
PARKER, Fanny 146
  Judith 81
  Keziah 67
  Mary 146
  Sally 90
PARMER, Judah 165
PARISH, Jane A. 100
PARRISH, Frances 26
  Joannah 11
  Judah 47
  Lucy 50
  Pauline R. 87
  Rebecca 125
  Sophia 3
  Susannah 46
PARSON, Mary 159

Q

QUINN, Agness 114
   Margaret 66

R

RAFE, Elizabeth 79
RAGAN, Sarah 174
RAGLAND, Martha 8
RAGSDALE, Elizabeth 175
   Elizabeth M. 175
   Harriet L. 24
   Louisa 175
   Mary 132
   Patsy 134
   Phebe 25
RAILEY, Lettice 11
   Mary 96
RALEIGH, Sally 24
RAMSEY, Betsey 101
   Elizabeth 31, 104
   Sally 111
RANEY, Manerva 22
REAGAN, Amanda G. 116
REARDIN, Nancy 54
REIGER, Polley 61
REYNOLDS, Anne 138
   Demarius 112
   Elizabeth 51, 90
   Haridice 3
   Mary 121
   Matilda 30
   Milley 20
   Nancy 16
   Polley 14
   Sally 51
RICE, Nancy 15
RICHARDS, Nancy 123
RICHARDSON, Agnes 86
   Elizabeth 129
   Fanny 96
   Kitty 97
   Salley 61
RICHEY, Sally 94
RICKEY, Elizabeth 113
RIDDLE, Eadey 6
   Elizabeth 47
   Fanny 99
   Susanna 63, 118
RIEGER, Polly 61
RIGHT, Frankey 33
RIGNEY, Sally 44

RITCHER, Polly 136
RITCHIE, Jane 147
   Sally 136
RITCHEY, Sally 136
ROACH, Catharine 103
   Jane 20
   Mary 65
   Nancy 117
ROBERTS, Elizabeth H. 167
ROBERTSON, Anna 139
   Edith 23
   Elizabeth 58, 142, 146
   Judah 127
   Louisa 48
   Lucy 82
   Mary 5, 148
   Milley 29
   Mourning 9
   Nancey 24
   Nancy 29
   Nancy P. 59
   Polley 92, 133
   Roselanard 171
   Rosillamond 171
   Sally 57, 102
   Susannah 29
ROGERS, Sally 71
ROLAND, Frances 101
   Pheby 22
RORER, Catharine 35
   Polley 158
ROSSON, Catharine 90
   Polley 154
   Rachel 177
ROWLAND, Elizabeth 65,
   92, 171
   Francis 87
   Ruth 23
   Sarah K. 27
ROYALL, Elizabeth 32
   Judith 148
   Susan 49
ROYSTER, Susan 145
RUMLEY, Edith 2
   Patsey 86
RUSSELL, Elizabeth 91
   Lucy W. 129
   Nancy 102
   Sally 174

SADLER, Salley 101
SANDERS, Mary 77
   Rachel 103
SANDS, Peggy 109
SAUNDERS, Mary 77
   Oney 45
   Peggy 167
   Polley 79
   Susanna 32
SAWYERS, Polley 24
SCARCE, Mary 98
SCOTT, Jane 10
   Keziah 122
SCRUGGS, Nancy 52
SEA, Stirah 78
SEAMORE, Sarah 97
   Wilmoth 30
SEAMOREL, Caty 116
SELF, Seany 75
SEMONES, Anna 161
SEYMORE, Mary 128
SHACKLEFORD, Jane 152
   Milley 152
   Polly 95
   Rhoda 64
SHAW, Bathina 25
   Lucy C. 70
   Martha 121
   Susanna 78
SHELHORSE, Polly 176
   Sally 87
   Susan 120
SHELLHORSE, Catharine 75
   Jane 109
SHELTON, Anna 134
   Anna R. 110
   Anne 140
   Chloe R. 133
   Dolly 35
   Eddy 68
   Eleasure P. 141
   Elizabeth 133
   Elizabeth G. 58
   Elizabeth I. 54
   Frances 19
   Gilliam 39
   Gillion 39
   Isabel W. 132
   Isabella M. 137
   Jane 100
   Jane A. 166
   Jane H. 68
   Judith 70

SHELTON, Lettice 75
   Letty S. 142
   Louisa 47
   Lucy 77
   Martha 176
   Martha H. 73
   Martha L. 120
   Mary M. 142
   Miranda 139
   Marinda W. 139
   Nancy 26, 138, 169
   Nancy C. 141
   Nancy W. 165
   Pamelia 141
   Patsy 176
   Patsy H. 60
   Patsy S. 64
   Pheby 21
   Polley L. 141
   Polly 70
   Rachel 74
   Sally G. 95
   Sarah 22
   Sarah B. 93
   Sarah H. 51
   Susa 59
   Susan H. 51
   Susanna 23
   Susan Robertson 21
   Tempy C. 89, 112
   Winifred 95
SHEPHERD, Anne R. W. F.
   132
SHEPPARD, Elizabeth 38
SHIELDS, Jane 32
   Lucy 9
   Mary 60
   Sarah 9
   Susanna 43
SHOCKLEY, Peggy 64
SHORT, Dicey 27
   Nancy 33
SHUMATE, Nancy 102
SIKES, Lucinda 6
SIMPSON, Celina 136
   Mary Ann 42
   Rachel M. 77
   Selety 145
   Stacey 43
SKATES, Eddy 37
   Eddy S. 37
SLATE, Ony 108
SLAYDEN, Apphia 70

THORNTON, Mary 157
  Mildred 93
  Polly 28
  Susan 65
THURMAN, Ailcey 130
  Oney 84
  Susanna 8
THURMOND, Bethaney E. 122
TIFFEN, Mary 65, 157
TIFFIN, Elizabeth 163
  Lucy 109
  Nancy 45, 65
TOLBART, Phoebe 58
TOMPKINS, Mary 67
TOSH, Catharine 121
  Polly 12
TOWLER, Catharine 129
  Elizabeth 143, 158
  Jane 156
  Judith 41
  Mary 41
  Mourning 132
  Nancy 45
  Polly 12
TOWNES, Ann E. 52
TRAVIS, Elender 149
  Elizabeth 55, 100
  Frances 121
  Martha 121
TRIBBLE, Frances 2, 38
  Sarah 149
TRIGG, Dianna 63
TROTTER, Catharine C. 108
TUCKER, Betsy 78
  Jane 141
  Martha H. 126
  Nancy 134
  Nancy H. 59
  Patsey 65
  Polly 106
  Sibby B. 139
TUGGLE, Nancy I. 115
TUNSTALL, Ann 160
  Eliza B. 158
  Sarah P. 5
TURLEY, Dorcas 92
  Elizabeth 55
  Lucindy 83
  Patsey 160
  Polley 112
  Sophea 64
TURLY, Zepora 92
TURNER, Delila 155

TURNER, Henrietta 161
  Judith C. 74
TWEDWELL, Massey 22
  Polley 168

U

UHLES, Catharine 49
  Susannah 162

V

VADEN, Sarah H. 106
  Winifred 2
VANCE, Elizabeth 71
  Polley 34
VASS, Celia 25
VAUGHAN, Fanny 92
  Francis 45
  Judith 162
  Martha 5
  Mary 61
  Metildy 107
  Nancy 56, 91
  Sally 123
VAUGHN, Mary 147
VOSS, Sarah 172

W

WADDILL, Betsey 130
  Sally 130
WADE, Salley 13
  Sarah 77, 107
WADDLETON, Mary T. 36
WAGGONER, Anna 7
  Milly 81
  Sally 81
WALDEN, Elizabeth 20
  Jane D. 139
  Lucinda 27
  Lucy 4
  Mary 35
  Polley 162
WALKER, Anna 55
  Betsy 149
  Elizabeth 51
  Judith 155
  Mary 10
  Patsy 154
  Sally 10, 91
  Susanna 34, 51
WALLACE, Jain 49

204

ATKINSON, Charles W. 60
  Henry 101
  Jesse 43, 57
  John W. 37
  Josiah 42, 57, 60, 164
  Lewis 72
  William 16, 62, 68
AUSTIN, Daniel B. 7
  Jeffrey 131
  Stephen 7, 39, 86
  William 106, 162

B

BABER, Joice 12
BAGGERLY, David 7
  John 7
BAGWELL, John W. 145
BAILES, Elizabeth 5
BAILEY, Charles 170
  Christopher 98
  James 75, 139
BALAS, Elisha 52
BALL, John 24, 75
  Samuel 75
BANKS, Gerard, Jr. 7
BARBER, Coleman 15, 81
  Elisha 157
  Hezekiah 84
  Joseph 5, 44
  Matthew 32, 84
  Molley 6
  Reuben 5
  William 8, 65, 76
BARBOUR, David 8
  Elisha 169
  John 8
BARDIN, James 55
BARKER, Green 71, 149
  Martha 73
  Moses 9, 21
  Nancy 21
  Stephen 161
BARKSDALE, Claiborne B. 14
  Claiborne W., Dr. 9
  Eliza 14
  Molley 123
  Molly 65
  Peter 2, 161
  Wm. H. 65, 123
BARNES, John 22, 24
BARNETT, Joseph 3
  Nathaniel 41

BARNETT, Thomas 150
  William 22
BARRET, John 162
BARNETT, John 10, 45
  John B. 131
BASKERVILL, George H. 40
BASS, Susan 137
BATES, Isaac 138
  Matthew 178
BATTLES, James 58
BAYES, John 2
BAYLES, Elisha 136
BAYLISS, Elisha 7
BEACH, Judah 58
  Samuel 58
BEADLES, Lewis Y. 172
BEASLEY, Stephen 55
  Warner 55
BEAVERS, Joseph 172
  William 19, 43, 61
BECK, James 11
  Lucy 81
  Richard B. 11, 39, 81, 133
  Robert 34, 101
  Samuel 12, 22, 115, 149
  William 12, 15, 16, 34, 83, 101
BEGGERLY, Henry 147
BELL, John 85
BENNETT, Bluford E. 144
  Coalman D. 36, 39
  Jane 157
  John 144
  Lewis B. 157
  Macager 15
  Palmerin 6
  Peter 12
  Reuben 163
  Richard 117, 134
  Travis 157
  Walden 4
BENSON, Selby 28
  Silby 86
BERGER, Daniel 40, 66, 159
  George 106, 150
  Jacob 40, 106, 150
  Jacob, Jr. 66, 141
  Jacob, Sr. 159
  John 12, 35
  Samuel 148
BETHELL, Alfred M. 77
BETTERTON, Wm., Jr. 93

BETTERTON, Wm., Senr. 93,
    174
BIBA, Benjamin 87
BILLENS, Patsey 115
BILLINS, Elisha 23, 115
BINGHAM, Edmond 78
    Edmund 119
BINGUM, Edmund 143
BIRTHWRIGHT, Samuel 146
BISHOP, Landon I. 64
BLACK, Eleanor S. 160
    Margaret S. 160
    Nathaniel 160
    Susanna 13, 160
    Thomas 160
    Thos. 160
BLACKWELL, Robert 84
BLAIR, James 16, 35, 129
    Josiah 60
    Samuel 1
    William 60, 144
BLAKE, Thomas 54
BLANKS, Anthony 137
    Henry 116
    Henry, Jr. 105
    Joel 14
    John 30, 44
    Jos. 131
    Joseph 14
BOAZ, David 15
    David R. 35, 145
    Edmund A. 14
    James 15, 108
    Lydia 108, 143
    Shadrach 88
    Shadrack 37, 129
    Thomas 58
BOBBETT, Randolph 84, 123
BOBBITT, William 129
BOBET, Charles 15
BOHANNON, John 86
    Joseph 4
    Ludwell 16
    Nancy 16
    Nathaniel 9
BOLEN, Joseph 31
BOLIN, John 118
BOLLIN, John 171
BOLLING, George 110
    John 124, 125
BOOKER, Richard 14, 74,
    124
BOOTH, Epaphroditus 16

BOOTH, John 16
    John, Jr. 16
    Mary 16
    Merady 16
    Nancy 147
    William 74
BOOTHE, Merady 16
BOSWELL, Charles 176
    Nacey 17
BOWLIN, John 14
BOWLING, Joseph 110
BOYD, George 170
BRADLEY, Daniel 3, 13,
    141
    Isham 105, 120, 128,
    138
    Samuel 25, 141
    Will 39
    William 134
BRADNER, Dozier 113
BRANSON, James 18
    Jonathan 21, 69
    Michael 121
BRAWNER, Ben 158
BRAY, Christopher 161
BREEDLOVE, David W. 30
    Pleasant E. 110
    Richard 15, 30, 110
    Richard P. 18
BREWER, William 101
BRIANT, Nelson 18
BRICE, Philip 33
BRIGHT, Joshua 157
BRISCOE, John 122
    Notley W. 18
BROOKS, Leonard 166
BROWN, Bird 92
    Burwell 70
    Daniel 10, 65, 88
    Henry 10
    John 33
    John E. 90
    Langston 19
    Lowden 65
    Lodowick 90
    Obediah 73
    Obediah H. 19
    Rebecah 19
    Richd 19
    Thomas 70
    Winston 16
BRUCE, Frederick 1, 53
    George 174

BRUCE, James 150
  John 36, 174
  Meredith 126
  Tabitha 53
  Thomas 64, 126, 140,
    150
  Ward 112
BRUMFIELD, Isaac 20, 80,
    116
  Thomas K. 58
  William 75
BRYANT, Elisha 170
  Fleming B. 110
BUCKLEY, Jesse 39
BULLINGTON, John 69
  Robert 15, 97
  William 21
BUMPASS, Benton 21
BURCH, Dandridge 10
  John 10, 26
  John, Senr. 26
  Robert 166
BURD, Robt. 176
BURGESS, Pendleton 99
  William 73
  Wm. 56
BURGISS, William 164
BURNETT, Benjamin 22
  Gilbert 7
  John 22, 54, 56, 85
  Joseph 10
  Malchijah 54
  Thomas 22, 35, 125
  William 56
BURNS, Harrison 93
BURTON, Elisha 73
  Isham 74, 90
  Nancy 11
BUSH, Lucy 33
BUTCHER, Benjamin 111
  Gincy 111
BUTT, Elizabeth 30
BYBEE, John 106
  Joseph 5, 106

C

CABANISS, Martha 38
  Matt 38
CAHALL, James 149
  John 5, 115
  Peter 5, 149
CALDWELL, Allen 18

CALLAHAM, Matthew 74
CALLAHAN, John H. 136
  Matthew 38
CALLAND, Eliza 145
  Elizabeth C. 88
  Eliza C. 107
  Samuel 155
CALLANDS, Eliza C. 142
CALLAWAY, Francis 138
CAMERON, Chloye 54
  Daniel 92
  John 140
CAMP, George 36, 66
  James 66
CAMPBELL, John 142
  Samuel 177
CAREY, Thomas, Jr. 107
CARMICAL, Robert 24
CARROLL, Ethredel 157
CARTER, Charles 127
  Charles E. 30
  Jesse 80
  John 134
  John R. 134
  Joseph 100, 132
  Lawson H. 123
  Levin 24
  Nathan 85, 119, 129
  Nathaniel 62
  Paskel 45
  Presley 146
  Rawley, Junr. 25
  Spencer 70
  Taleferro 60
  Talliaferro 167
  Thomas 24, 38
  Thornton 146
  William 11
CHADMAN, Elizabeth 120
  Robard 120
CHAINEY, Abraham 126, 131
  Charles 53
  Moses 26
  Reubin 25
  Samuel 53
CHAMBERLAIN, Britton 120
CHAMBERS, Thomas 20
CHANDLER, Allen 125
CHANEY, Charles 21, 105
  Elijah 25
  Josiah 26
  Joshua D. 171
  Moses 25, 26, 69, 70

COUSINS, Peter G. 148
    Willis G. 142
COVINGTON, David 161
    Fanny 61, 162
    Harrison 7
    John 167
COX, Elizabeth 72
    Elizabeth S. 4
    George 105, 131
    James S. 40, 106
    Samuel 81
    William 78
CRADDOCK, Asa 123
    John T. 33
    Samuel 165
    Samuel, Sr. 165
CRAFT, George 7, 17, 49
    Philip 38
CRAIN, Susanna 125
    Thomas 125
    William 147
Craine, Jacob 160
CRANE, Henry 84
    John T. 66, 115
CRAYNE, John 92
CREWS, Andrew 44
    Chrischana 174
    John 29
    Josiah 87
    Susannah 29
    William 69
CRIDER, Andrew 158
    Henry 34
    John 40
    William 75
CROFF, David 34
CROSS, Arthur 20
CROWDER, Langley B. 59
CULLY, Samuel M. 114
CUMLEY, Thomas 99
CUNNINGHAM, Nathan 71
CURREY, John 88
    Thomas 88
CURRY, James 77
    Thomas 81
CURTESS, Reubin 101
CURTIS, Reubin 20
    Thomas 101
CUSTARD, James 133
    William 39

D

DABUSSE, Martha 100
DAINGERFIELD, Elizabeth 81
    John 81
    Wm. 81
DALLIS, Robert 22
    Terry 22, 77
DALTON, Benjamin 36, 43, 116
    Charles P. 20
    Elijah 123
    James P. 90
    Jarrett P. 12, 37
    John 112, 118, 158
    John S. 118, 158
    Lewis, 15, 122, 150
    Littleberry 36, 131
    Milly 123
    Thomas 35, 81, 118
    William 12, 34, 36, 118
DALY, John 80
DANCE, Stephen 126
DANGERFIELD, Henerham 105
    Herinham 154
    John 166
    William 105
DANIEL, George 57, 98
    Jonah 98
    Marey 68
    Martin 165
    Matthew 67
    Thomas 101
DARBY, Hugh 175
DAULTON, Martin 120
DAVE, Landford 41
DAVIS, Asa 42, 43, 122
    Benj. 104
    Benjamin 31
    Frances 134
    Francis 6
    Garrett 78, 104, 156
    Israel 38
    James 31
    James G. 168
    John 55, 111, 117
    Jordon R. 38, 64, 83
    Joseph 38, 71, 73, 117
    Joshua 95
    Mercy 117
    Sarah (Meadow) 142
    Sarahann 95
    Thomas 64, 77, 83, 99, 104, 142

GALARBY, James 152
GALDING, Andy 49
GAMMON, Drury 60
   William 7, 136
   Wm. 60
GARDNER, Bere C. 54
   Daniel 106
   Hath 41
   Isaac 51
   Nathaniel 95
   Silvan 60
   Silvany 42, 106
GARLAND, James 154
   Nicholas A. 167
GARNER, William 143
GARRETT, Jesse 120
   John 61
   John, Jr. 32, 47
   Levi 3, 108
   Thomas 52, 75, 121, 160
GAULDEN, Pegy 162
GAULDIN, Auda 174
   Samuel 61
   Wm. 174
GEESLING, Sarah 16
GEORGE, Hugh 66
   Jordan 61, 75
GIBSON, Bailer 139
   Joel 139
   John 62, 112
   Thos. Geo. 62
GILBERT, Cornelius 159
   George 37, 159, 160, 164
   James 49
   Jeremiah 37, 160
   John 160
   Preston 62
   Themuel 62
GILES, Ephraim 109
   Ephriam 25, 118
   George 158
   Hezekiah 40
   John 63, 100, 128
   Smith 175
   Stephen 62, 63, 88, 158
   Thomas 46, 87
   William B. 155
GILMORE, Samuel S. 126
GIVEN, Littleberry 102
GLASCOCK, Eliza 4
   Mary 148
   Thomas 4, 73

GLASCOCK, William H. 138
   William L. 108
   William S. 134
GLASGO, William 76
GLASGOW, Robert 51
GLASS, Johnson 164
   Willis 86, 124
GLENN, David 56, 116, 140, 171
   John S. 64, 109
GLOVER, John 88
GOARD, Jemima 8
GOAD, Jemimah 158
   Sarah 129, 163
GODLEY, Hiram 71
   Rockhill 71
GOING, Anna 64
GOODMAN, David 9
GOODWIN, Beale 98
   Jane 29
   Walker 154
GOSNEY, Benjamin 111
   Henry 36
   Lewis 113
   Richard S. 65
GOURLEY, Robert 66
GOVER, John 19
GRADY, Philip L. 44
GRANT, Anna 85
   Robert 57
   Salla 85
GRAVELEY, William 99
GRAVELLY, Francis 91
GRAVES, Peyton 67, 85
   William 13
GRAVILLY, James 99
GRAY, Adin 125
   Jeremiah 91
   John 13, 66, 114
   Nancy 66, 91
   Narby 13
GREEN, Berryman 66
   James 73
   John 66, 98
GREGORY, John K. 89
   Robert T. 47
GRIFFEY, Nathan 18
   Sally 67
GRIFFY, Isham 3
GRIFFIN, Isham 172
GRIFFITH, Salley 78
   Willis 67
GRIGG, Marthy 101

GRIGGS, Peter 91
  William D. 120
GRIGSBY, Moses 2, 31, 58,
  67, 153, 161
GRISHAM, Laban 7
GROF, William 82
GROFF, Henry, Junr. 176
  Henry, Senr. 176
GRUBB, Jesse 70, 137
  Jesse I. 114
GUNNELL, Anderson 80
GUNTER, Thomas 18
GUTREY, Denet 38
GUY, Samuel 135, 153
GWIN, Jesse 51
GWINN, Edmond 114
  Holmes 6, 94

H

HADEN, John 68
  John, Sr. 139
HAGOOD, Lewis 109, 118
HAILEY, Archibald 68
  Edward 76
  John 25, 26, 117
  Joseph E. 23
HAIRSTON, Robert 69
  Samuel 69
HAISLIP, James 52
  Polly 84
  William 69, 84
HAIZLIP, Mary 93
  William 64, 93
HALEY, Ambrose, Jr. 173
  Francis 137
  Joseph E. 153
  Jos. E. 69
  Matthew 52
  Samuel 54
  Temple 153
HALL, Anderson 69
  Benjamin 83
  Edward 114
  George 173
  Henry 101
  James 140
  John 70, 75, 141, 142
  163
  Reubin 3, 13, 72
  William 16, 19, 66, 80
  William H. 70, 141
HALY, Lovelace 52, 172

HAM, Obadiah 137
  Thomas 117
HAMBRICK, Sitha 87
HAMLETT, Robert 67
  Stephen B. 71
  William 67
HAMM, Thomas 78
  Willis 78
HAMMACK, John 104
  Spencer 104
HAMMOCK, John T. 154
HAMORE, John 117
HAMPTON, John 125
  Thomas H. 125
HAMRICK, David 28, 167
  Sitha 61
  Sytha 106
  William 28
HANCKS, Thos., Sr. 59
HANKINS, William 112
HANKS, John M. 59
  Thomas 34
  William 34
HARAWAY, James 176
HARDEY, Jesse 56
  John 167
HARDY, Banister 17, 41
  Elijah 79
  James 95
  Jesse 1
  Robert G. 111
  Thomas 147
  Vincent 71
  Wesley 167
  William 166
HAREFIELD, William R. 4
HARMAN, James 32
HARMON, James 72
  Mary 92
  Nicholas 92
  Samuel 72
HARP, Philip 16
HARPER, James 60
  Jesse 94
  George 137
  Nancy 102
  Nicholas 102
HARRIS, David 93
  Elizabeth 9, 175
  Fuller 73
  John 3
  John, Jr. 23
  John, Senr. 23

214

HARRISS, Peter M. 41, 69
    Rebeckah 93
    Samuel 59
HARRISON, Ashworth 39
    Joshua 39
    Josiah W. 6
    Meredith 79
    Nathaniel 74, 129
    Ro. 6, 111
    Robert 95
    Washington M. 80, 152
    Will P. 112
HARRISS, Austin 19
HART, James 137, 162
    John M. 65
HARVEY, Nancy 97
    Richard 38, 77
    Samuel 123, 168
HARVILL, Joel C. 136, 163, 166
HARVILLE, Joel 61
HASKINS, John 41
HATCHETT, Archibald 62, 74
    Edward 11, 62, 107
    William 55
HAWKER, Ambrose 47, 69, 102 130
    Ambus 47
    Cloary 47
    James 47, 102
    Philip 28, 74, 146
HAY, Ambrose 113
    Reubin 113, 127, 161
    Thomas 137
    Woodson 161
HAYMORE, Daniel 131
    John 27
HAYS, James 37
    John 75
    Thomas 53
HEADSPETH, William 17, 76
HEDGPETH, Holland 108
HEDRICK, George 7
    Philip 7
HEDSPETH, Lewis 42
HEMSON, Solomon 110
HENDERSON, James 92, 107
HENDRICK, Alexander 107
    Ezekiel 92
    Jane 159
HENRY, Benjamin 6
    Francis 37
    James W. 58

HENRY, John 66
    Martha 58
    Mary 6
HERNDON, Hannah 124
    Moses 21, 124
    Reuben 124
HERRING, William 76
HIGH, David 156
    Freeman 64, 69, 72, 94
HIGHT, Edward 156
HILER, Mary 9, 71
HILL, Ann 138
    Ezra 1
    Joseph 26, 121, 139, 141, 151, 153
    Thomas W. 75
HILLSON (Hittson), Alexander 26
HINES, James 3
    Nancy 35
    Thomas 35
HINTON, James 23
HODGE, Fleming 48
    Morton 48
HODGES, David 121
    Edmund 15, 100
    Elizabeth 121
    James 2, 67
    Jesse 15, 68, 81
    Lyon 78
    Moses 78, 154
    Nephanon 15
    William 68
HODNETT, Ayres 145
    Daniel 168
HOLDER, Delaney 116
    Delany 159
    Peter 112
HOLLAND, Catherine 49
    Joseph 79, 139
    Kitty 83
    Richard 77
HOLLEY, James 115
HOLLOWAY, John 56
HOLT, David 40
    James 161
    Lucy 103
    Matthew H. 103
    Miles 58, 161
    Sally 161
    William 15, 119, 166
    Wm. 15, 174
HOPKINS, Reubin 3, 54, 110

HOPPER, Terrell 16
HOSKINS, Elisha 79
 Hannah 79
 Hiriam 74
 Hyram 79
 James 70, 79, 89
 Johnson 80
 Richard 80
 Thomas 74, 79, 119
HOW, William 32
HOWARD, John B. 161
HOWERTON, Joshua 169
HUBBARD, Hezekiah 82, 125
 Moses 115, 129
 Reuben 87
HUDSON, John M. 36
 Sally 8
 William 165
HUFFMAN, John 37
HUGHES, Elijah 31
HUGHEY, Allen 162
 Robert 162
HUNDLEY, Caleb 59
 John 117, 135, 163
 Joseph 117, 135
 William 59
HUTCHERSON, Saml. 82
HUTCHINGS, Samuel 29
 John 129, 164
 M. 158
 Moses 164
 Stokley 158
 William 49
HUTCHISON, Elijah 82
 Mary 89
 Nathan 67
 Susanna 89
HYLER, Joseph 163

I

INGE, John 79, 126
 John M. 18, 73, 108
INGRAM, Elizabeth 142
 Garland 39
 George 142
 George D. 43
 Katherine 43
 Larkin 43
 William 142
INMAN, Betsy 15
 Henry 15, 146
 William 15, 108

IRBY, Anna 106
 Charles 83, 164
 Francis 109
 George 116
 Martha 109
 Peter 106
 Thomas 8, 20
 William 8
 William R. 1
 Zachariah 65

J

JACKSON, Alexander 7
 Ephram 46
 Ephriam 17, 50
 John 13
JACOBS, Aaron 84
 Henry 28, 37, 64,
  84, 132, 158
JAMES, Jesse 69
JEFFERSON, John 17
 Noton 128
 Saml. A. 85
 Samuel A. 18
 Thomas 85
JENKINS, Daniel 106,125
JENNINGS, John 122, 124
 Joseph 130
 Meredith 144
 Robert 121, 122, 130
 Susannah 121
 William H. 86
JOHNS, A. B. 159
 Anthony B. 159
 Daniel 52, 98, 159,
  164
 Danl. 52, 137
 Janiel 98
 John 160
 Mary 164
JOHNSON, Champness W. F.
 86
 Franklin S. 172
 Geo. W. 14, 107
 James 99, 167
 Josiah 42
 Nancy 14, 107
 Richard 23, 49, 55, 70
  154
 Thomas 151
 William 26, 140
JONES, Buck 67

LINDSEY, John 84, 96
LINN, William 56, 144
　Wm. 86
LINTHICUM, Rice B. 109
LOGAN, David 9
LOVE, Daniel 99
　James K. 46
　Robert 39, 75
　William 177
LOVELACE, Atkinson O. 39
　James 20, 96
　Thomas 123
LOVELL, John 124
　Sarah 124
LOVERN, John 96
LOWELL, Samuel M. 41
LUCAS, Charles 41, 129
LUCK, James A. 124
LUCY, Charles 42
LUMPKIN, Moore 51
　Nancy 63
LUMPKINS, George 63
　Peyton, 83
LYNCH, Charles H. 44
　Elijah 41
LYON, Nicholas 101, 150

Mc

McALASTER, James 107
McALISTER, John 40
McDANIEL, Aaron 98
　Ann 42
　Clement 42
　Geo. 108
　George 134, 173
　Gwilliams 67
　James 117
　Moses 61
　Randolph 61, 98
McDONALD, Aaron 151, 152
　Clement 43, 98
　Randolph 151, 152
McGLASSON, Francis 36
　Matthew 161
McGRIGOR, William 44
McHANEY, John 159
　William 159
McKINZIE, Absalom 46
　Elizabeth 46
McLAUGHLAN, Henry 176
McMILLION, John 143
　Joseph 31

McNEALEY, William 24
McNEALY, William 11, 173
McNEELEY, William 33

M

MADING, Robert 112
MADDING, John 19, 140
　Rachel 112, 153
　Rawley 99
　Robert 100
　Sarah 140
　Thomas 72, 95, 153
　William 86
MAHAN, David 129
　Edmund 73
　John 85
　Pleasant 21, 61
　Thomas 52
MAHON, Thomas 65
MALICOAT, John 91
MANN, Harrison 177
MARKHAM, Peter 41
MARLER, John 148
MARRABLE, Joel 4
MARSHALL, Thomas 37
　Unity 42
　William 61
MART, Fanney 131
MARTIN, Abraham 86
　Bailey 171
　Joel 3
　Robert 156
　Salley 171
MASE, Fleming 11
MASON, Martin 167
MATHERLEY, Israel 108
MATHERLY, Joel 133
　Shadrack 133
MATHES, Luke 68
MATNEY, John 177
MATTHEW, Thomas 47
MATTHEWS, Thomas 46
MATTOX, Coley 102
　Mary 102
　Polly 131
　Samuel B. 27
MAY, George 102
　James 102
　Susanna 50
MAYES, Armistead 83
　Frances 83, 100
　Gardner 103

219

MUSE, Thomas   24, 31, 71,
   163
   Thos. O.   128
MUSTAIN, Avery   36, 45,
   141
   Drury   36
   James   136
   John   139
MYERS, George   175
   John   111
   Stephen   149
   William   27, 97, 111

N

NANCE, James   11
   James, Capt.   111
   William M.   94
NAPIER, William A.   128
NASH, John   78, 153
NEAL, Abraham   34, 143
   Boling   169
   John   7
   Simon   169
   Stephen   11
NEEL, John   43
NELSON, John   15, 49, 143
   William   71, 78
NEWBEL, John   55
NEWBILL, John   10
NEWBY, Asa   143
NEWLIN, Sherod   134
NEWMAN, Henry   11
NEWTON, William   57, 68,
   96
NICHOLAS, Chas.   22
NICHOLS, Dudley   109
   John   54, 80, 165
NICKLES, Charles   104
   Michel   104
NOBLE, John   63
NORCUTT, Janiel   113
NORMAN, Marshall   150
NORTON, Drury   113, 137
   Jacob   28
   Prior E.   114
NOWLIN, Bryan W.   88
   Bryant W.   48
   David   40, 44, 52, 78,
   88, 145
   James   134
   John   155
   Sherwood   142

NOWLIN, Wade   44
NUCHOLS, Levi   59
NUCKOLS, Levi   59
   Levy   59
   Milly   59

O

OAKES, Catherine   3
   Elizabeth   115
   George   82
   James   115, 176
   Jesse   90, 128
   Presley   139
   Robert   17
   Will   115
   William   3, 18, 31, 82,
   115, 124, 142, 157
OAKS, Isaac   31
OLIVER, John I.   115
OLVIS, Shadrack   122
ONEAL, John   79
O'NEAL, John   48
ORANDER, Pleasant   140
OTENEAL, John   136
OVERBY, John H.   127
   Thomas   9
OWEN, David   11, 14, 78,
   97
   James   36
   John   97, 117
   Julius   1, 31
   Oba.   97
   Obed   62
   Pleasant   116
   Pleasant B.   131
   Thomas   116
   Salley   116
   William   62
OWENS, Peggy   97
OWING, John   173
OWN, David   78

P

PANNILL, Saml.   105, 119
PARISH, Peter   100
PARKER, Alexander O.   146
   David   6, 146
   James   90
   William   81, 90, 122
PARMER, Cloe   165
PARRISH, Abraham C.   82

PRICE, John 72
  Major, Sr. 15
  Samuel 170, 172
  Thompson 133, 145
  William 72, 120, 122,
    147, 170
PRITCHETT, John 126, 159
  William 18, 73, 83,159
PRUITT, Joseph 38
PUCKETT, John 126
PUGH, Overton 126
PULLIAM, Drury 65, 72, 89

Q

QUIN, Margarett 114
QUINN, Peggy 66
  Redmond 66

R

RAFE, Lewis 79
RAGAN, Daniel 174
RAGLAND, Row. 46
  William 60
RAGSDALE, John 25, 127,
  175
  John B. 75
  Pascal W. 52, 97
  Thomas 24, 132, 175
RAILEY, William W. 96
RALPH, Lewis 49
RAMSEY, Frances 101
  Hailey S. 31, 104
  Haley 104
  Noton 104, 111
  Rachel 104
RANEY, Mary 22
RATLIFF, John 12, 41, 168
  Pendleton 128
  William 97, 127, 128
RAWLINGS, Thomas 72
RAWLINS, E. 49, 57, 87
  Eldred 57
READ, Thomas H. 146
REAGAN, Danel 116
REYNOLDS, Burton 128
  Hugh 106
  Jesse 51, 121, 138
  John 128
  John D. 3
  Sarah 51
RICE, Benjamin 15

RICE, David 175
  Davis 122
  Hawker 6
RICHARDS, David 72, 123
  Joseph 123
RICHARDSON, Elijah 86
  Fanny 96
  Frances 129
  George 30
  John 61, 90, 97, 145
  Luce 61, 86
  Thomas 61, 86, 129
  William 96
RICHEY, James 94
  James H. 113
RICKEE, David 113
RIDDEL, Basel 130, 131
RIDDLE, Basdel 130
  Bassel 130
  Reubin 99
  Thomas 147
  Zach. 109
  Zachariah 130
rIGHT, George 10
RIGHT, Milley 33
RIGNEY, John 44
RITCHER, Benjamin 107,136
RITCHERSON, David 152
RITCHEY, Robert 131
RITCHIE, Benjamin 147
ROACH, Burdett 20
  Burdill 117
  Burditt 131
  Henry 65
  James 103
ROARER, David 12
ROBERTS, Michael 167
ROBERTSON, Arthur 161
  Christopher 29, 132,
    146
  Christopher, Jr. 59
  Christopher, Senr. 24
  Christopher, Sr. 57,82
  David 5
  Edw. 92
  George 29, 142, 171
  James 29
  John, Jr. 5
  Joseph 127
  Nathaniel 80, 146
  Peter 57
  Samuel 73
  William 127, 148

ROBINSON, George 102
    Saly 102
RODDEN, Spencer 69
RODGERS, Charles B. 97
    William 158
ROGERS, James B. 44
    Joseph 71
    William 23, 71
ROLAND, Jesse 101
    Robert 40
RORER, Abraham 134, 157
    Abraham, Jr. 9
    Betsey 158
    John 35, 134
    Rudolph 132
ROSS, Robert 107
ROSSAN, Jerome 6
ROSSON, Joram 90
    Joseph 90, 154, 177
    Molly 90
ROWLAND, Elizabeth 27
    Frances 87
    Jesse 23, 87, 92
    John 27, 65, 171
    John, Sr. 65
    Nimrod F. 27
ROY, John B. 80
ROYALL, Eliza 32
    Elizabeth 49, 134, 148
    Frs. L. 142
    Nathaniel R. 49
ROYSTER, William 145
RUSSELL, William 91, 102
RYNER, Jacob 83

S

SADLER, Creed 135
SANDERS, Jesse 103
    Nathaniel B. 135
SAUNDERS, George 135
    Jacob 167
    Jane 32
    Jesse 45
    Joshua 5
    Nathaniel B. 136
SAWYERS, James 24
SCARCE, Geo. 136
    George 136
    Thomas 136
SCATES, Zebulon 18
SCOTT, Asa 167
    Jeremiah 10

SCOTT, Nimrod 122
    Niven 10
    Pinkney 129
SCRUGGS, Drury 52
SEAL, Charles 126
    Joel 137
    Solomon 137
    William 137
SEAMORE, Parham 97
    William B. 52
    Zachariah 116
SEEMSTER, John 76
SELF, Burwell 75
    Thomas 75
SEMONES, John 161
SHACKLEFORD, Garland 64,95
    John 137
    Nancy 95
SHAW, Evan 164
    Even 78
    Jesse 25, 26, 121
SHELHORSE, Barnett 176
    Henry 120
SHELLHORSE, Barnett 75, 109
    Jacob 75
SHELTON, Abner C. 144
    Abraham C. 133
    Benjamin 140
    Bennett 141
    Beverly 59
    Booker 21
    Coleman 64, 75, 140
    Creed T. 17
    Crispen 141
    Daniel 23, 74, 89
    David 21, 92
    Dudley 99
    George 140
    Henry 51
    John 100, 148
    Leroy 47, 73, 133, 165
    Leroy G. 54
    Lewis 68, 141
    Margaret 137, 138
    Moses 141
    Noah 153, 169
    Richard 35, 141
    Richard I. 6, 70, 88,
        174
    Richard J. 174
    Robert 5, 70, 132
    Robert H. 51
    Robertson 132

SHELTON, Spencer 140
  Tavner C. 107
  Taviner C., Doct^r 142
  Thomas 19, 51, 60, 77
   100, 143
  Thomas S. 77
  Thomas, Sr. 142
  Tunstall 7, 58, 89
  Vincent 21
  Vincent H. 110
  Washington 139, 170
  Wesley 109, 142
  W. H. 144
  William 19, 39, 86, 110,
   139, 142, 160, 176
  William H. 142
  William I. 133
  Willis 142
  Young 68
SHEPPARD, William 38
SHIELDS, Anderson P. 138
  John 116, 174
  Pleasant 32, 42, 43,
   60
  Thomas 9
  Unity 42
  William 9
SHOCKLEY, Thomas 64
SHORT, Robin 27
SHORTER, John 143
SHUMATE, Tolison 102
SIKES, Joab 6
SILCOCK, Amos 66
  Jane 66
SIMPSON, Lewis 42, 145
  Thomas 43, 136
  William 8, 86, 95, 144
   145, 161
SLAUGHTER, Robert H. 156
SLAYDEN, Christian 113
  Daniel 108
  James 15
  John 175
  Samuel 15
  William 42, 98
SLAYDON, John 77
  Thomas 51, 70
  William 112
SLATON, Daniel 123
SLAYTON, Daniel 160, 161
  Daniel E. 168
  Joseph 168
  Lucy 39

SLAYTON, Milley 30, 123,
  168
  Sarah 39
  Thomas 17, 103, 163
  William 160
SMITH, Allen 39
  Ewel 38
  Hezekiah 87
  Hezekiah, Jr. 46
  Jabez 110
  John H. 146, 159
  John, "Minor" 157
  Jno. 157
  Joseph 19, 38
  Joshua 50, 96, 133
  Marthy 87
  Orlando 146
  Ralph 28
  Randolph 129, 145
  Thomas 1, 19, 60, 80,
   147, 167
  Thomas D. 79
  William 79, 145, 166
SMITHSON, Hezekel P. 10
SMOTHERS, John 28, 88,
  109
SNEED, Dabney P. 44
SNODY, John 28, 74
SNOW, Daniel 105
SOURS, W. B. 9
SOVERN, Asa 96
SOYARS, Alexander B. 165
  James 11, 13, 24, 48,
   57, 81, 165
  John 165
  Samuel 27
  Thomas P. 146
SPARKES, Anderson 114
  Elizabeth 114
  Thomas 7, 114
SPARKS, Caty 147
  John 46
  Thomas 7
SPENCER, William 16, 32
SPRATTEN, Geo. 147
STAMPS, Leyanner 164
  Timothy 30, 96, 153
  William 17, 42, 57, 77
STANLEY, James S. 120
  Luke 138
STEPHENS, William A. 148
STEWART, Thomas 25
STILL, James 18, 129

224

YATES, Joseph 176
   Stephen 176
   Stephen, Senr. 71
YATTES, Samuel 16, 17
YEAMAN, John 32, 37
YEATES, Charles 34, 58, 64
YEATTS, Sam¹ 77
YOUNG, Peyton 34

Z

ZINC, Jacob 4, 6

* * * * * * * * * *

www.ingramcontent.com/pod-product-compliance
Lightning Source LLC
Chambersburg PA
CBHW070407270326
41926CB00014B/2736